ASTRE

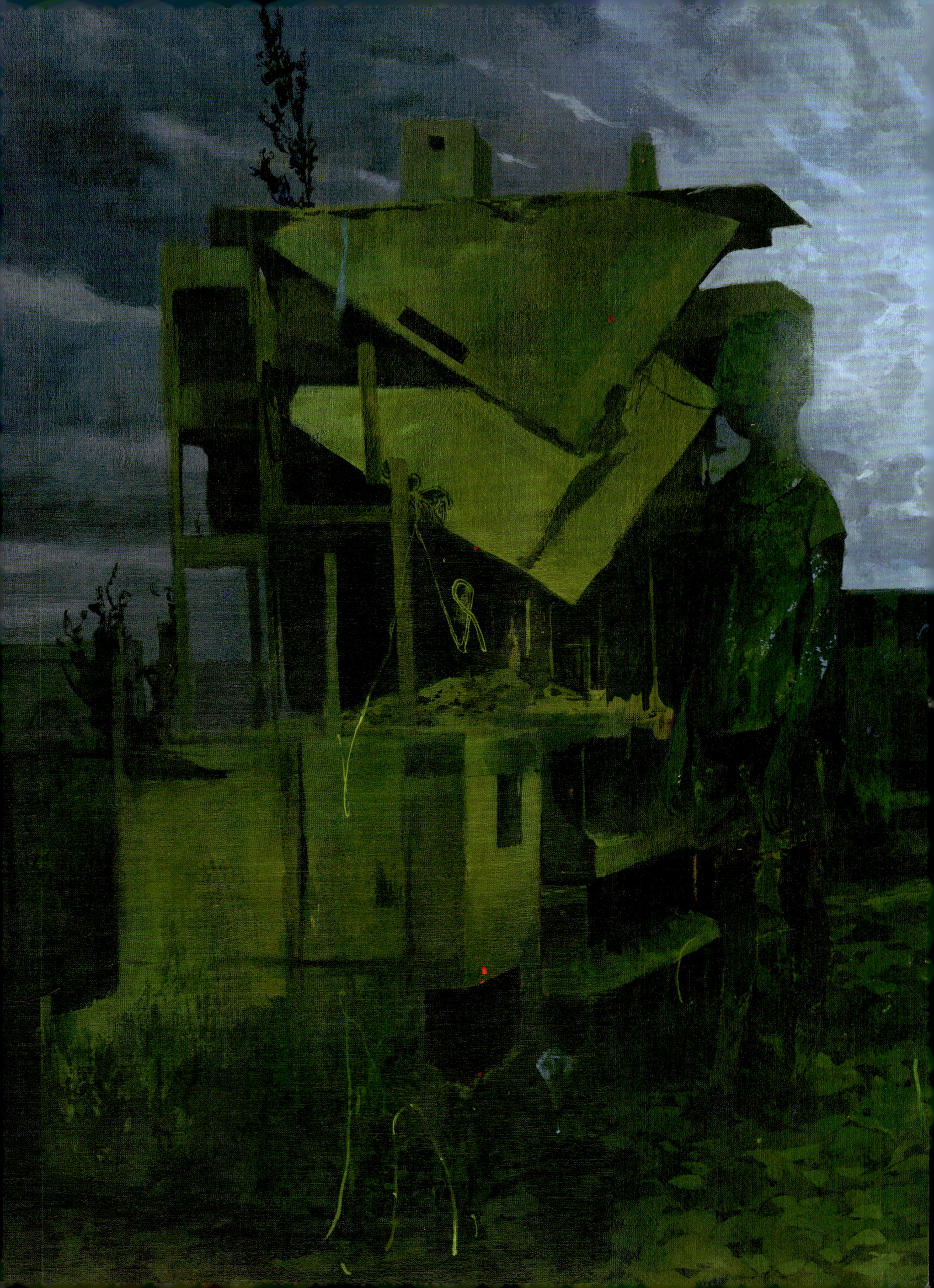

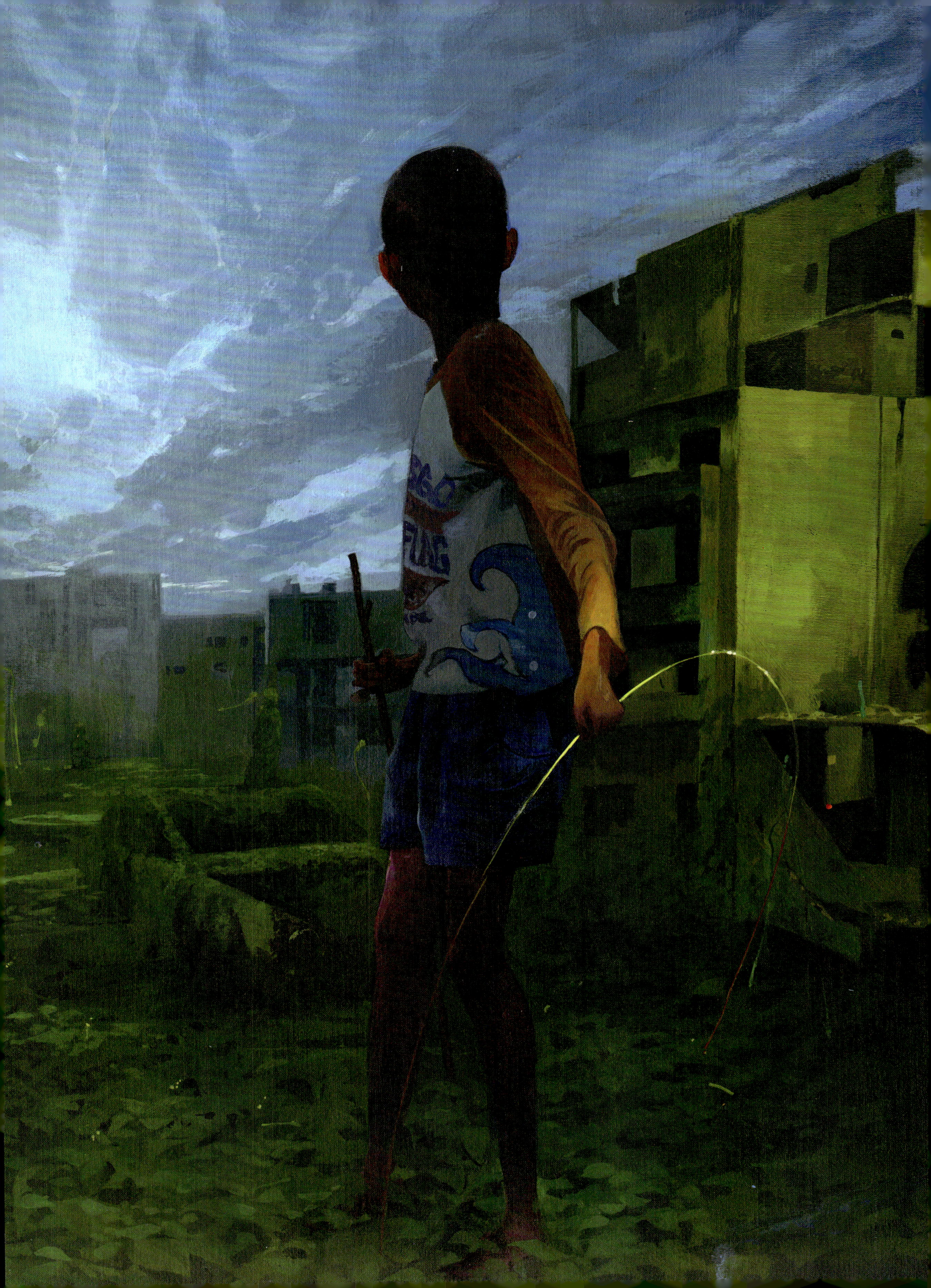

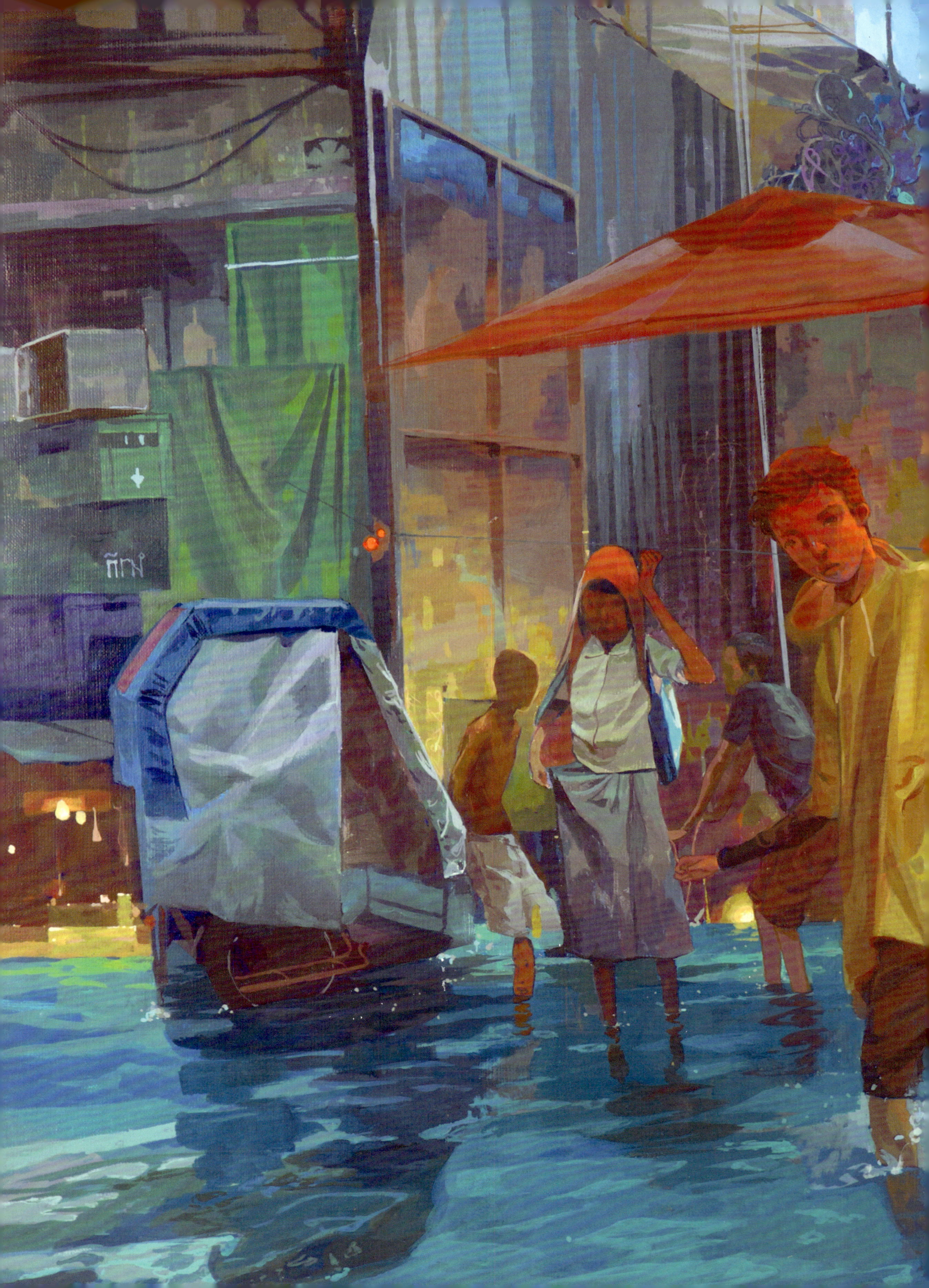

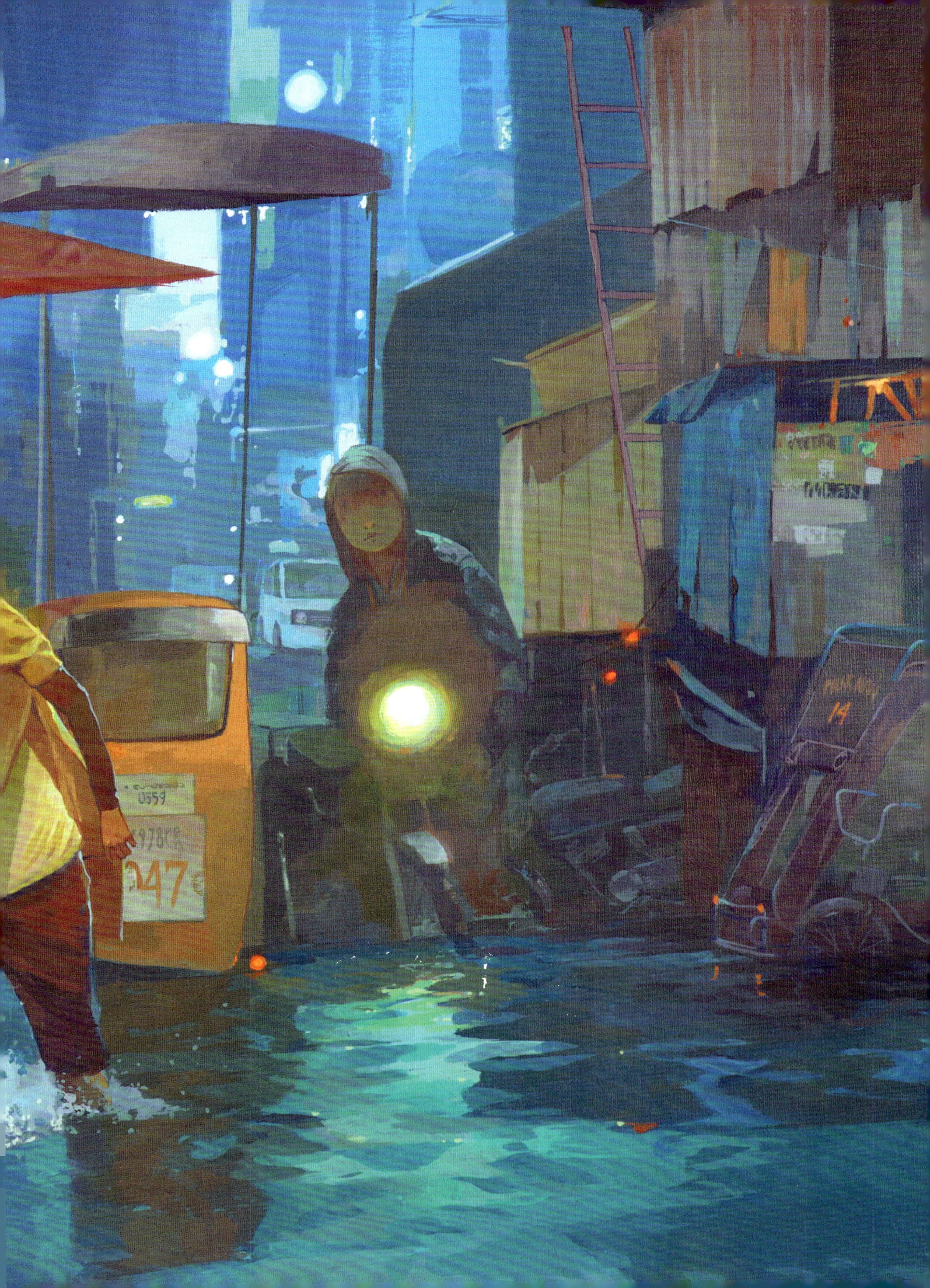
0559
978CR
047
14

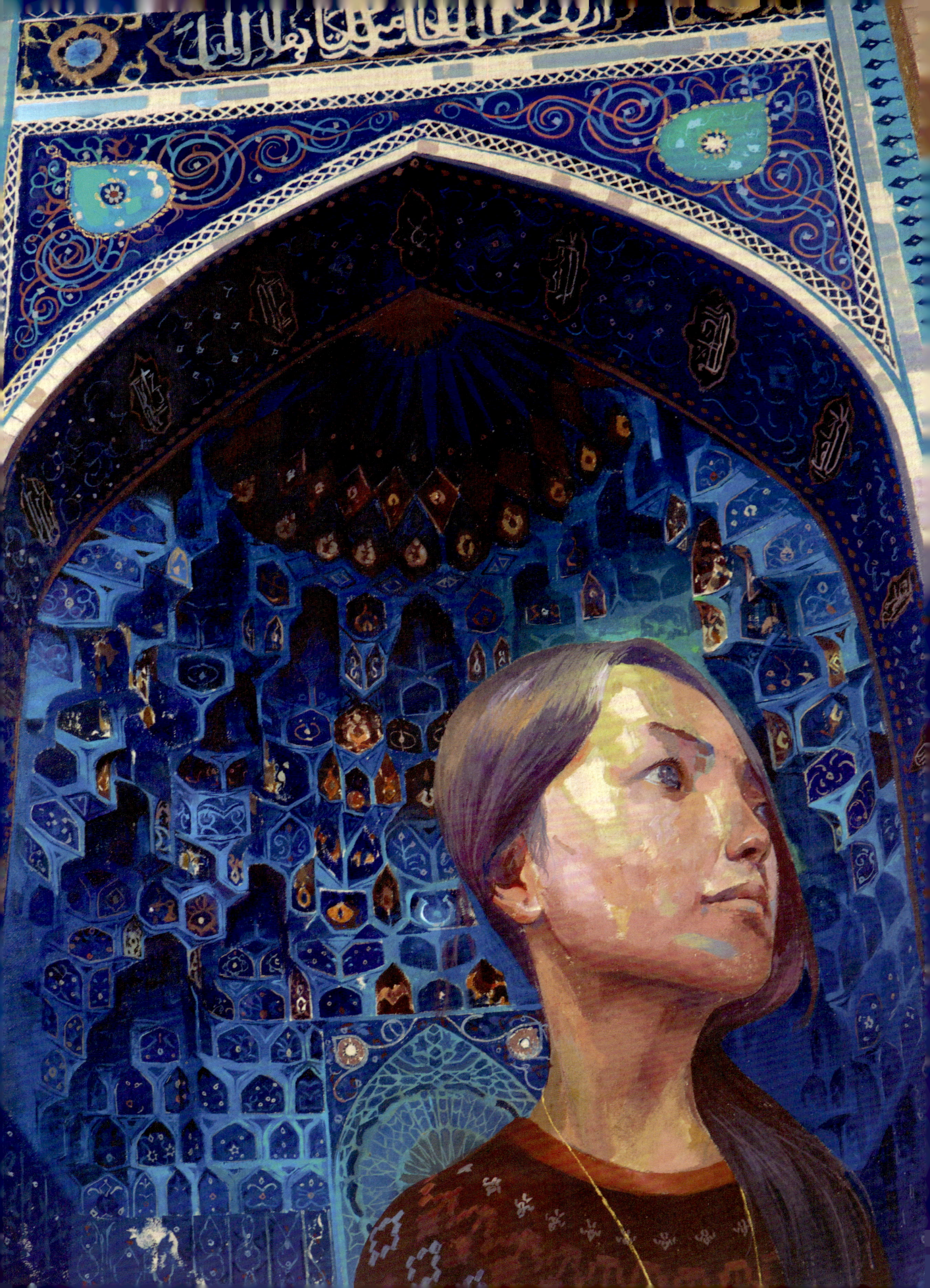

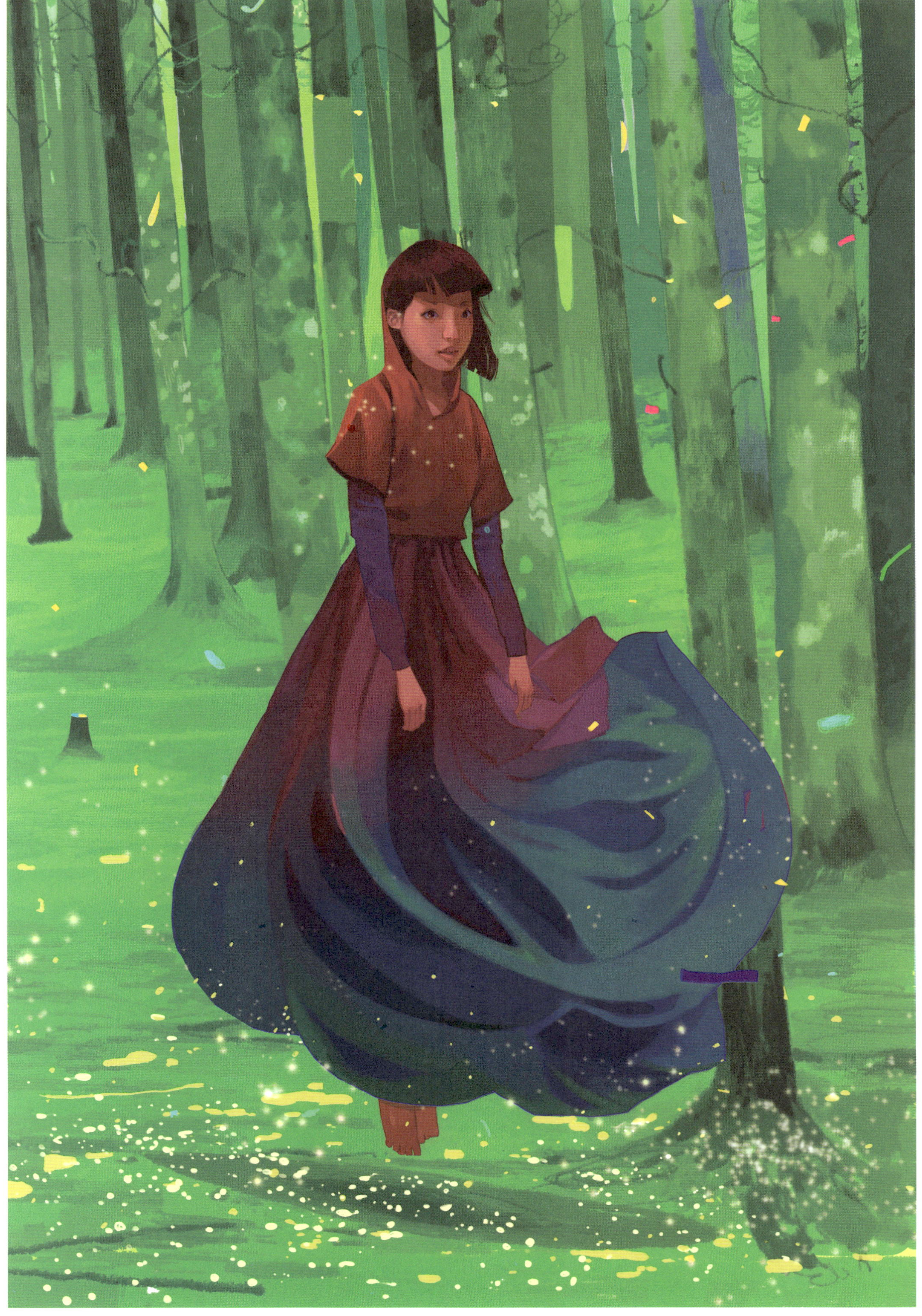

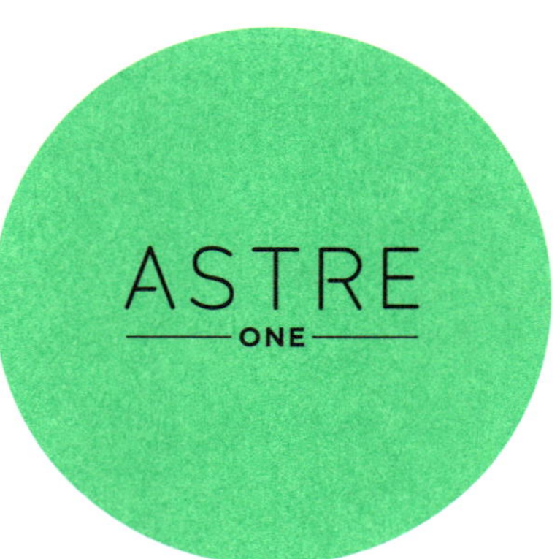

GREENERY BY ANDREW HEM

— ASTRE ORIGINAL PRINT —

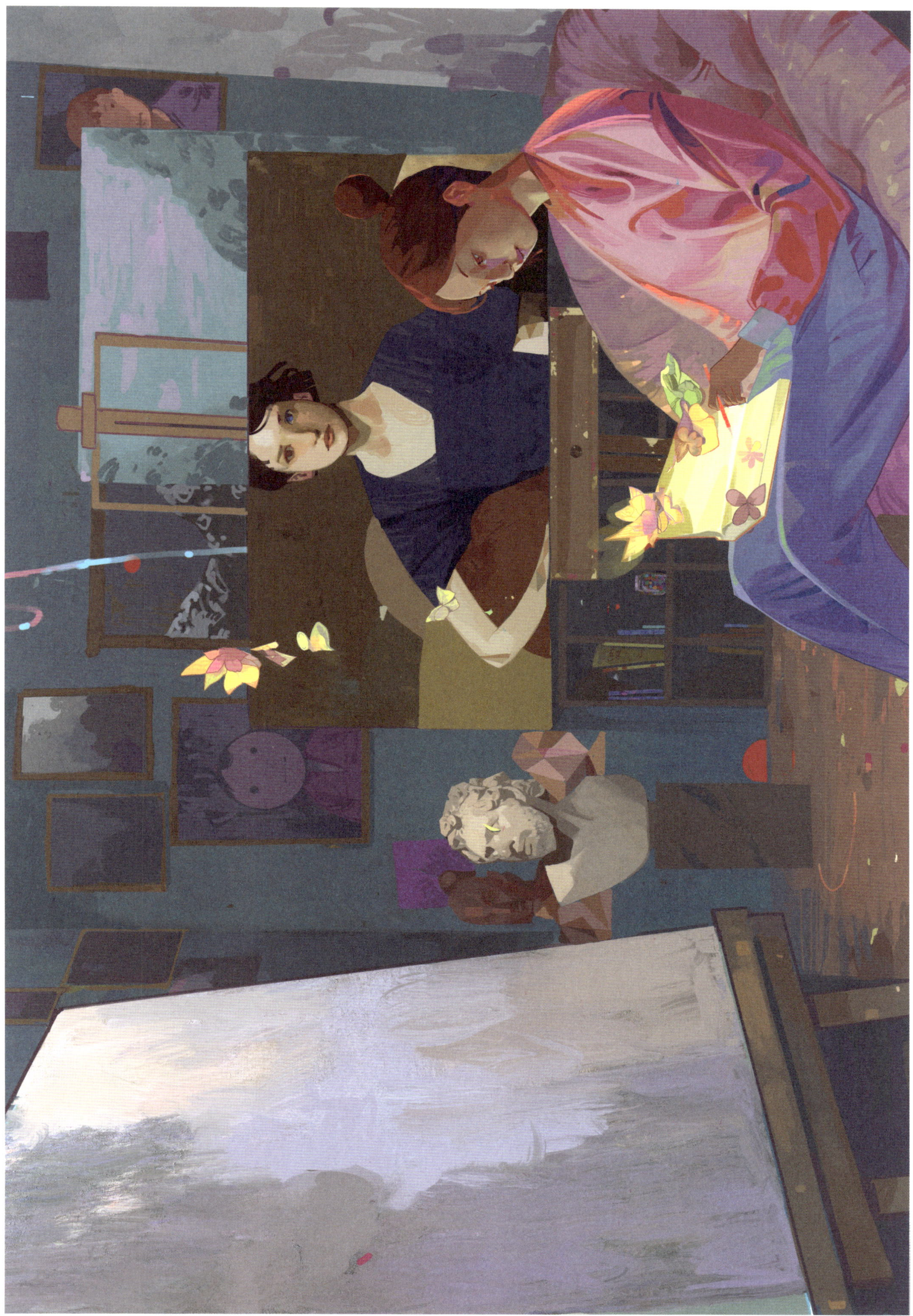

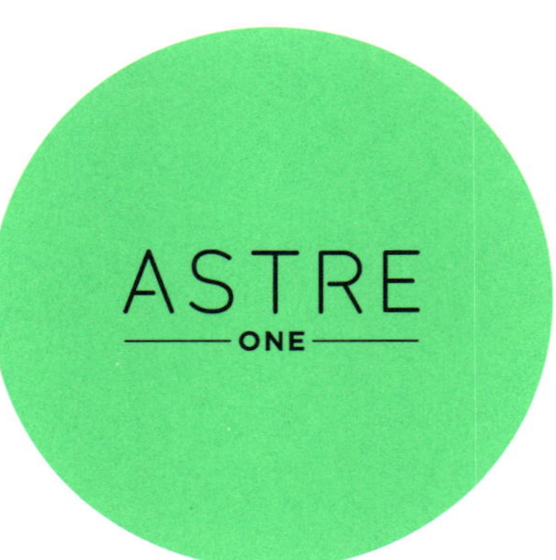

STUDIO 61 BY ANDREW HEM

— ASTRE ORIGINAL PRINT —

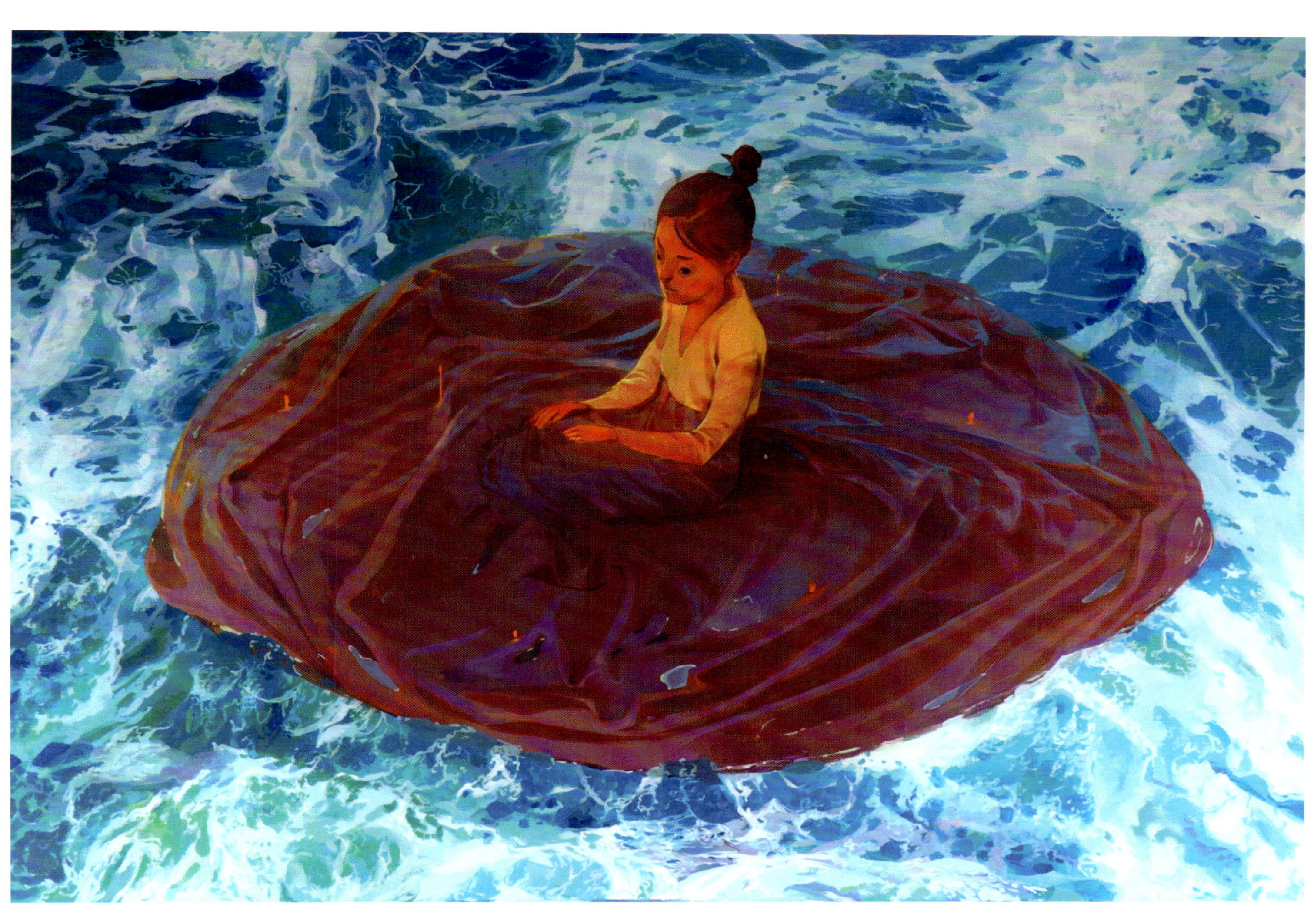

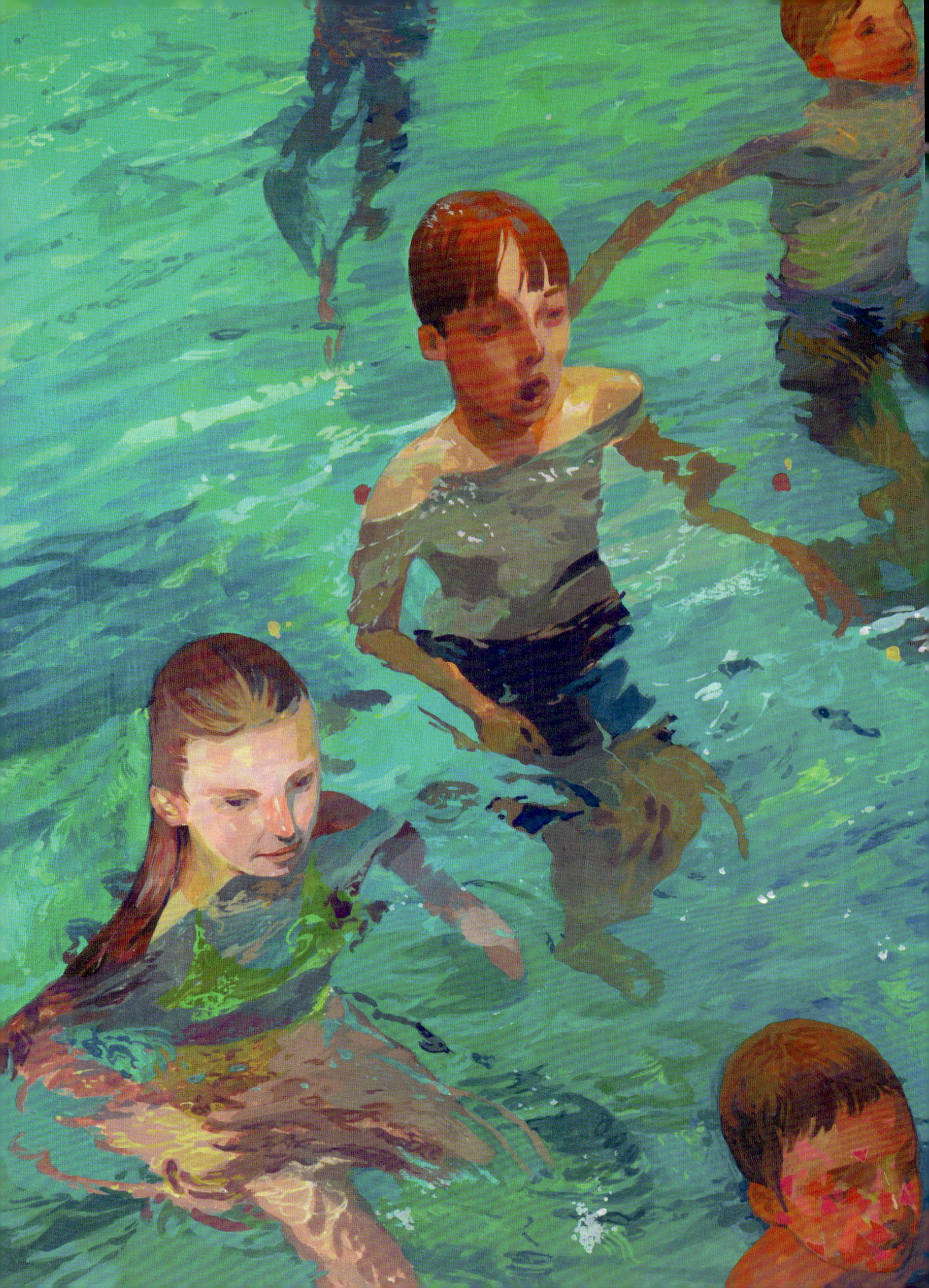

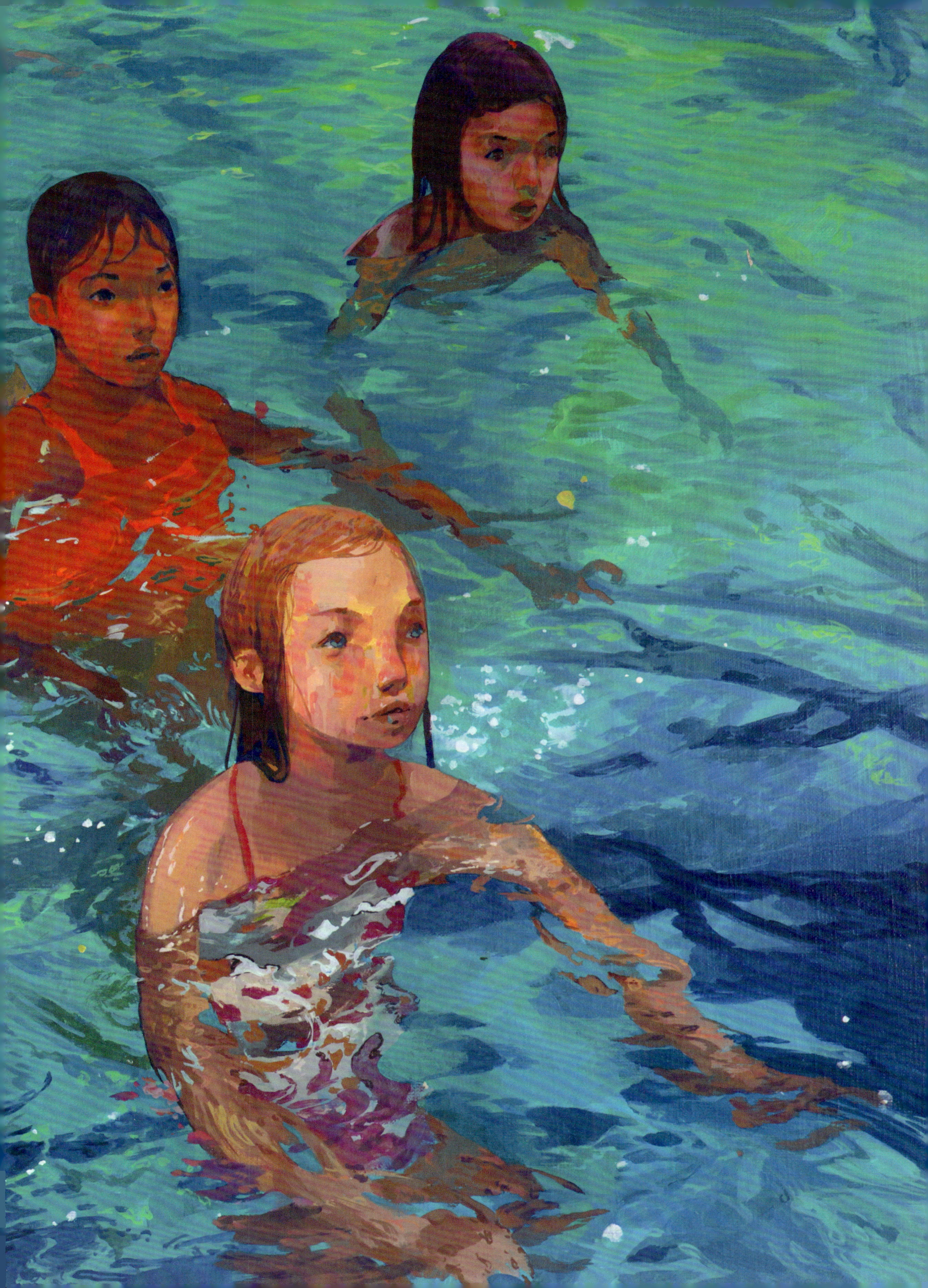

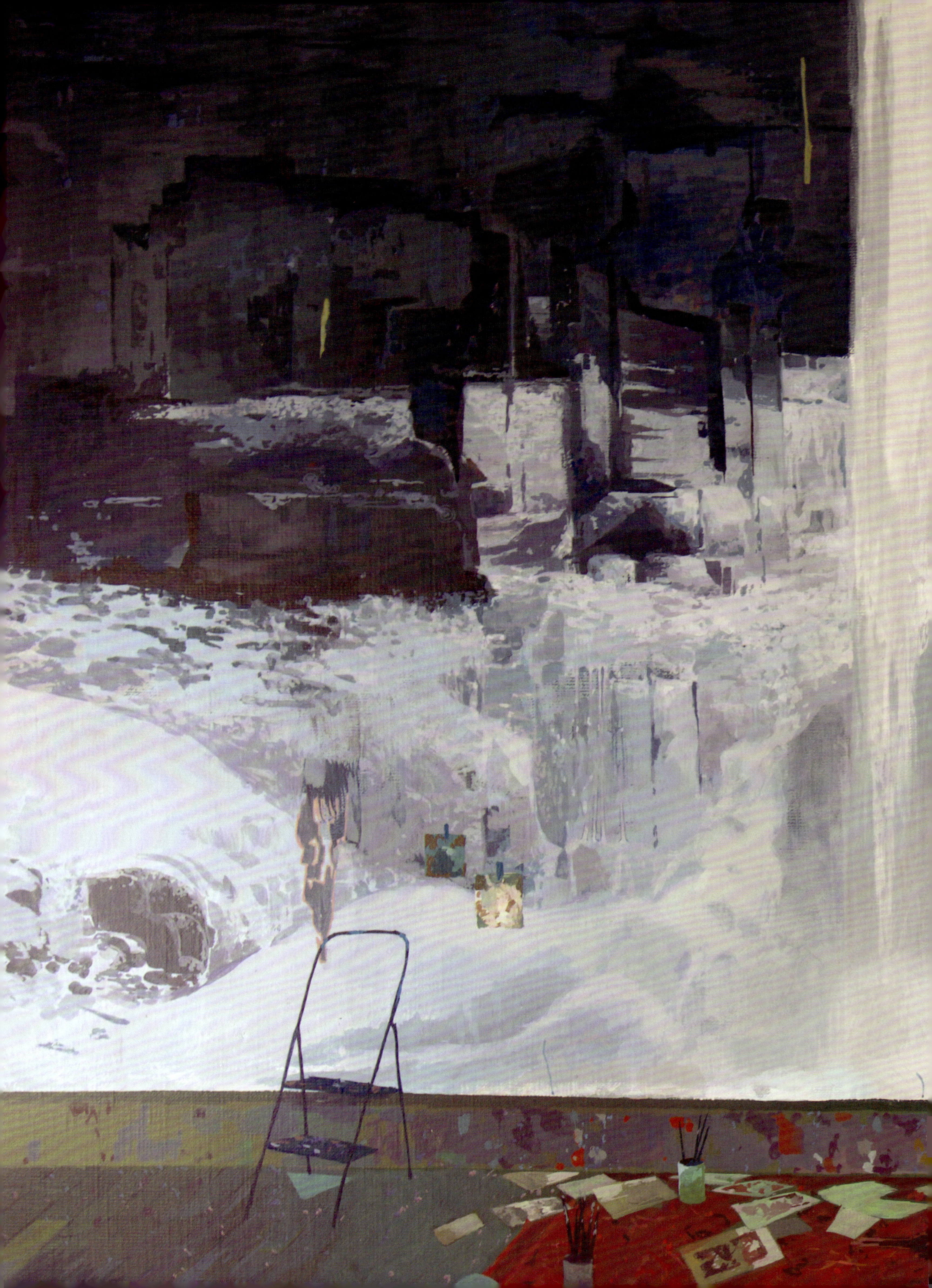

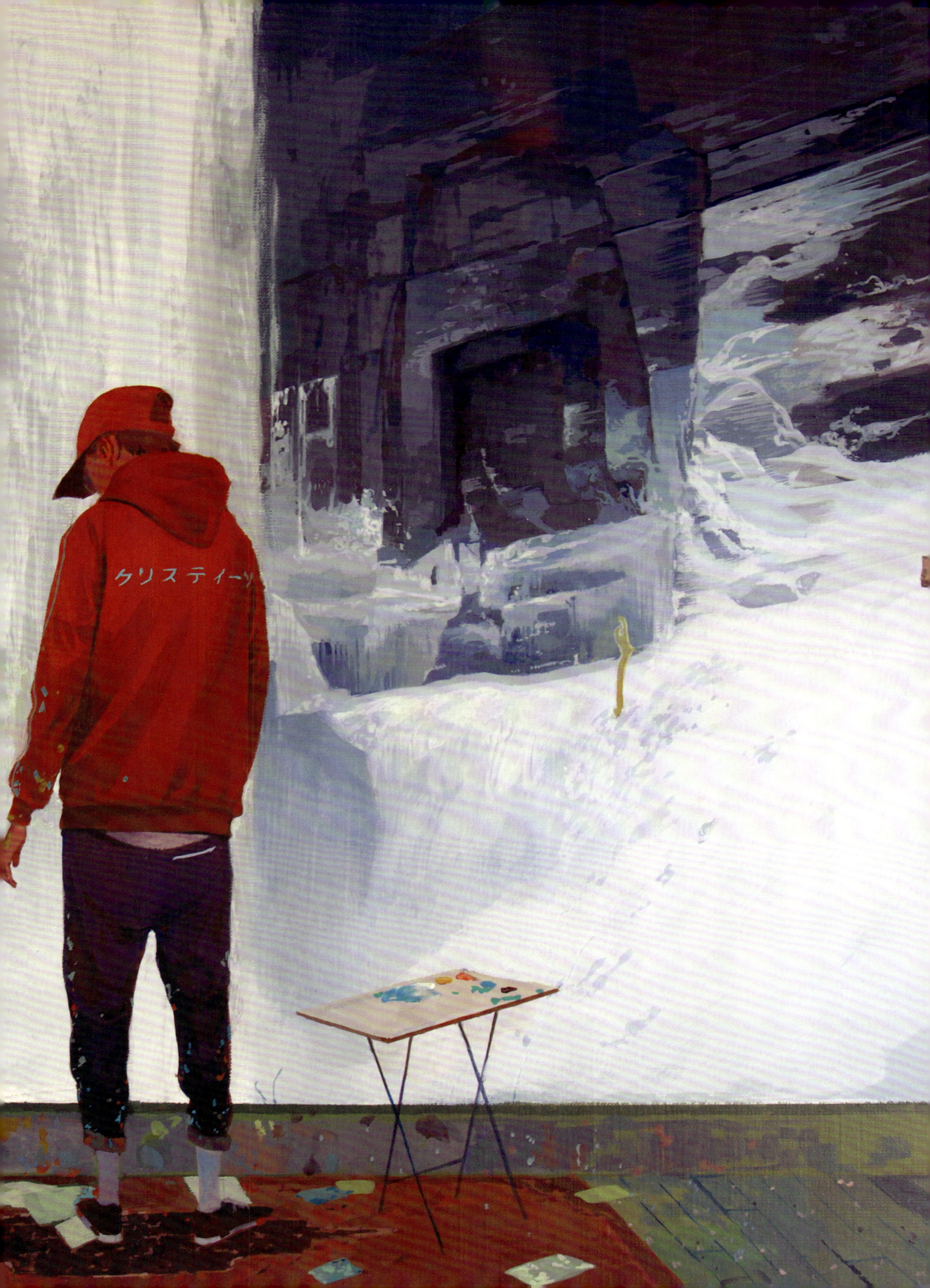
クリスティーン

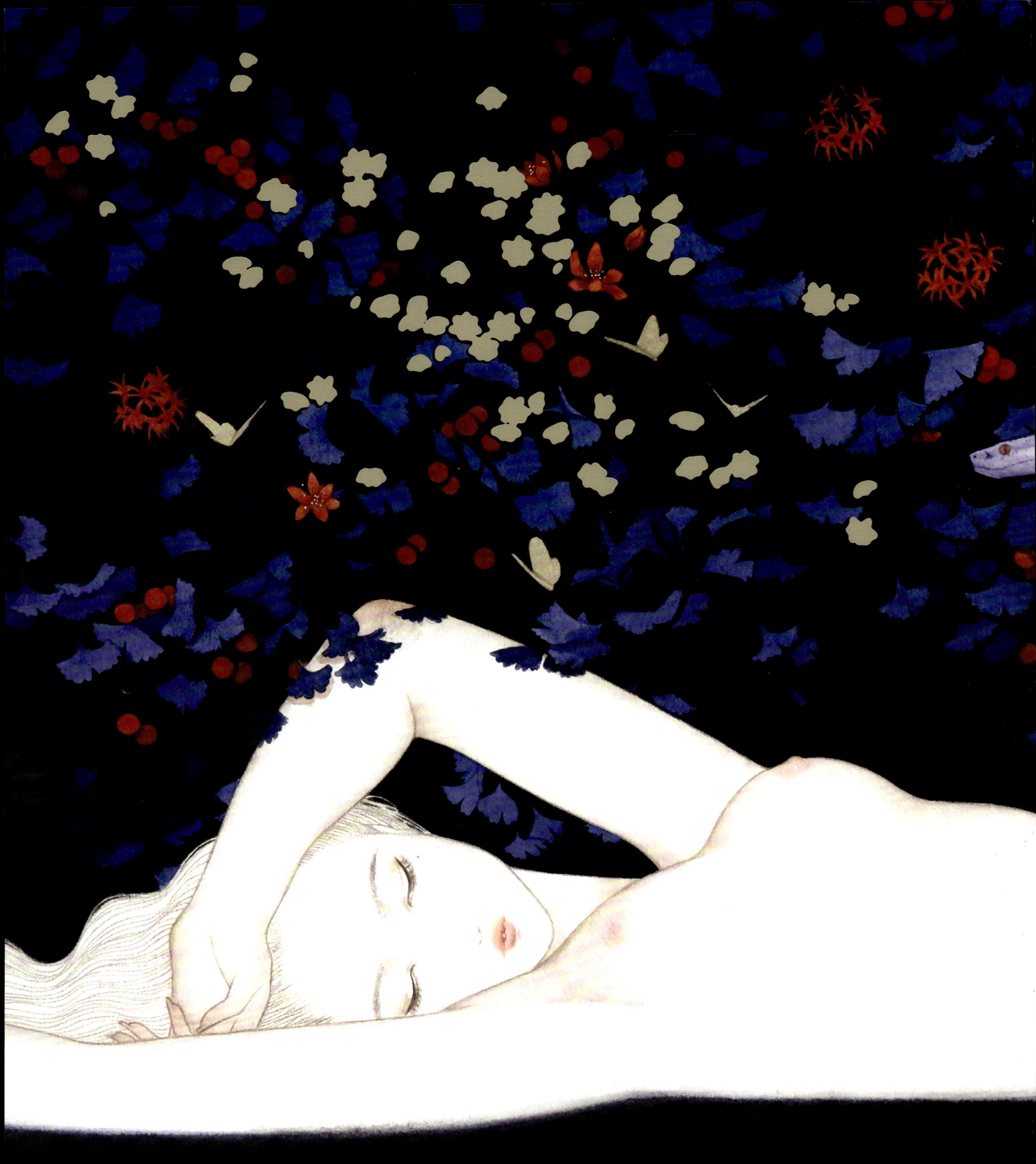

Janice Sung

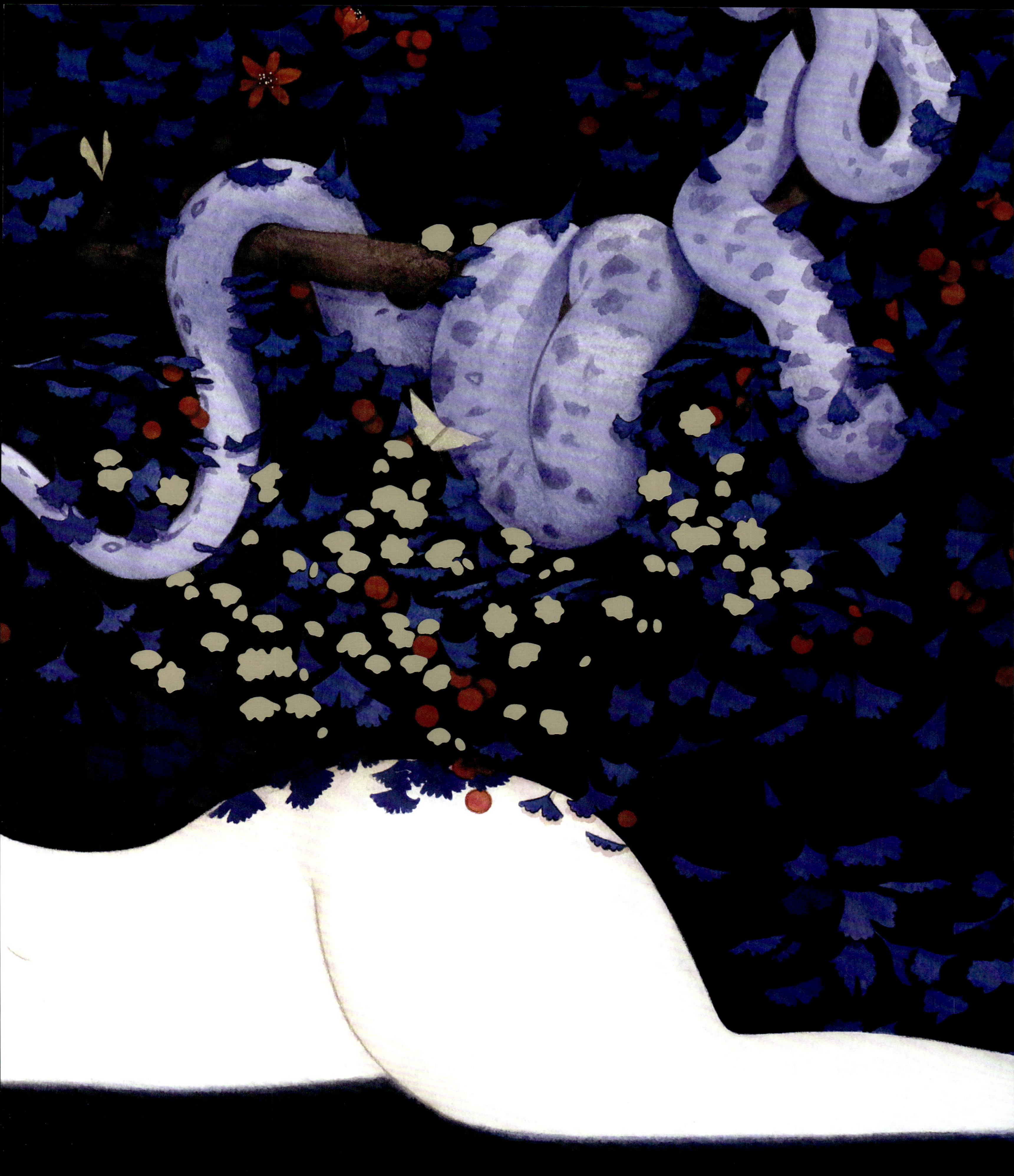

Inspiration

The lily of the valley is the focus of the print I have created for ASTRE**. This has been one of my favourite flowers for a while and I've wanted to incorporate it into one of my paintings for quite some time. While painting this piece, I wanted every aspect of the painting, from the character to the jewellery, to reflect the delicacy of the flower.**

The primary challenge for me, when working on this or any other piece, revolves around creating the initial concept. Defining the pose and selecting the colour palette demand a substantial investment of time dedicated to sketching and meticulous planning; even more so when dealing with larger-scale canvases. The planning phase tends to surpass the actual painting process in terms of time and commitment.

I'm frequently driven by the desire to evoke an enchanting sense of fantasy and intrigue in my paintings. I find that incorporating ethereal elements such as lush foliage and delicate creatures not only imparts a sense of tranquillity, but also infuses my work with a profound and captivating beauty. Identifying and developing my own instinctive style has always been a challenge for me. Just as my tastes and interests change often, so does my art. My artistic expression has always been about holding a mirror to my current passions and inspirations. I've embraced the notion that, much like my personal growth, my artistic style will naturally evolve as well and I'm content with embracing this continuous evolution.

After graduating from Sheridan College with a degree in animation, I worked in the entertainment industry as a concept artist in Toronto. After two years, I made the pivotal decision to transition into a career as an independent artist and illustrator. In this capacity, I've had the privilege of collaborating with brands such as Apple, National Geographic, Biossance, and many others. Throughout that period, I primarily created my artwork digitally. However, late in 2023, I made a significant shift, opting to transition to traditional painting with primarily watercolour, as I find this artistic process much more fulfilling.

ON PREVIOUS PAGE:
Pandora

RIGHT:
Andromeda

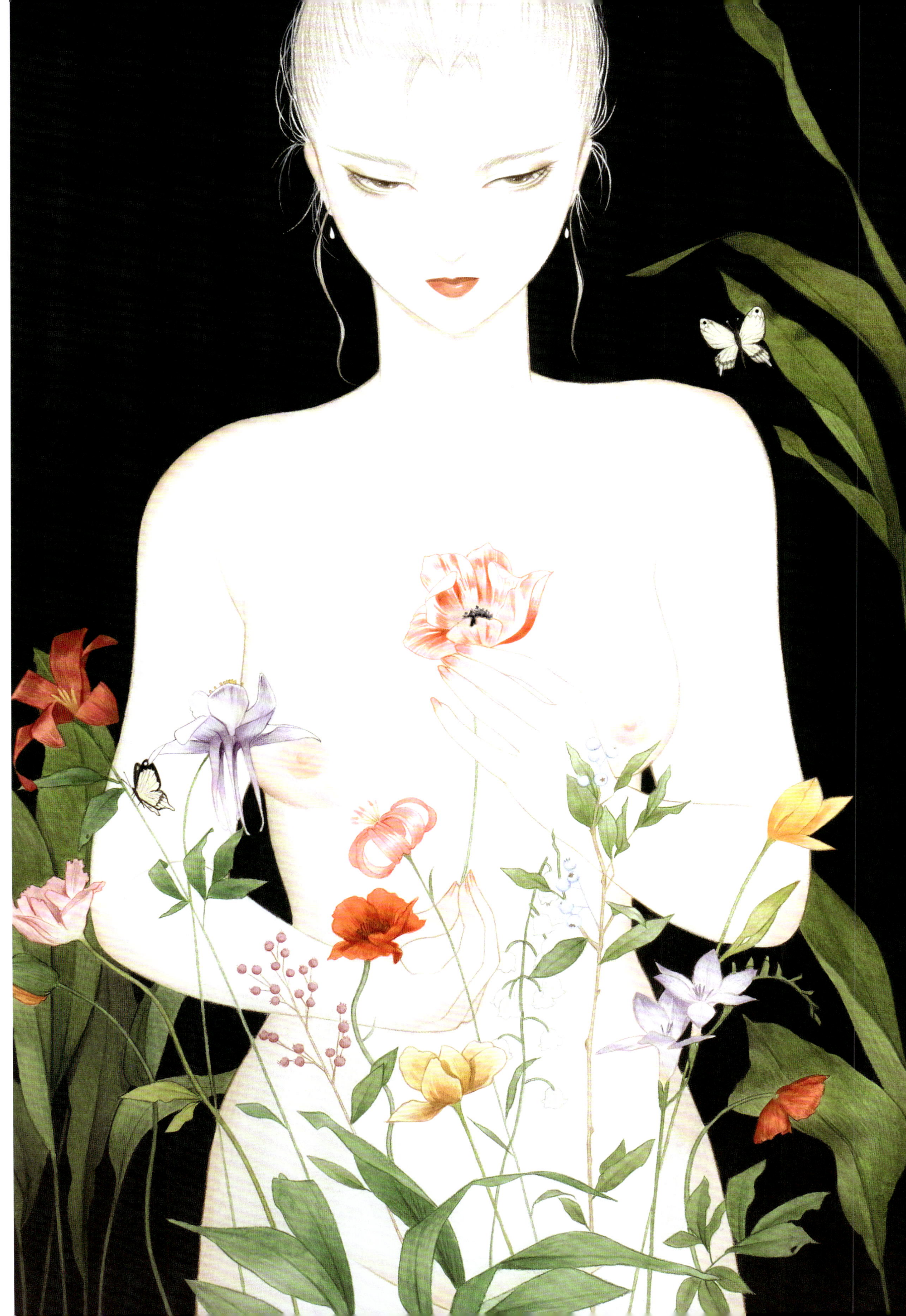

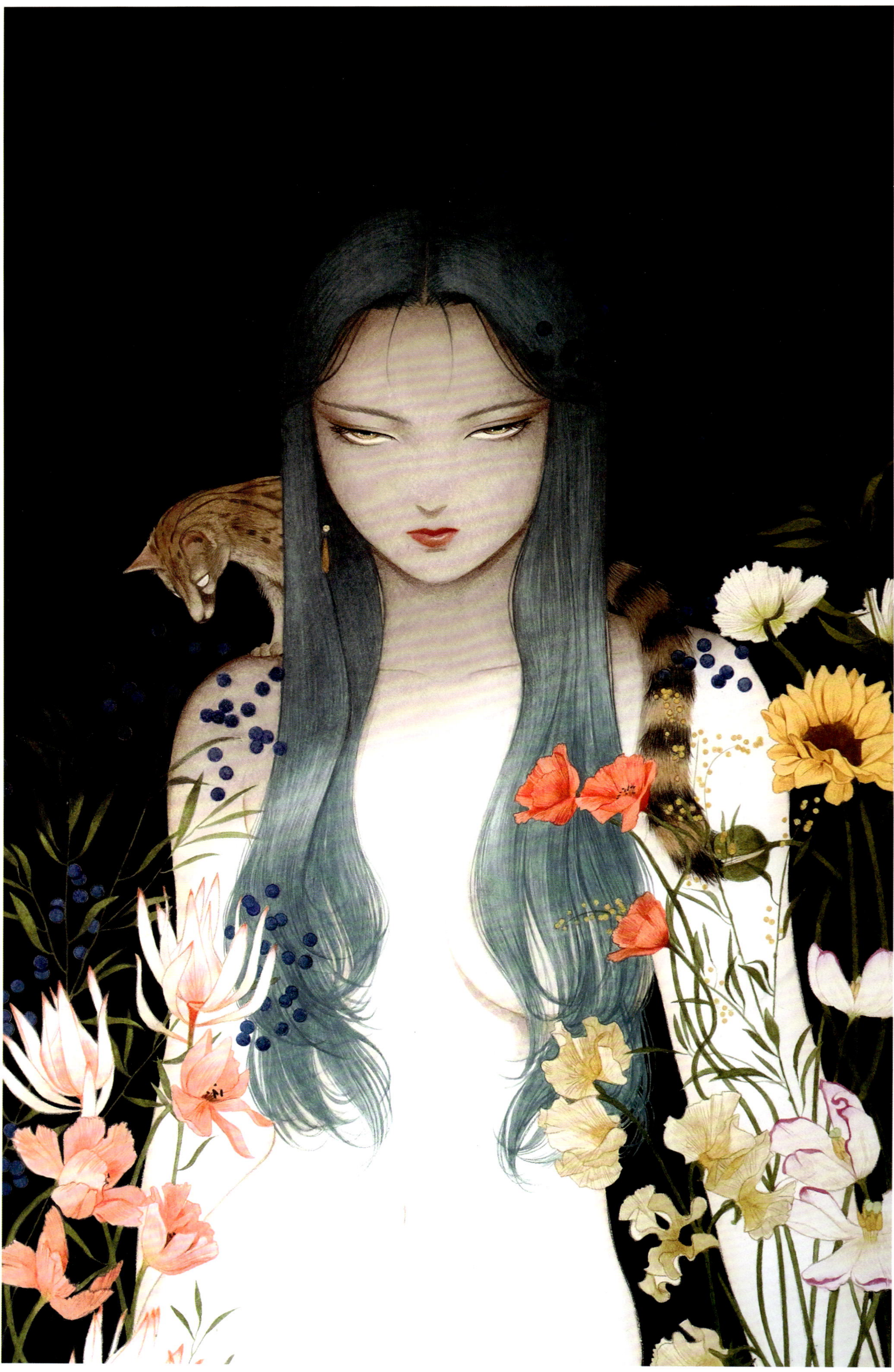

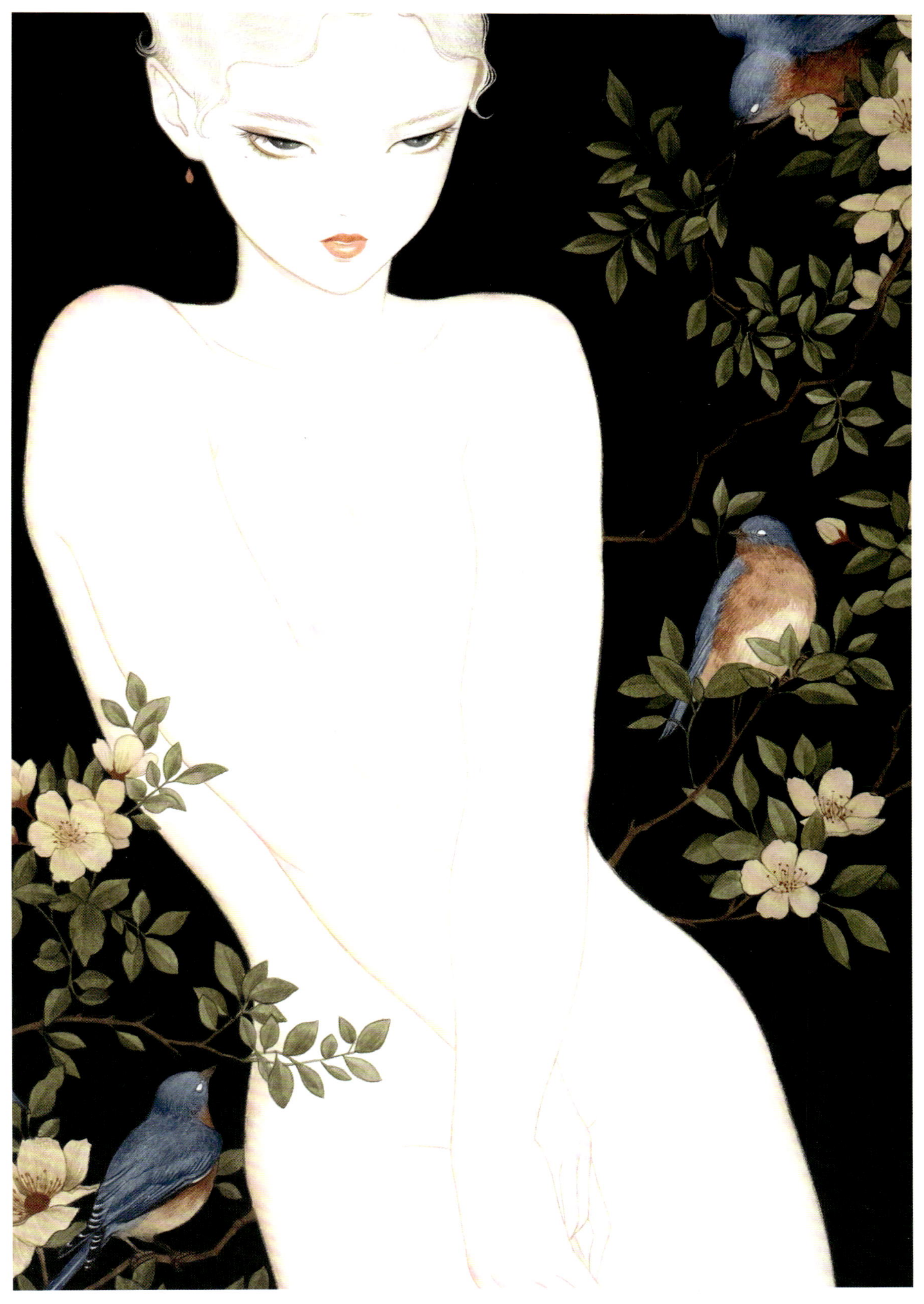

LEFT:
Diana

ABOVE:
Luna

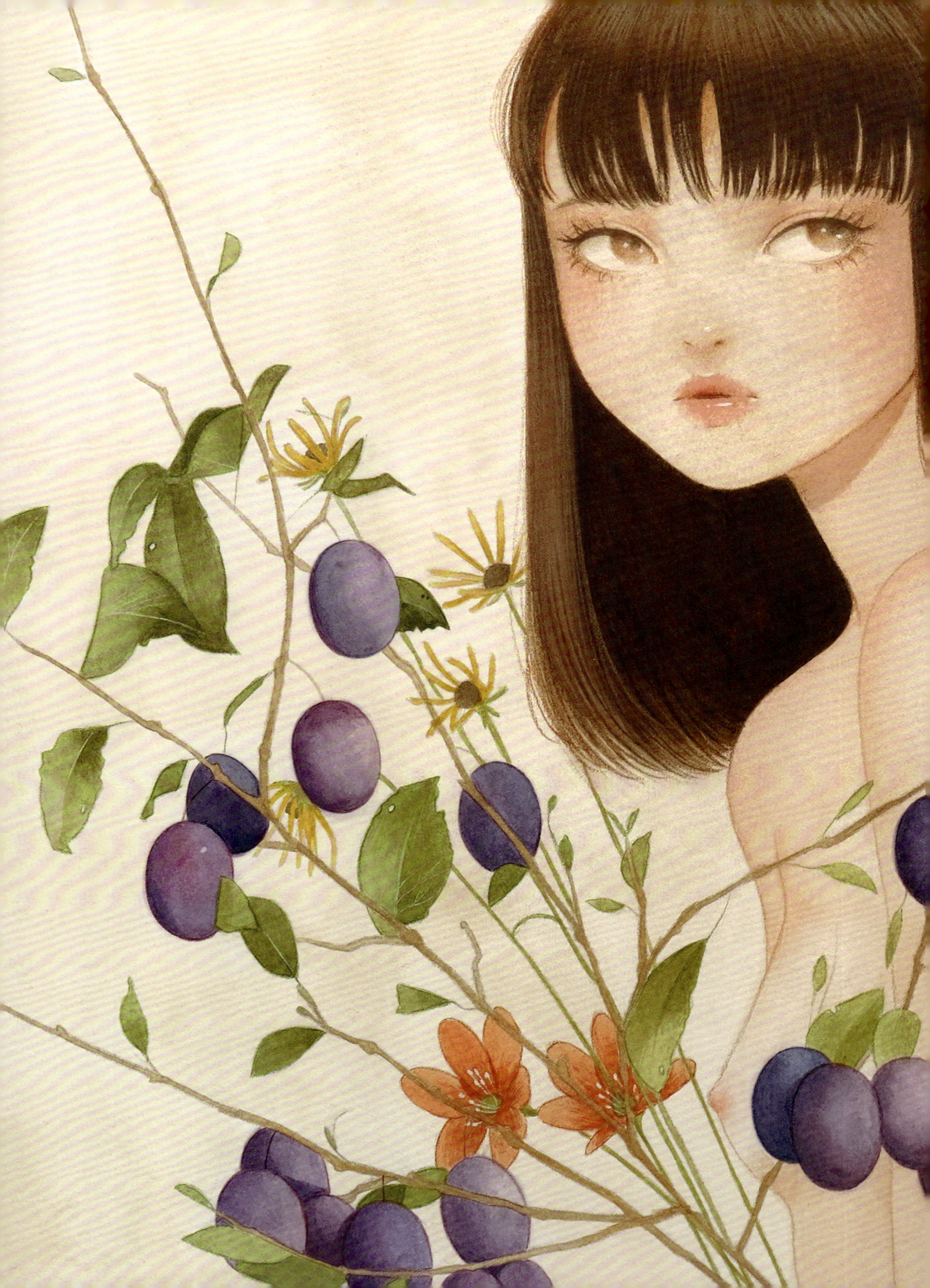

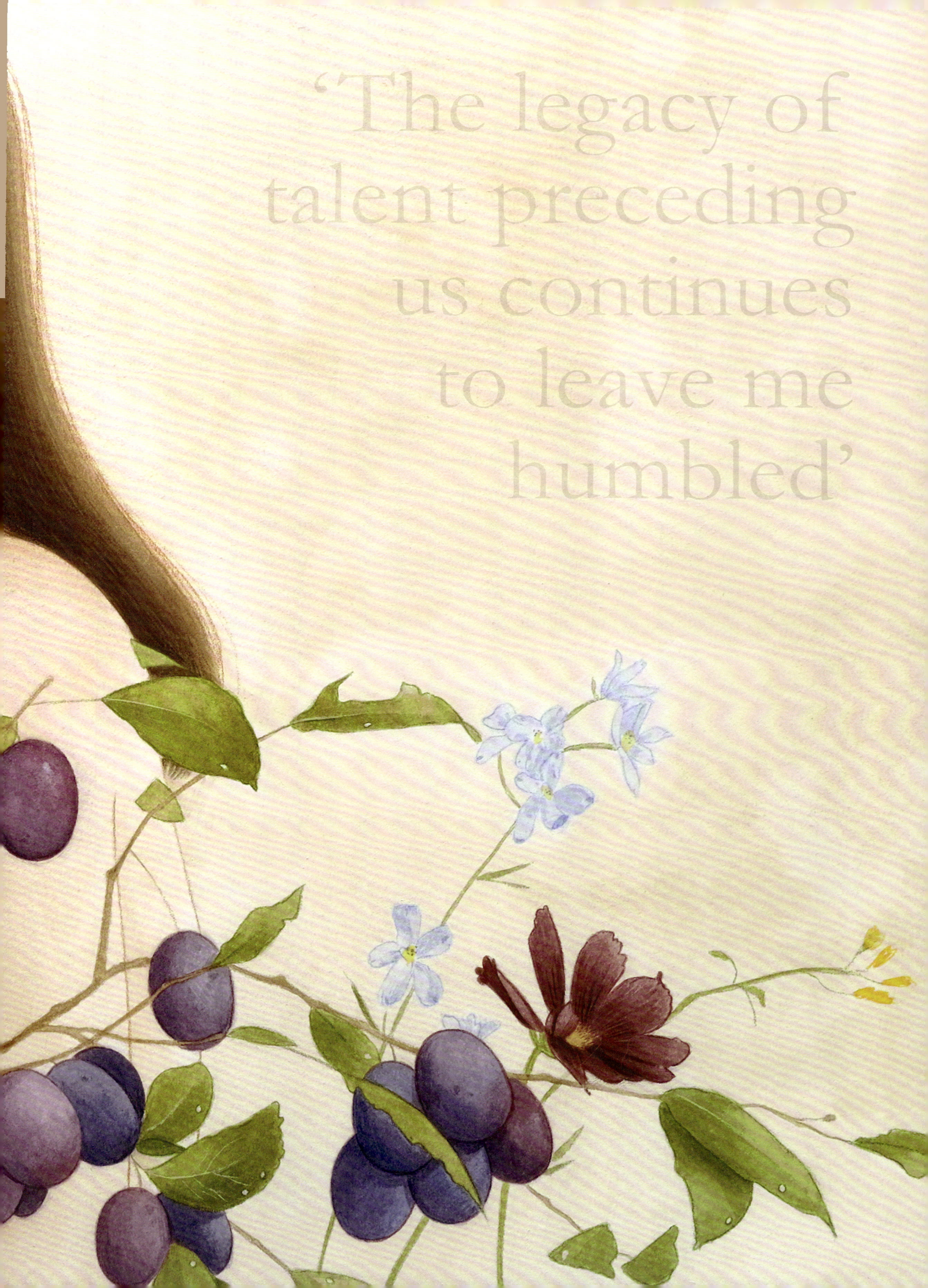

'The legacy of
talent preceding
us continues
to leave me
humbled'

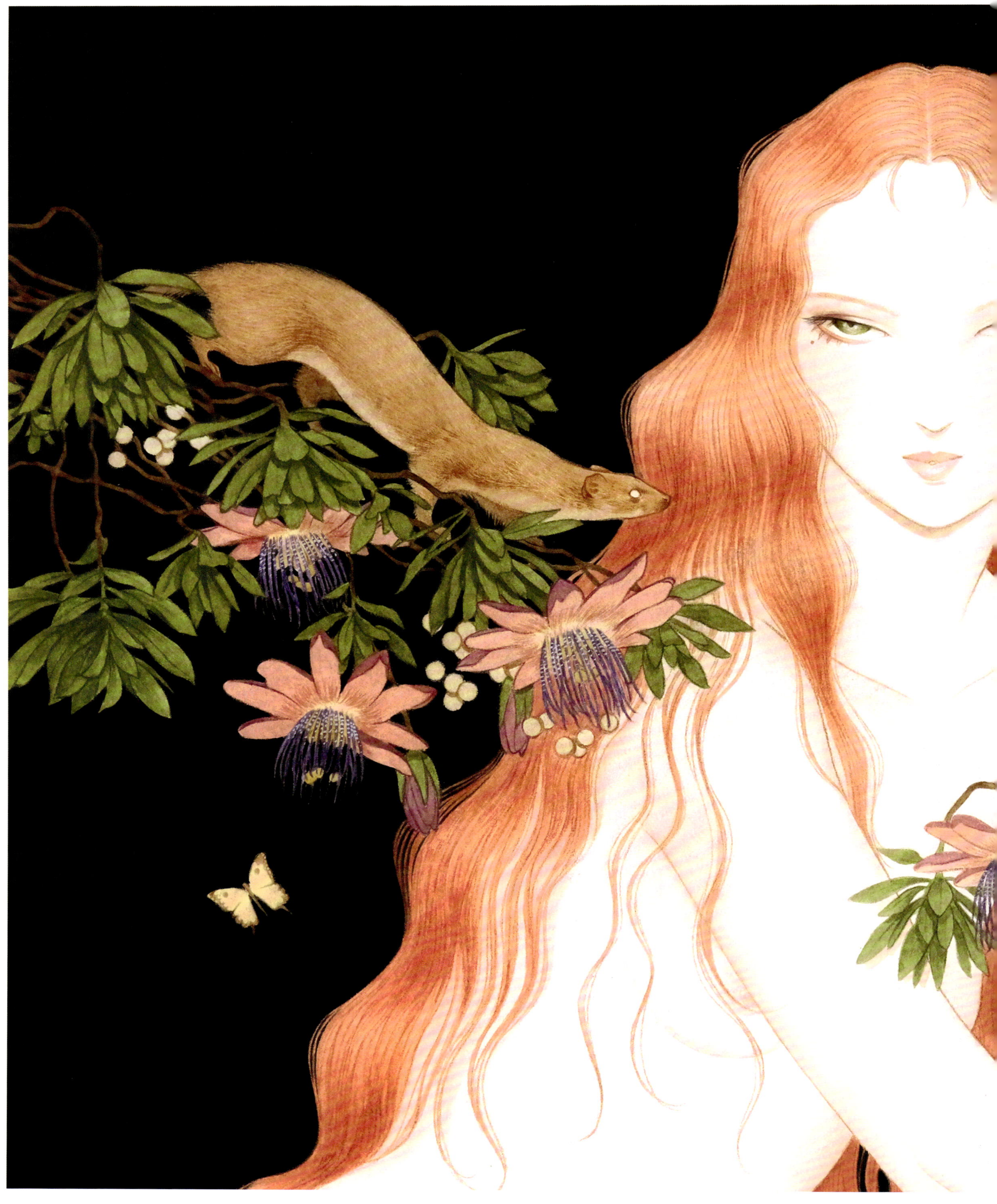

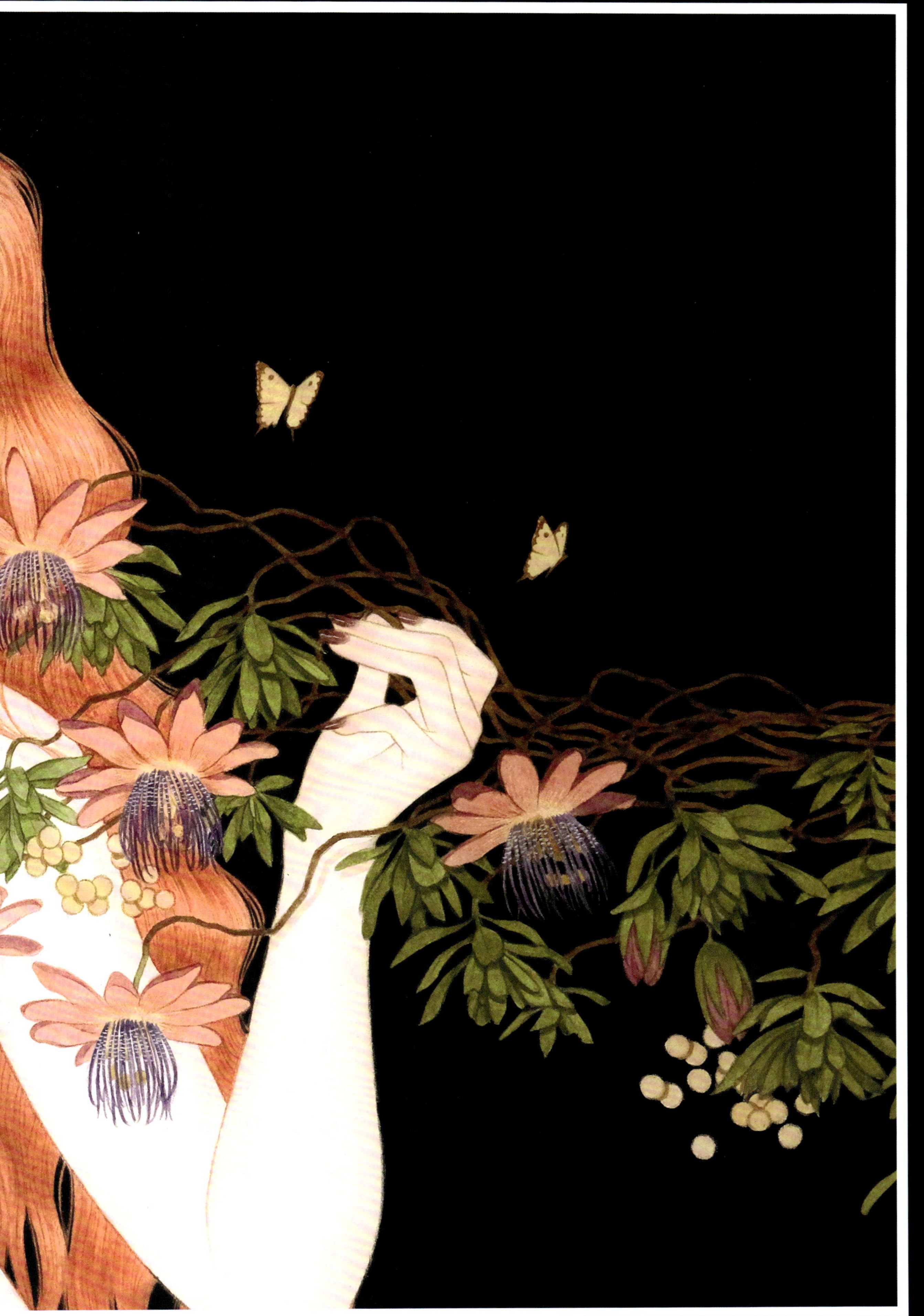

ON PREVIOUS PAGE:
Pomona

LEFT:
Hera and Galanthis

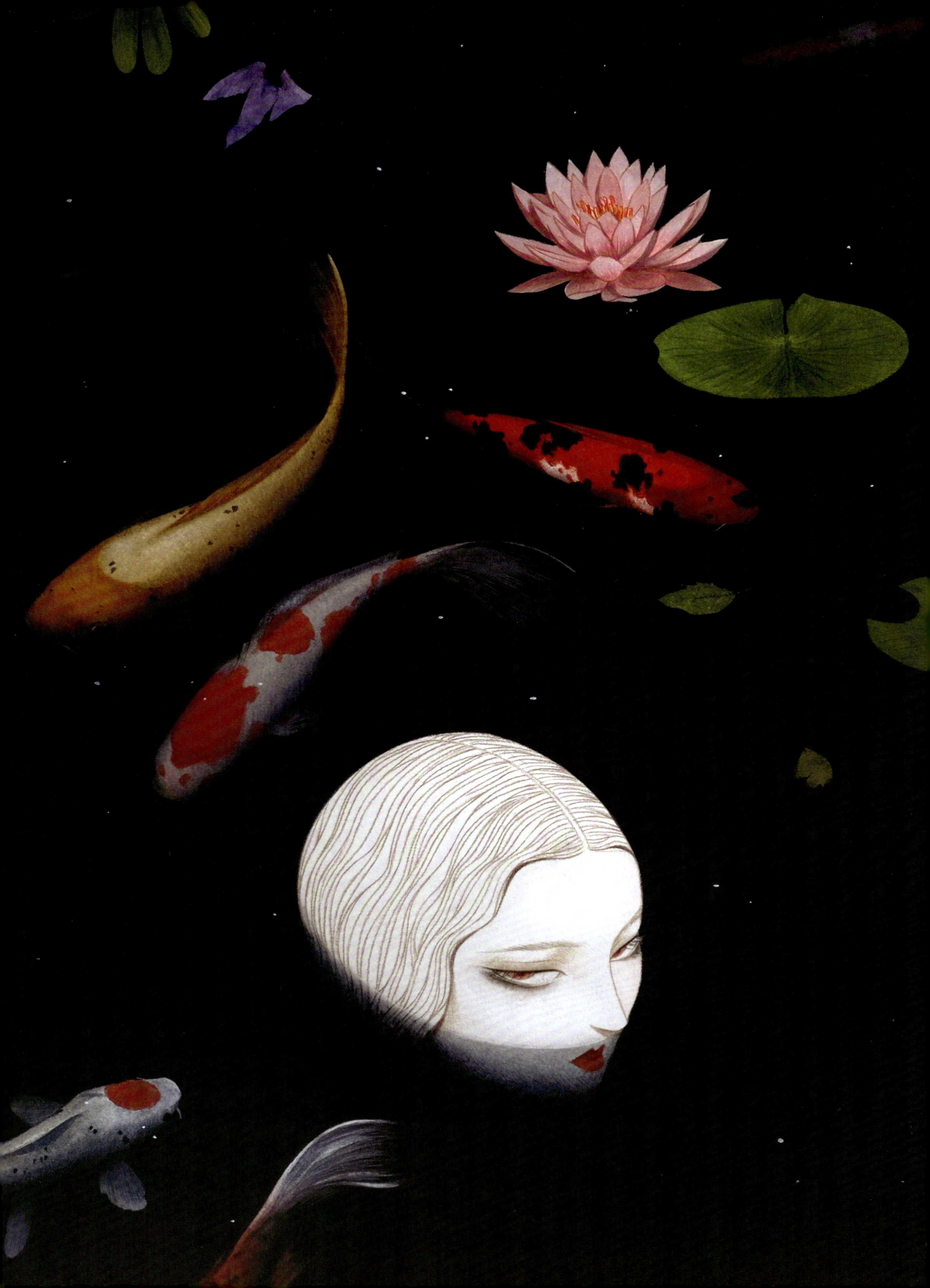

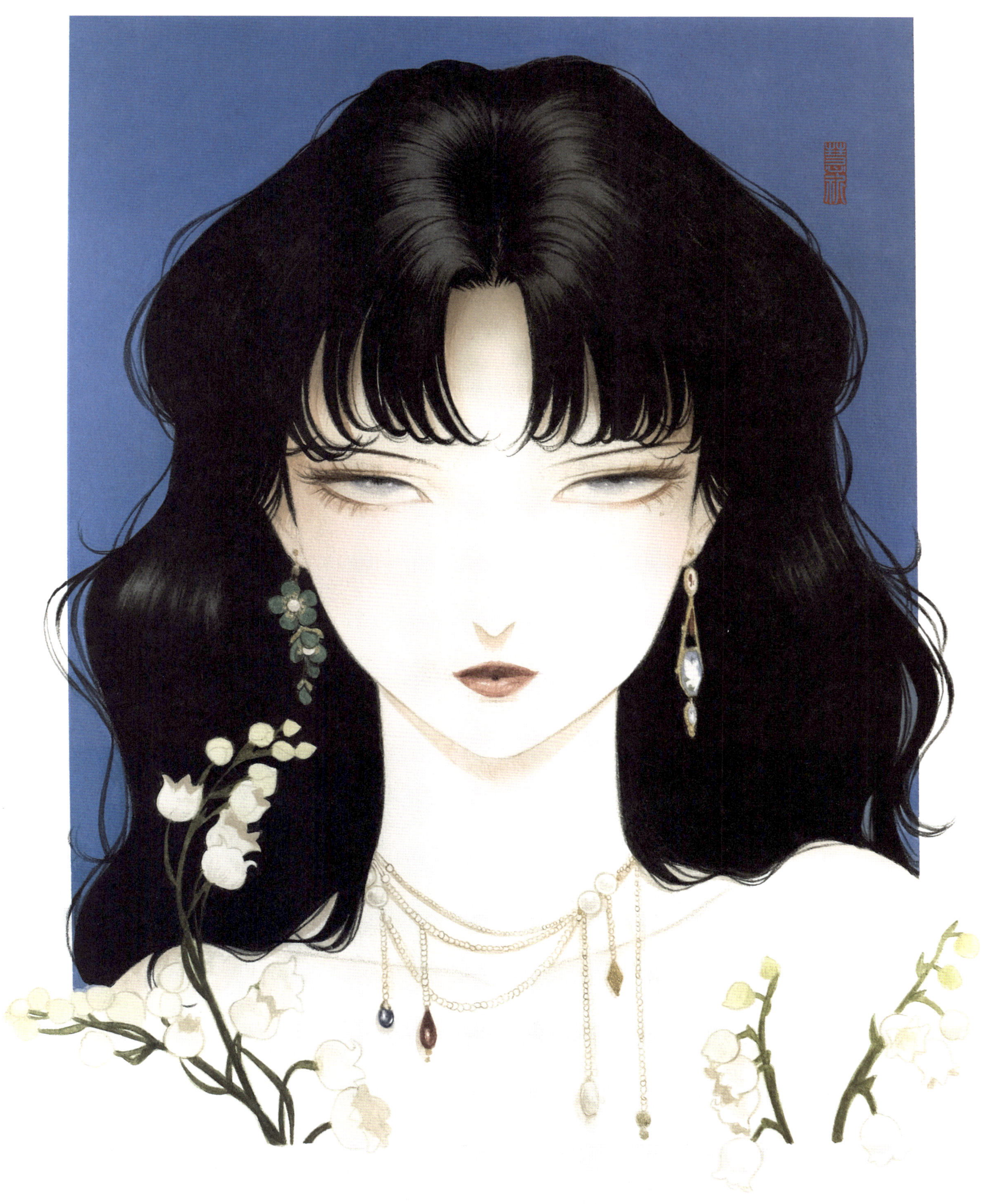

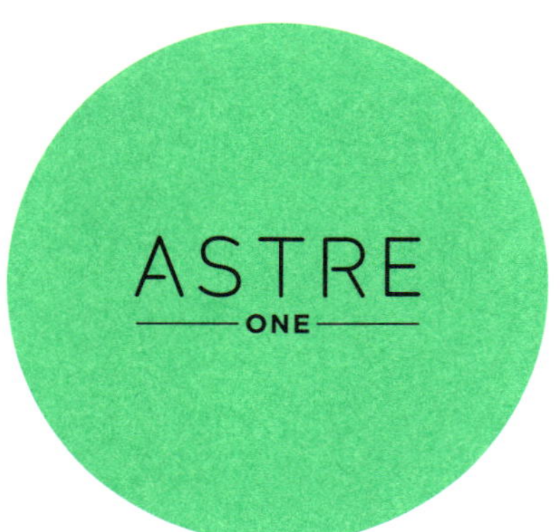

LILLIAN BY JANICE SUNG

— ASTRE ORIGINAL PRINT —

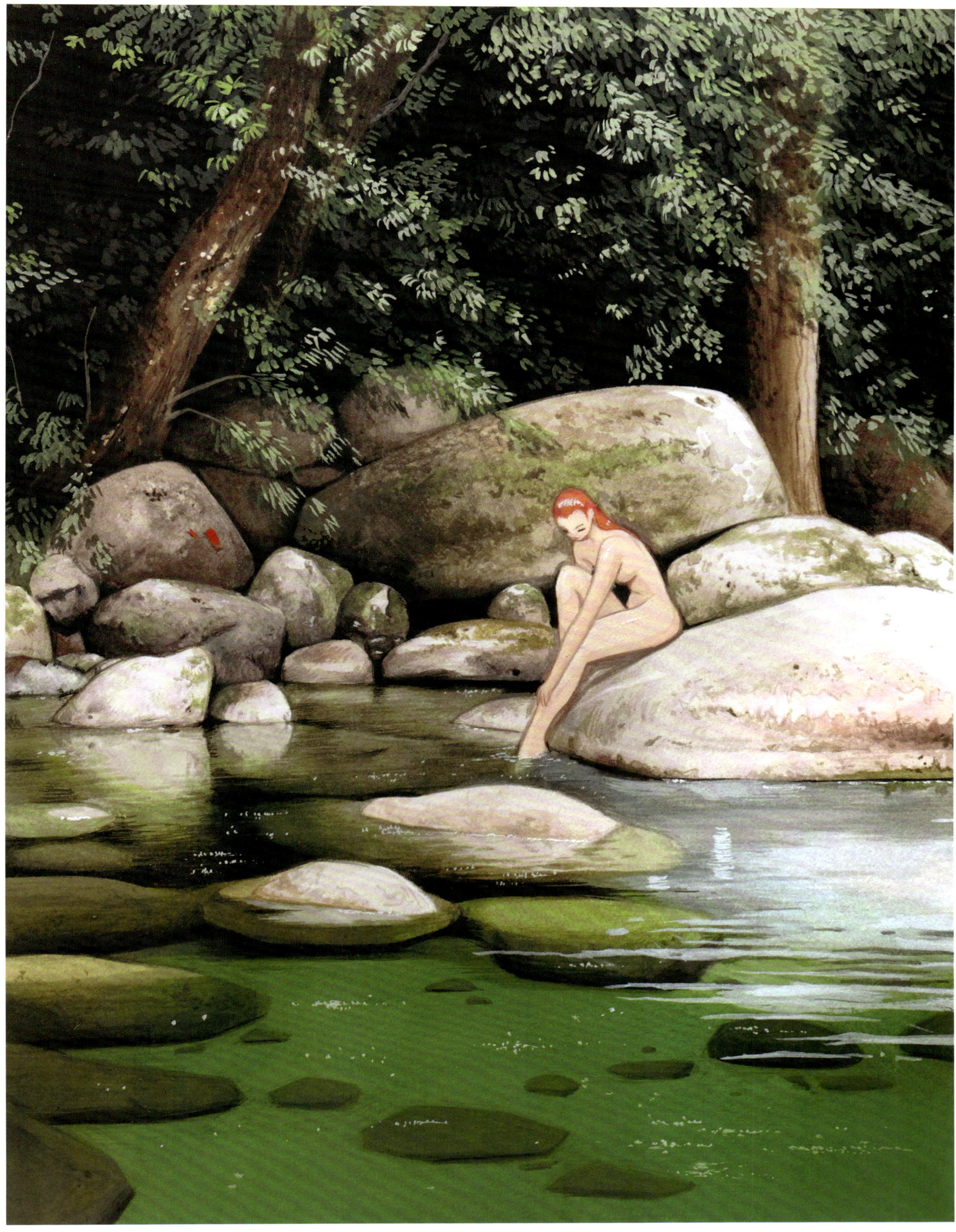

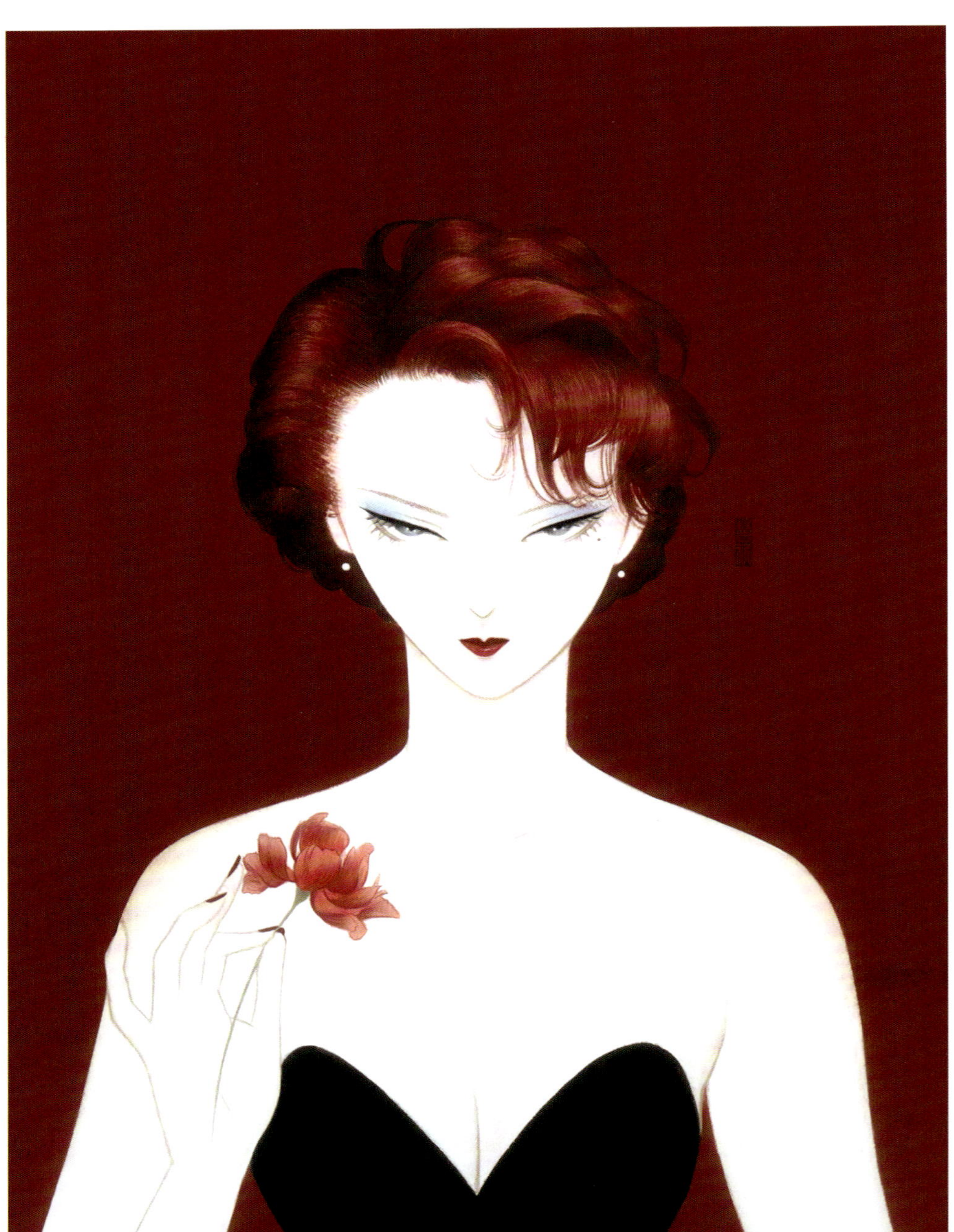

Frequently, I draw inspiration from the Neoclassical, Baroque, and Renaissance periods. I'm particularly enamoured by artwork showcasing ethereal women, their skin radiating an otherworldly glow, gracefully posed against dark backdrops that accentuate their presence. I also hold a deep affection for the landscape paintings of those eras as well. Above all, it's the remarkable craftsmanship and techniques employed during those times that truly ignite my creative spirit. The legacy of talent preceding us continues to leave me humbled and in admiration.

While my artistic preferences may undergo constant shifts, there are certain artists who will forever hold a place in my heart and serve as a wellspring of inspiration. Among these notable figures are Gustav Klimt, Ferdinand Keller, and John William Godward, to name just a few. Beyond their mastery, their creations possess a timeless quality that resonates deeply with me.

When I'm not working, you'll often find me hanging out with my partner and our dog. We have a love for venturing into the great outdoors, whether it's hiking or simply unwinding on the beach. I also love gardening – being able to grow our own fruits and vegetables lately has been so rewarding. As a naturally creative individual, I also dabble in various other artistic activities, including pottery and photography. I'm always on the lookout for fresh and imaginative outlets for my creativity. △

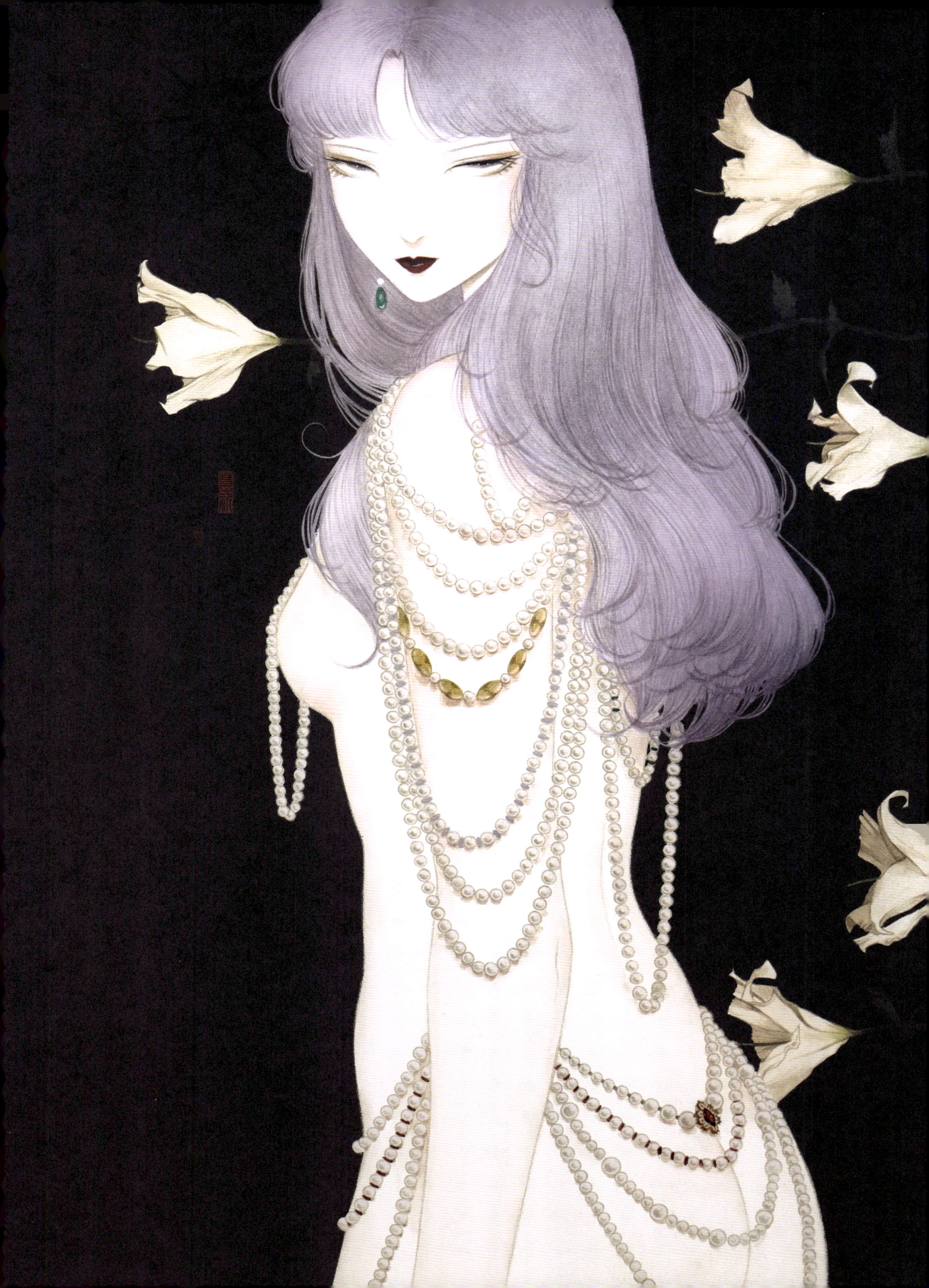

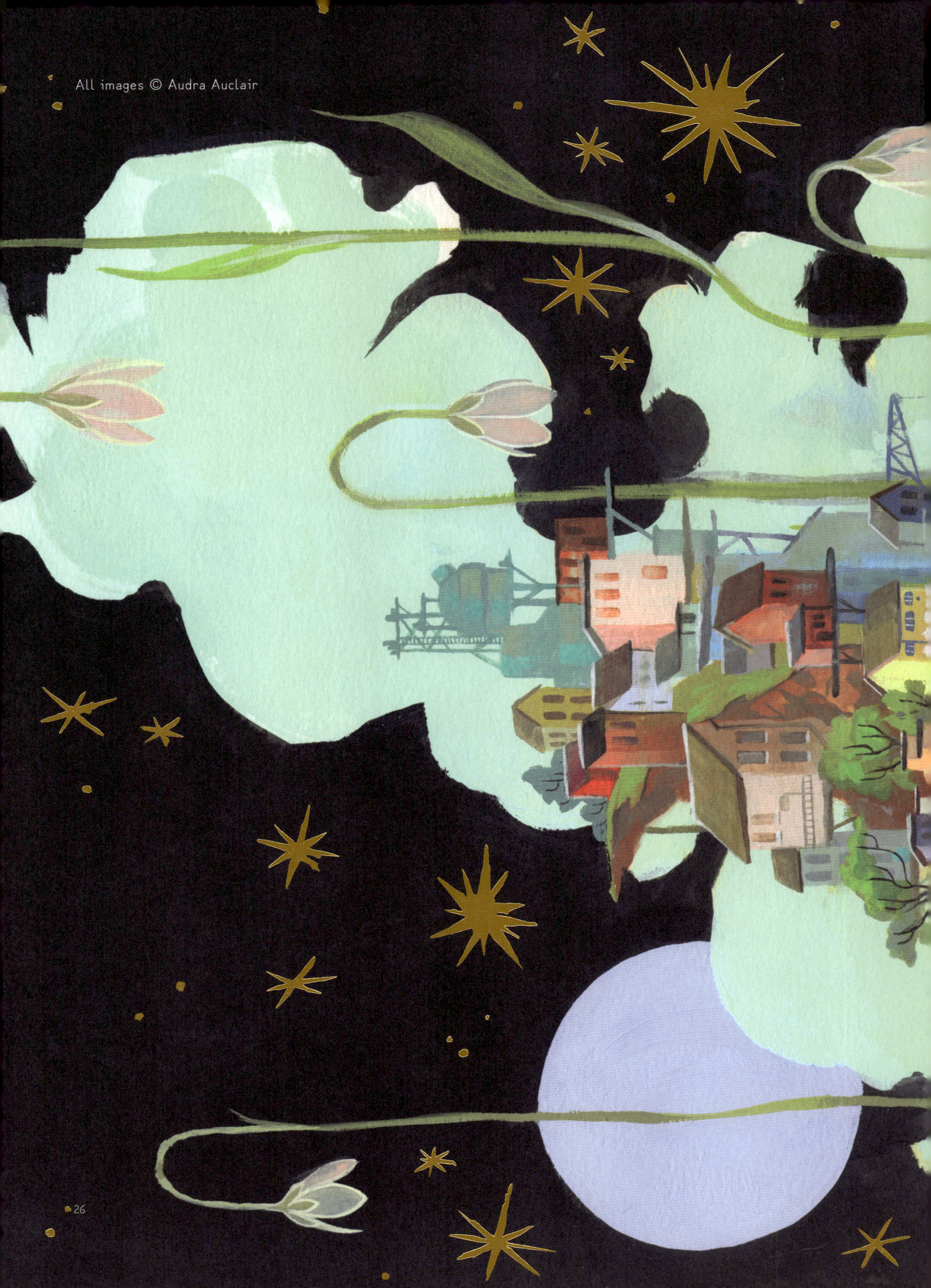

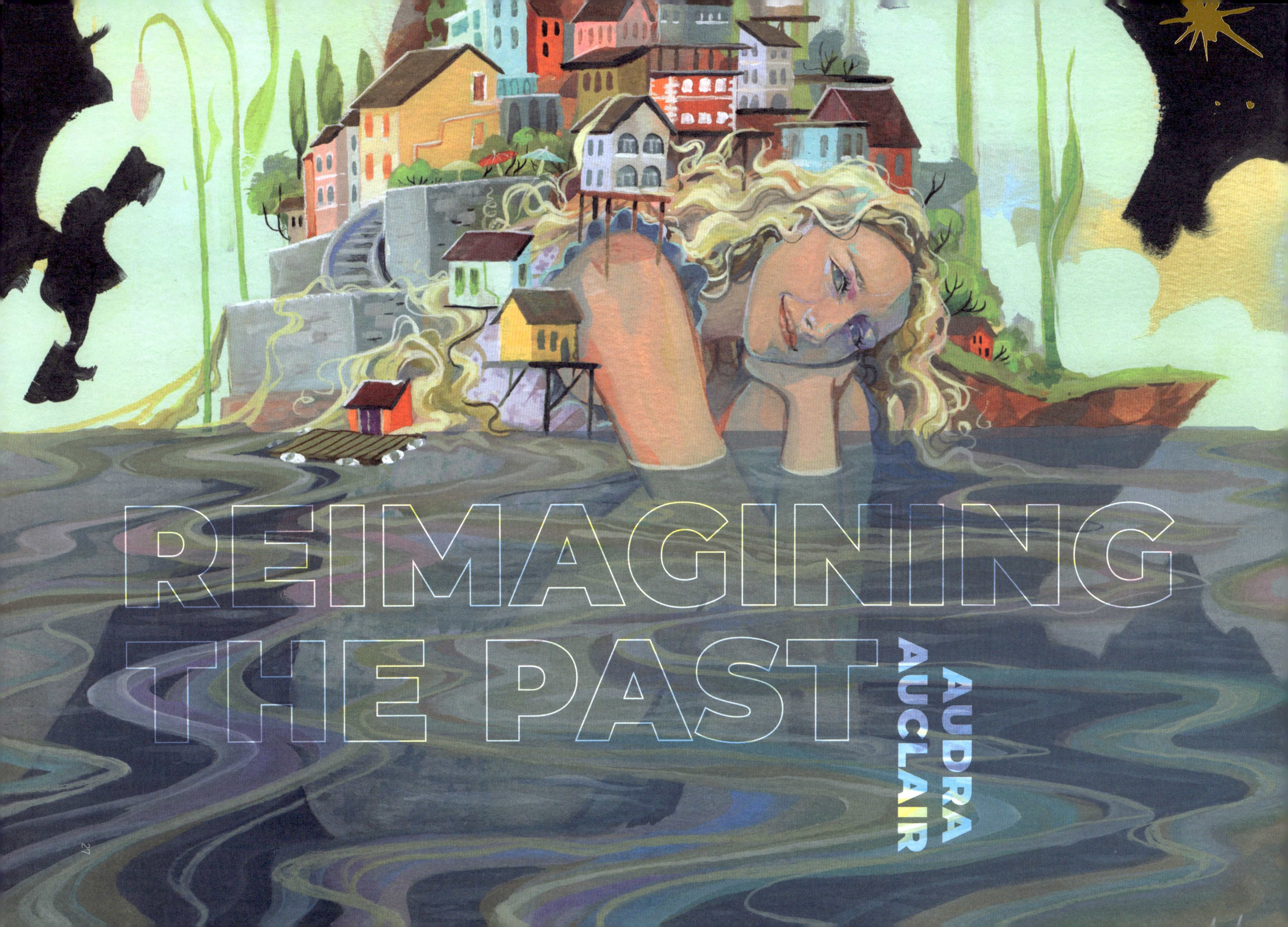
REIMAGINING
THE PAST
AUDRA AUCLAIR

For my ASTRE original print I wanted to recreate my piece *Under the Surface*, which I made back in 2012. It was a painting that depicted a woman as the foundation of a ramshackle island town. At the time, the meaning of the painting seemed clear to me, in that it was about someone feeling an immense amount of pressure. I think it was created from a place of feeling overwhelmed, a fear of adulthood, as well as some 'eldest daughter syndrome'.

I've always been fond of the original version of this piece. It was one of those works in my life that said to me, 'This is proof you are going in the right direction.' I felt it translated my emotions to the canvas in a way that felt understandable, but it was still a piece that could be put on a wall. Of course, as more time passed, I noticed flaws in the anatomy and there were stylistic choices I didn't appreciate as much. The concept was still so strong to me that I felt it deserved a rebirth and I was curious what that rebirth would look like. My first rendition of this concept was done in a totally different medium and it was very small, so the detail was limited. Back then, I was still afraid of colour, references, and shading, so the idea of painting it again on a bigger scale and with a different medium was exciting to me.

Revisiting a piece like this is something I hadn't done before, but it's a process I would love to do again if I could find the patience, as there are a few paintings of mine that I think deserve a revival. The process for this painting was a bit different than usual – because it was tied to a specific project, I took it more seriously, by printing out many references and getting my lovely niece to be my muse, for instance. Plus, I forced myself to work on it quicker than I normally would. I found myself enjoying the loose elements of the painting, like the stars, flowers, and the hair in the water. I can say that I'm fairly pleased with the outcome.

My revived version of *Under the Surface* (shown on the previous spread and pull-out print) was created with Holbein gouache and acrylic gouache on a large piece of watercolour paper. I wanted my new, revised painting to be more detailed and colourful than the original, while still maintaining the same concept. I took photos of my niece, Vienna, for reference, and gathered various photos of cliffside towns. I taped the reference images, the border of my Fabriano paper, a palette, and a piece of shop paper towel to my drafting table. I sketched the image out first on the large sheet of paper and, after some tweaks, I went ahead and began painting. I initially aimed to make a gouache-only painting with a sunset background, but after creating the sunset I decided to use acrylic gouache to make it a night scene – that way, the subjects would stand out more and create a mystical vibe. That mystical look became something I really wanted to imbue in the painting.

I made a mistake partway through the painting where some water dripped down the black of the sky. I was going to just paint over it, but instead it gave me the idea of creating large flowers to add an element of growth to the painting. The clouds were added for some extra colour and to make the background feel more dynamic. I wasn't entirely sure how I was going to render the hair, but I wanted it to have a lot of movement and colour to balance out the black of the sky, so it became a bit of a pastel rainbow. The houses were a gradual process of blocking out the colours, adding roofs, then windows, and then finally other little details, like drainpipes and barrels. I love featuring metallic elements in my paintings, so I added some stars to help break up the painting and get some shine on the paper.

My niece had a slight smile in the reference photo I was using and I pondered for a long time whether I wanted to keep it, because the painting was initially about struggle. The more I reflected on my life since the original painting, the more I recognized that keeping the smile was important. Like me, my niece is an eldest daughter and I see a lot of myself in her, despite not being related by blood. She faces her own struggles, but she is a smiley, creative, and funny kid. I am a goofball to my core and consider my humour my defining feature, aside from being an 'artist' – it's taken me a while to see that. I've always had moments of laughter, even in my darkest days, so it made sense to me to keep the smile in the painting, despite the weight on the subject's shoulders. I want this painting to show some contentment underneath the struggle.

Under the Surface | *This is the original version of my* ASTRE *exclusive print. I took inspiration from Picasso because I wanted to make her look crushed and crumpled under the weight of the house, almost like she was in a box. I'm glad that I kept the ramshackle grungy appearance of the city and the strings of lights and wires in the new piece*

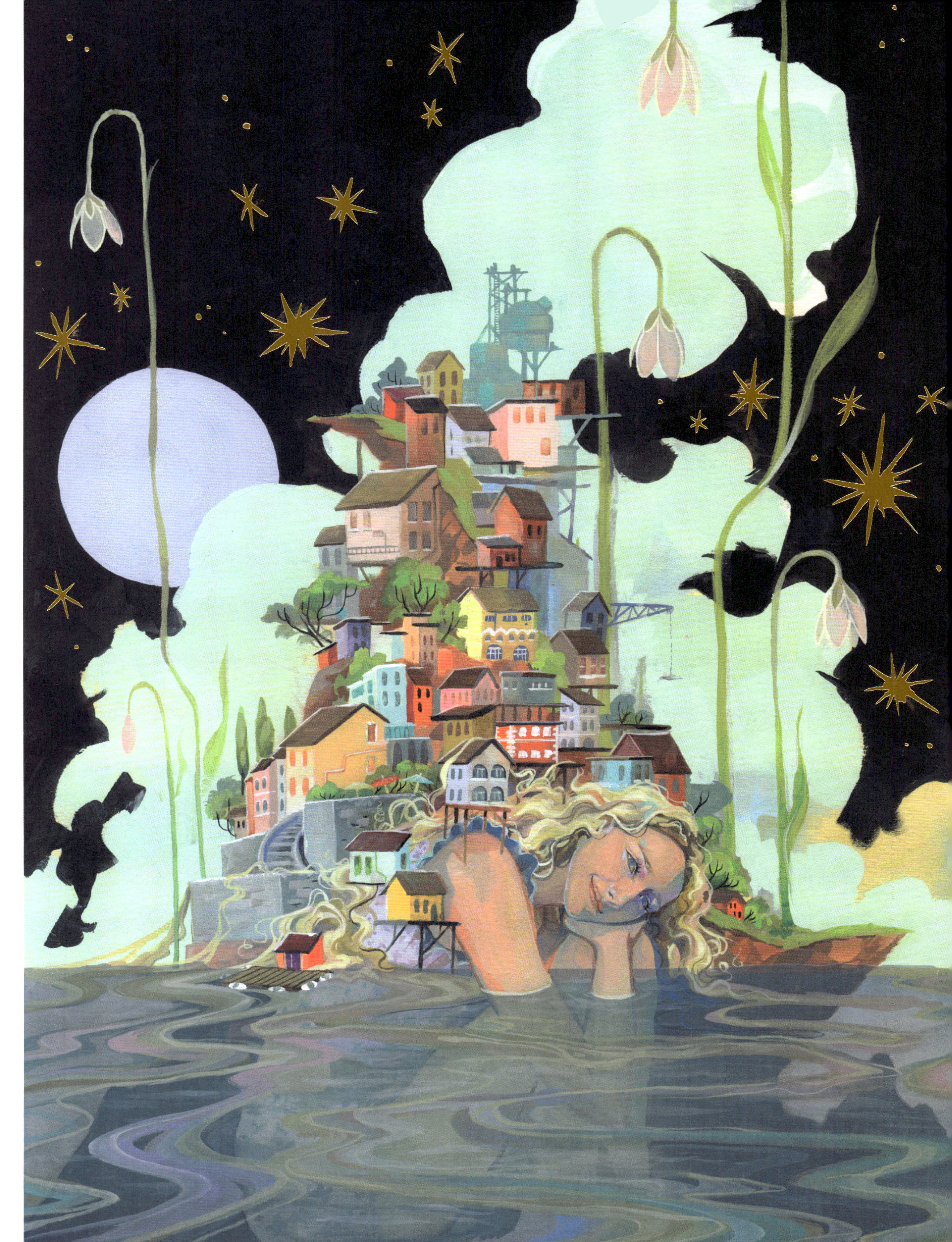

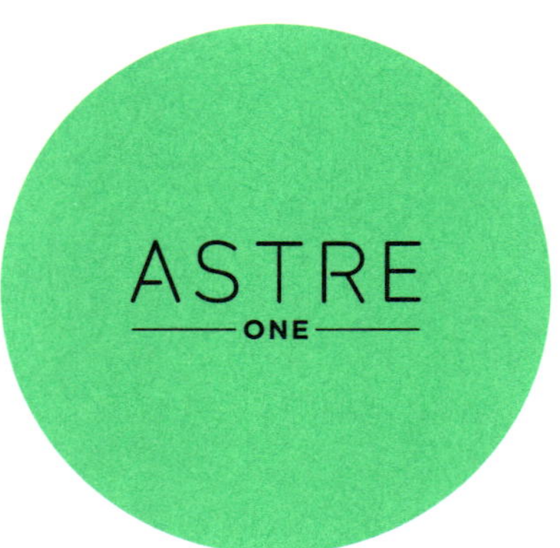

UNDER THE SURFACE BY AUDRA AUCLAIR

— ASTRE ORIGINAL PRINT —

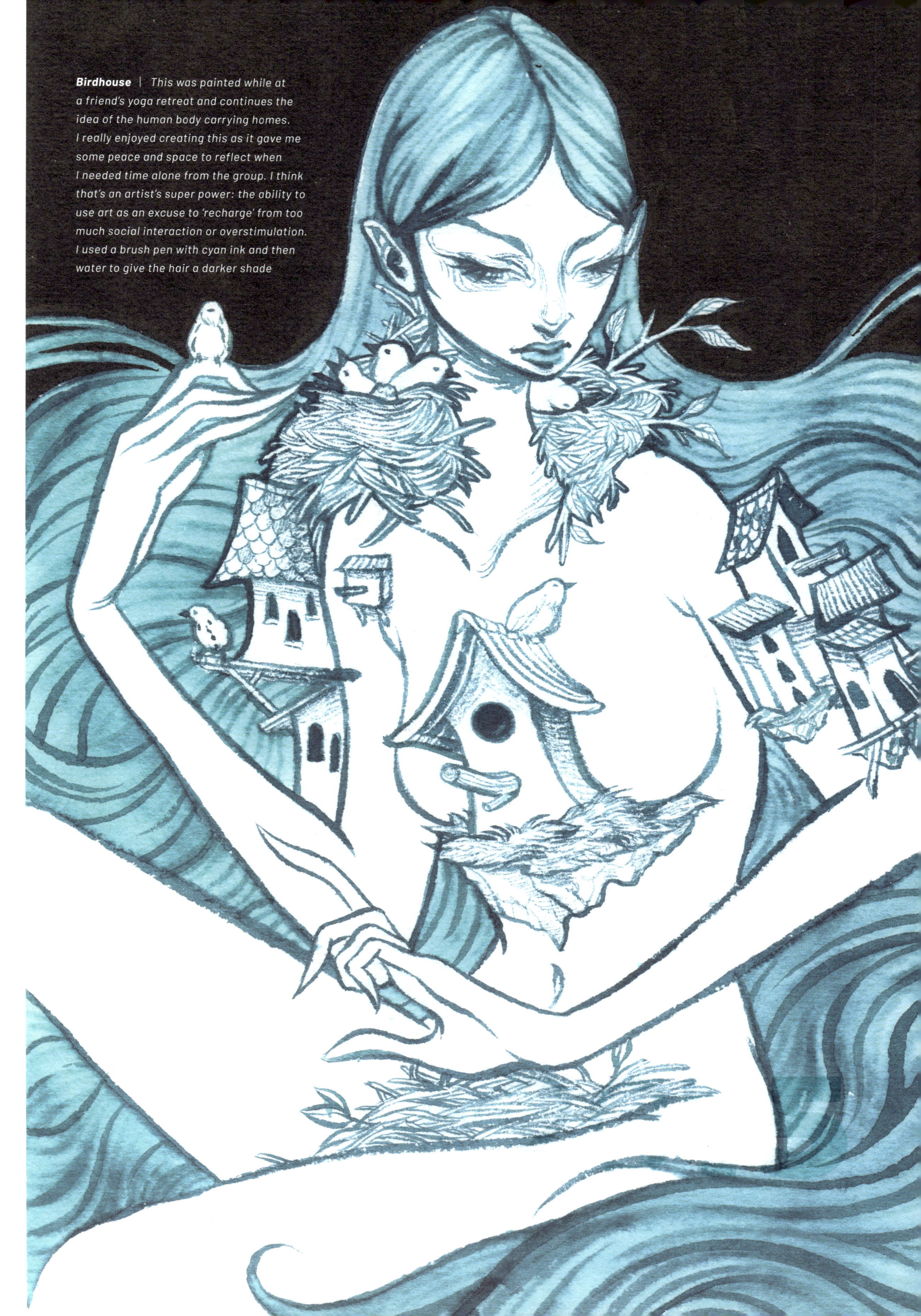

Birdhouse | This was painted while at a friend's yoga retreat and continues the idea of the human body carrying homes. I really enjoyed creating this as it gave me some peace and space to reflect when I needed time alone from the group. I think that's an artist's super power: the ability to use art as an excuse to 'recharge' from too much social interaction or overstimulation. I used a brush pen with cyan ink and then water to give the hair a darker shade

Tokyo Heartache | You can tell I started to use the themes of an urban sprawl on the human body more as my career developed. The thought that someone could carry around so many thoughts and ideas, and so much history really spoke to me. I'll be honest, I don't recall the original title of this one, but I do remember being influenced by my lifelong dream to travel to Japan (which I did later that year.) I used a standard ballpoint pen, which created very silky hair textures and lots of fun details. My friend worked at the local art store at the time and she delivered some Japanese papers to me, which I cut up and used for the kimono-inspired robe

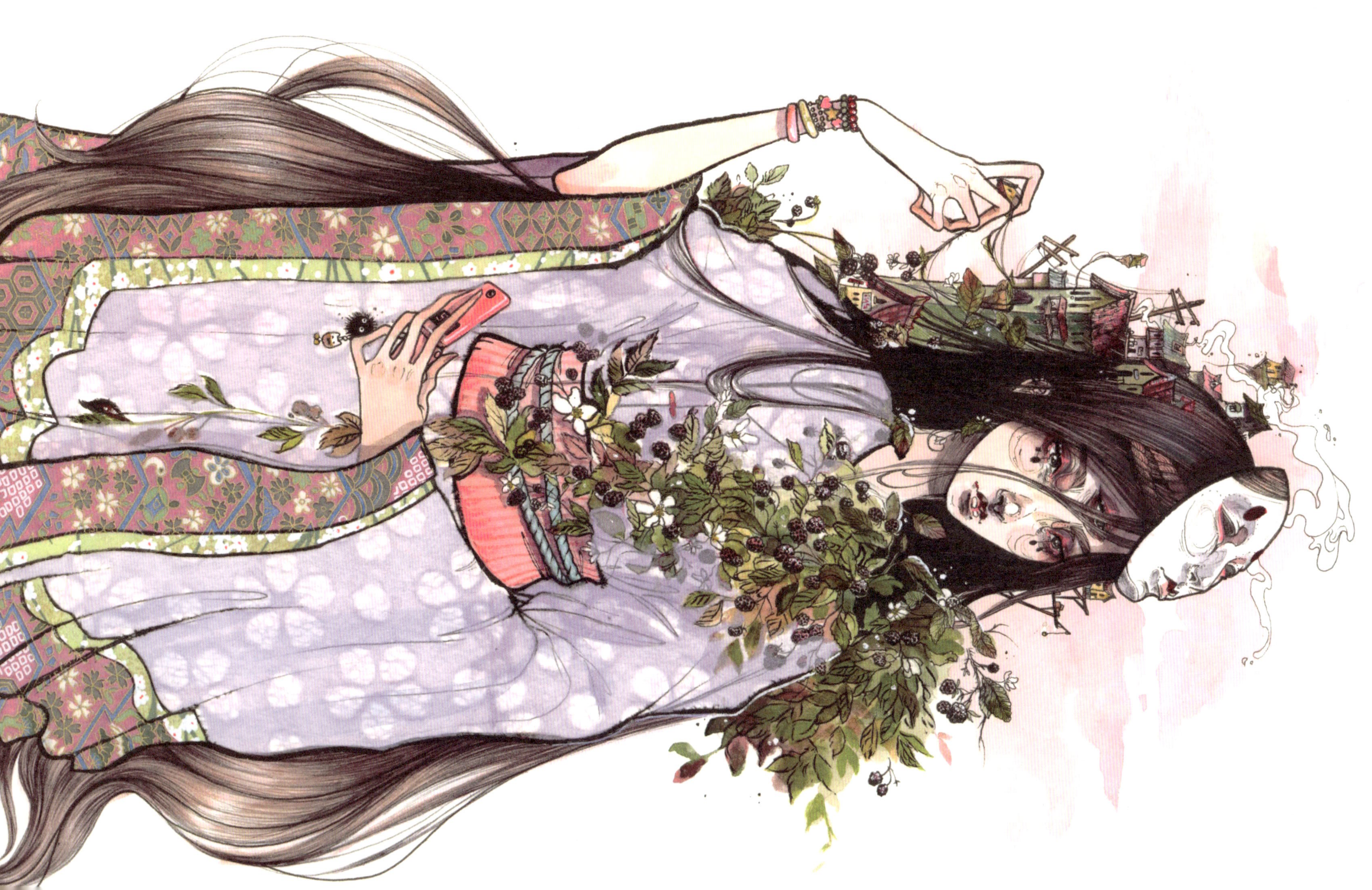

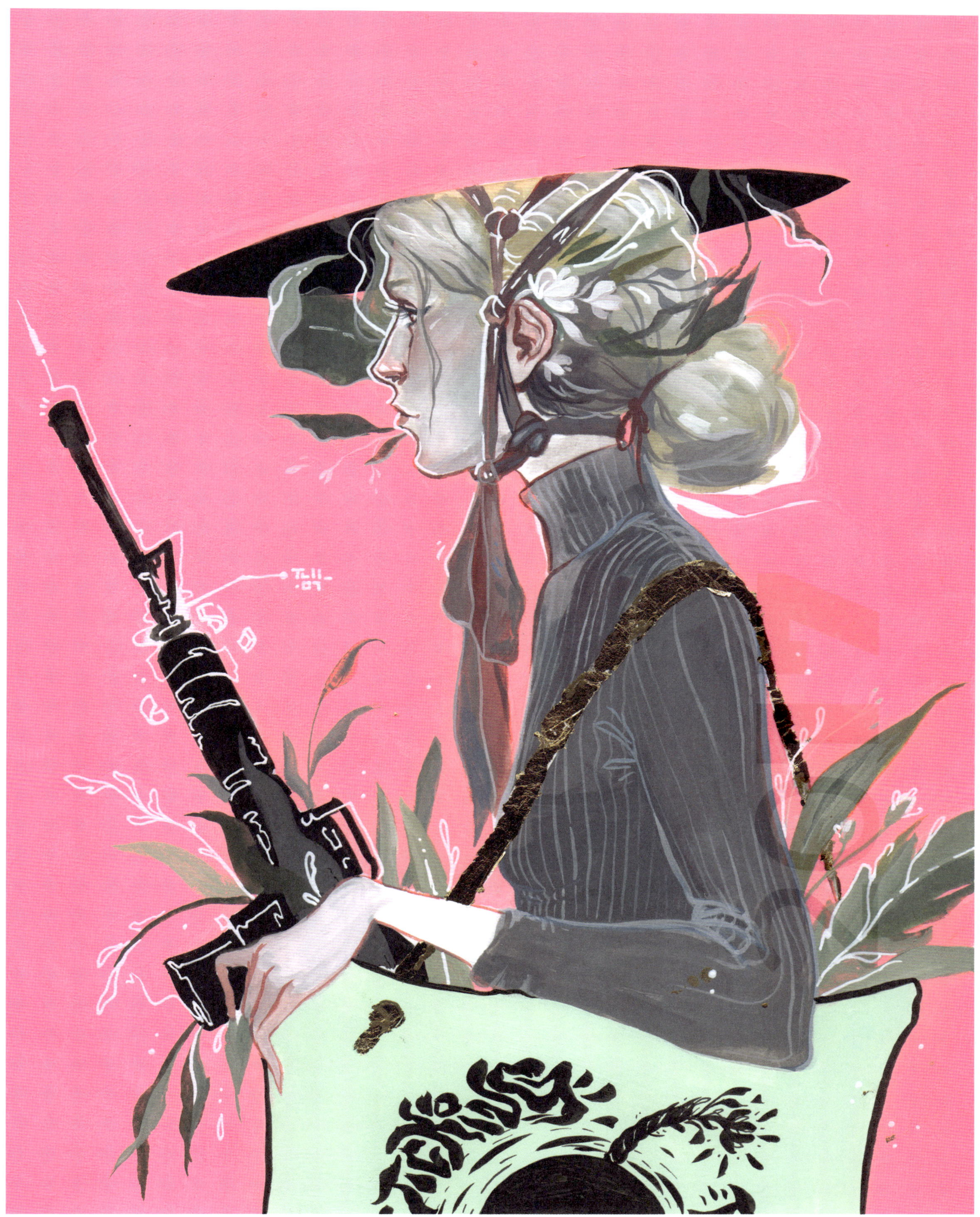

Beau Monde | *Here, I began experimenting more with creating realistic figures, while still distorting them to fit my desired composition. The title translates to 'fashionable society' – the painting was a tongue-in-cheek take on the strange gun culture in the US. With her head in a hole, this character is ignoring the harm guns can cause to innocents. I used gouache, acrylic gouache, white gel pen, black brush pen, and some roughly applied gold leaf on the shopping bag's handle*

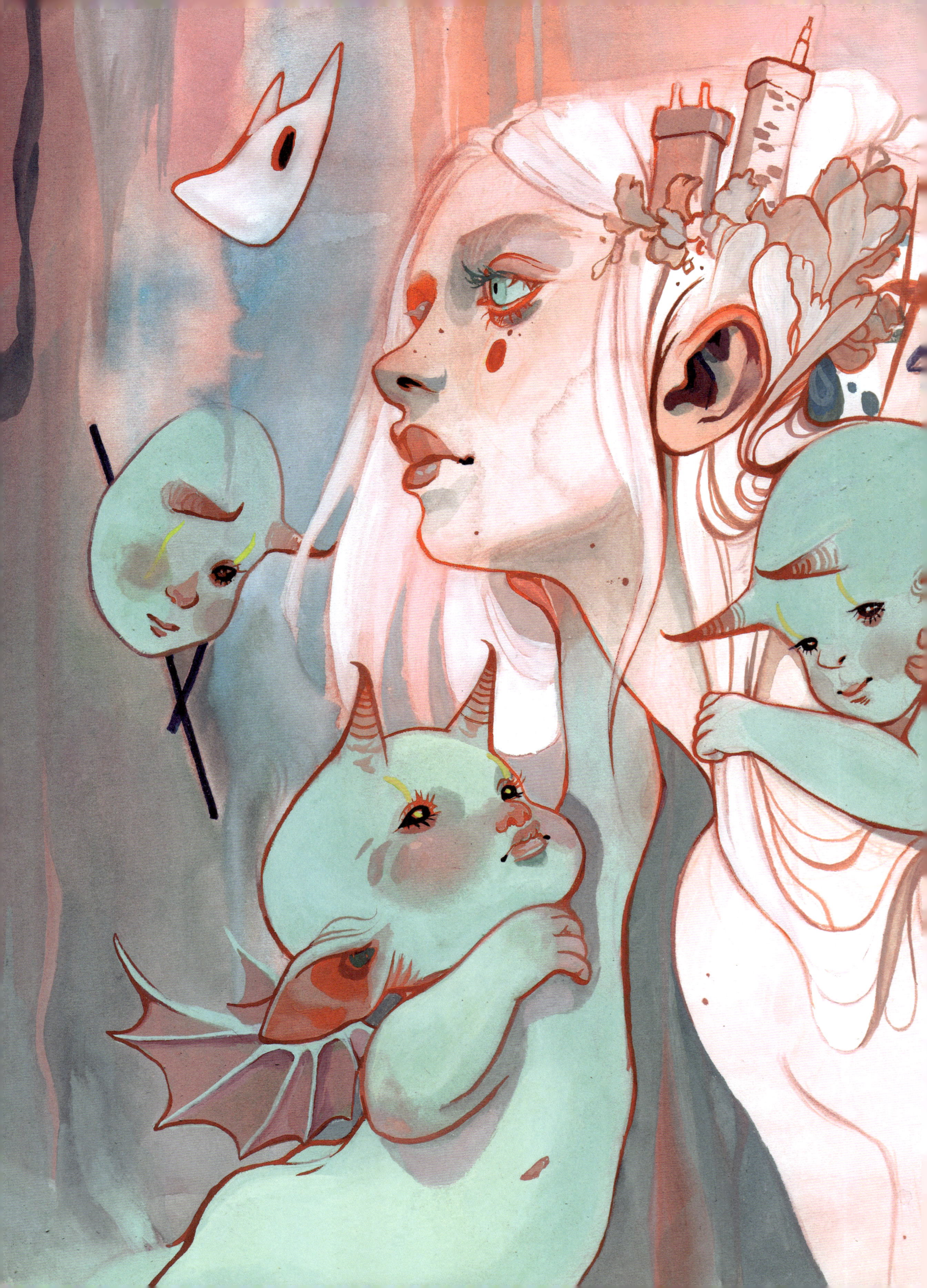

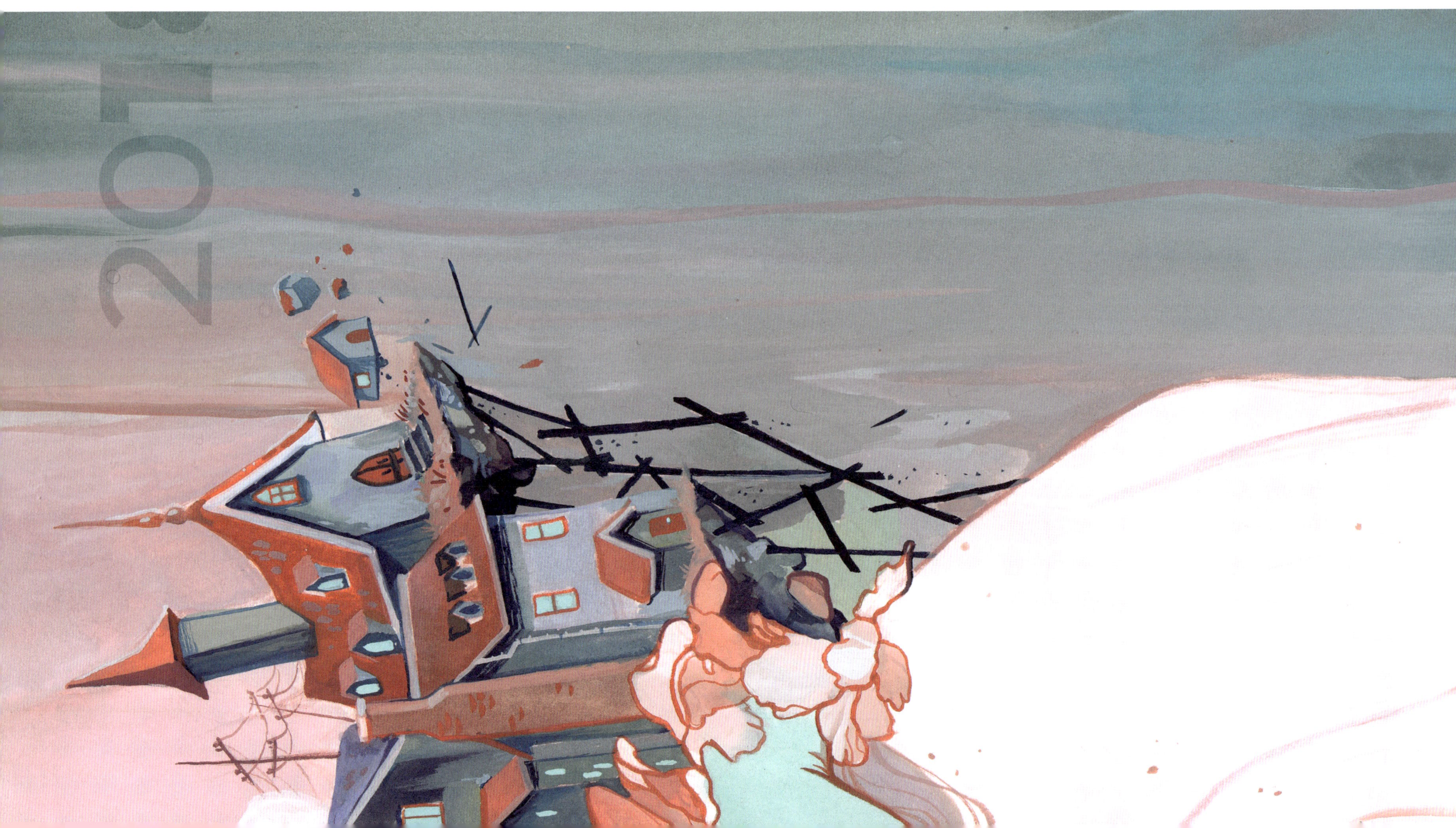

Scatterling | Again, I wanted to convey pressure with the vibe of this painting, but I also really wanted to try painting babies. I'm not sure why – I think this is the only time I've painted them. This was when I started experimenting more with dripping and blending gouache. I used watercolour and gouache for this but I used acrylic gouache for the base of the baby skin. You can tell from my work over the years that I really enjoy using this seafoam colour

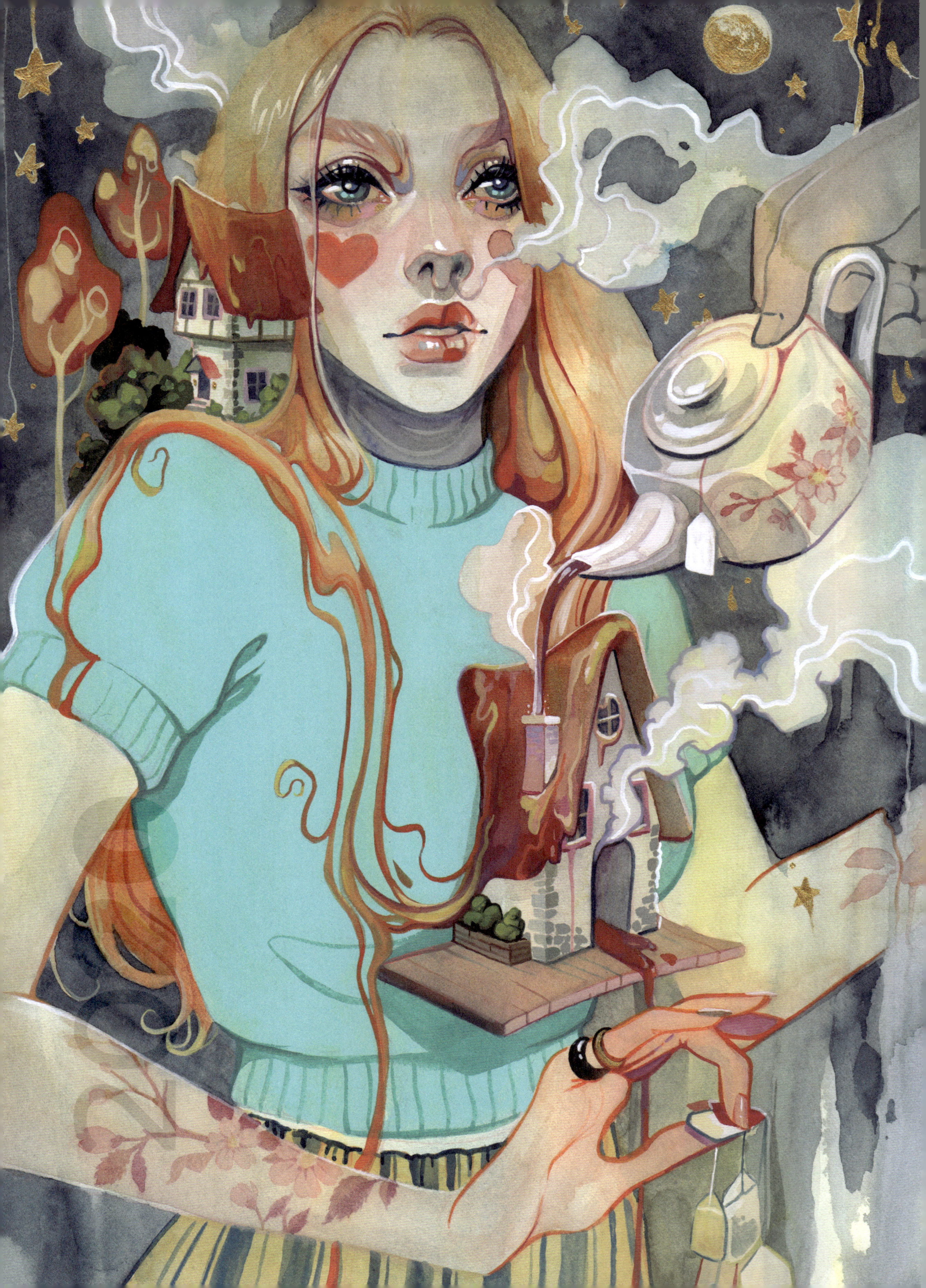

Autumn Tea | As time passed, I gradually
became more comfortable with adding more
detailed surroundings and took more risks by
painting things I wouldn't normally attempt
due to fear of failure. This was my first time
painting a teapot or something with that
texture. I began using nature and stylizing it
more because I was going out and doing
plein-air paintings. For this piece, I really
wanted to instil a cosy, sleepy vibe. I used
gouache, acrylic gouache, and gold gouache
to add a metallic shine to the stars and moon

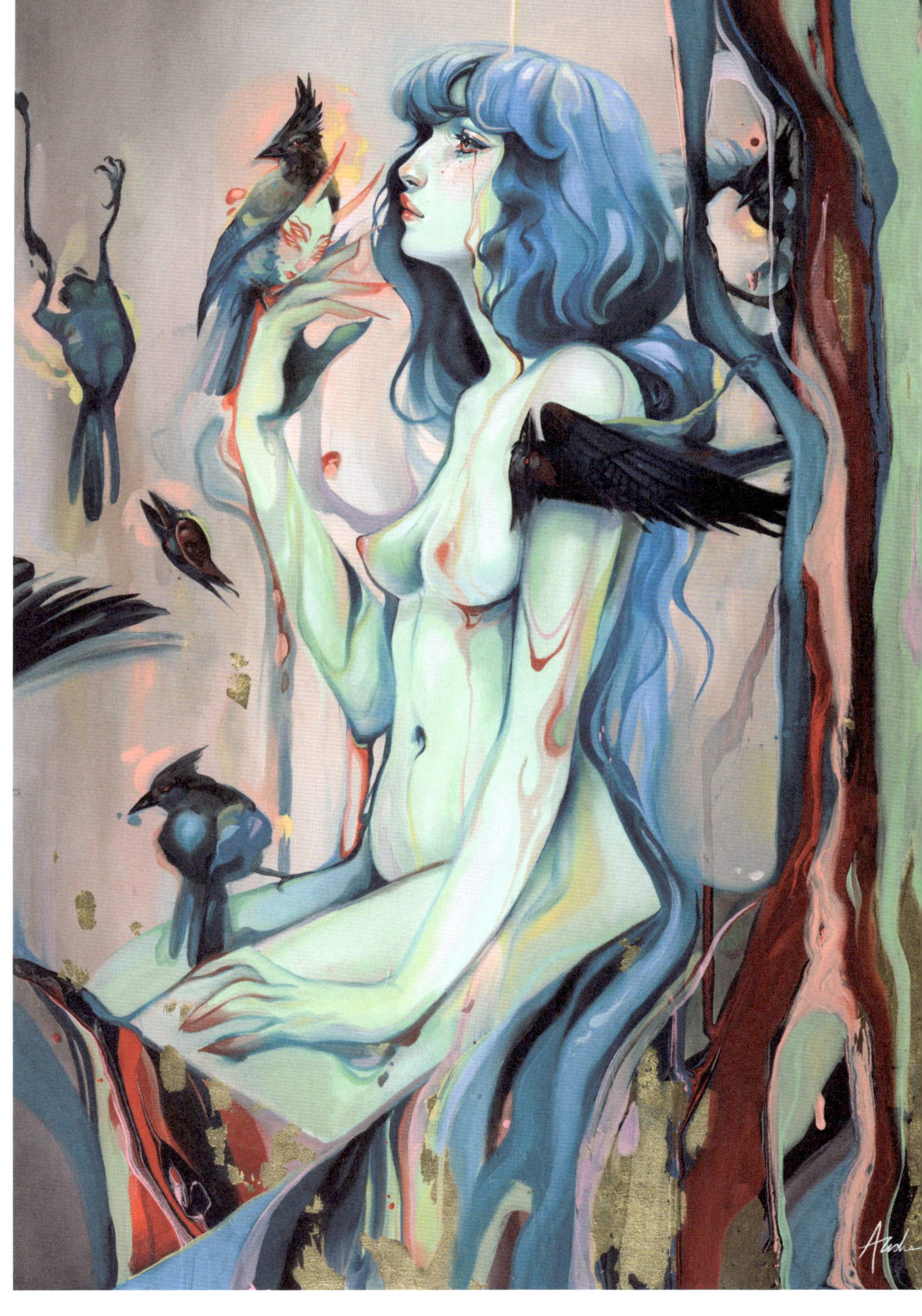

Death & Transformation | This was the first
and only time I ever used the acrylic pour
method. I'd seen it done many times, but not
with a painted subject added. I would like to
do more pieces like this, because I loved the
outcome. It scratched my itch for that sort
of dripping look, but my floor became a bit
of a mess in the process – it was challenging
to do in an apartment with cats! I painted
over the acrylic pour with oil paints. I was
becoming more comfortable with painting
animals, but I wish I could go back in time
and remove the face on the Steller's jay's
chest and add some clothing. I used to avoid
clothing because I wasn't confident with it,
but I think it would've been a great addition

Patience With a Wolf | *This was painted with gouache and acrylic gouache, and accompanied by a manga-style screentone on the hair. With this piece I spent a lot of time focusing on the face, aiming for a mix of bright colours in combination with a dark meaning. I spent many years painting wolves as a metaphor for depression. It's been interesting, while going through my old work, to see this collaboration between art and depression taking shape without me realizing. This motif began as a wolf carrying flowers, then became a wolf mask as the depression got worse, and then finally the wolf's maw surrounding the character's entire face, like in this piece*

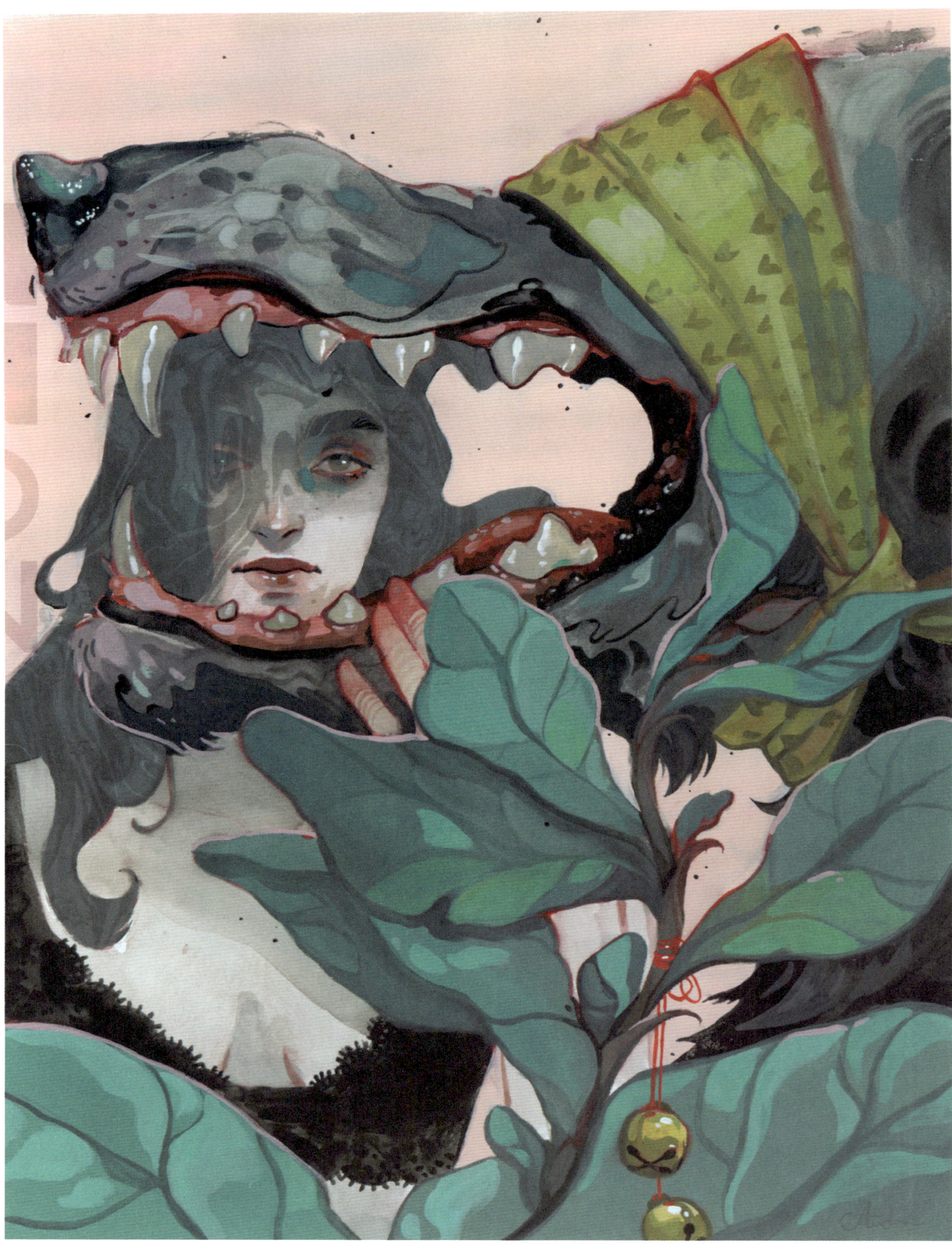

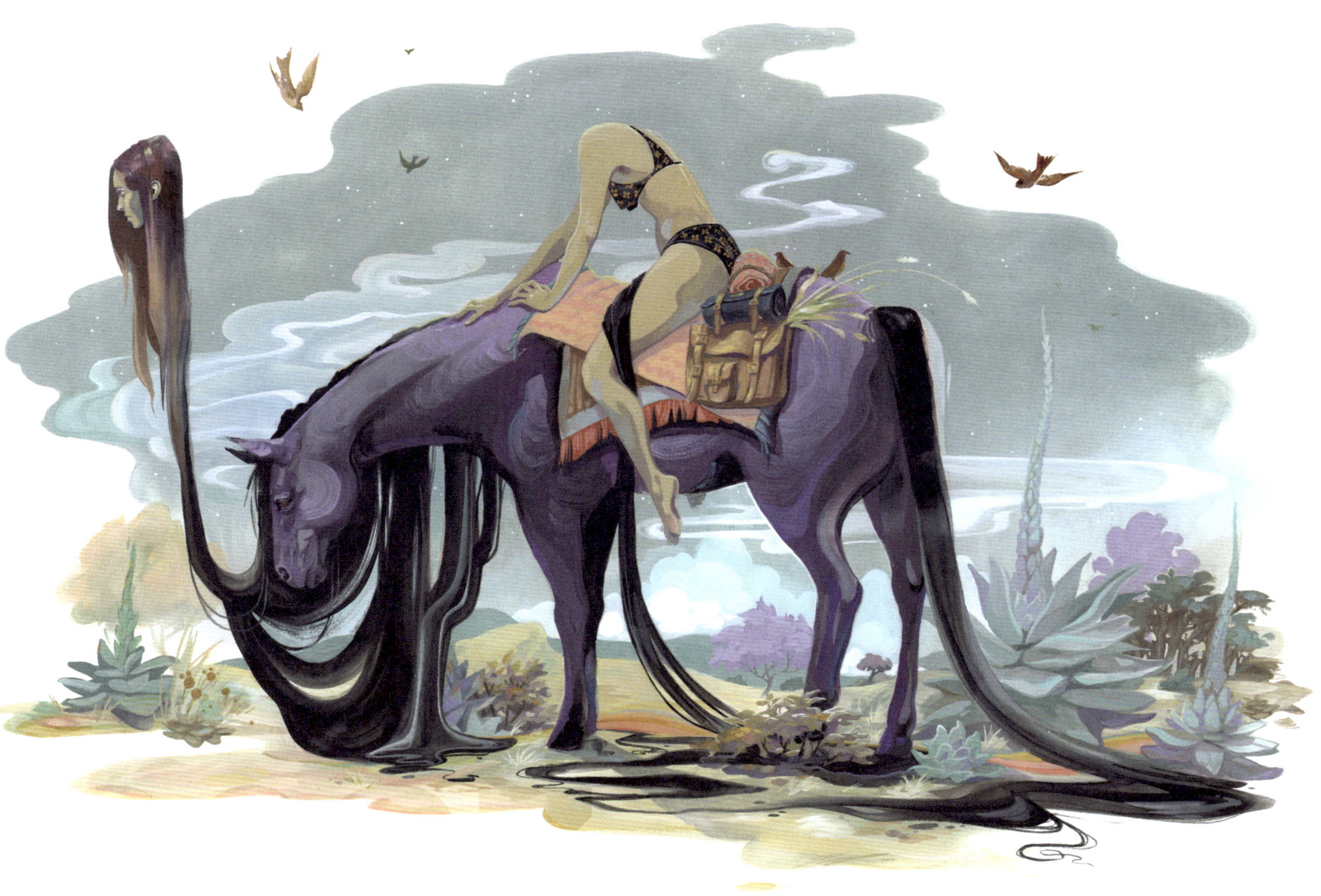

Growing up, I lived in small towns with little access to art, so the earliest works that inspired me were *Swans Reflecting Elephants* by Salvador Dalí, which my doctor had a print of in his office, plus *Sailor Moon, Final Fantasy, CardCaptors,* and Studio Ghibli. The rare times I managed to catch *Kiki's Delivery Service* on the Family Channel were like spiritual experiences for me. I've been inspired by so many artists since then it would be impossible to name them all but, if I had to name a few, I would say Dalí, James Gurney, William Morris, James Jean, Loish, Kim Jung Gi, J.A.W. Cooper, Alfred Liu, Eliza Ivanova, and many, many more.

I graduated during the 2008 recession, so my early career was a struggle. Often while working other day jobs, I tried applying my art to many different fields that never felt quite right. I've worked at tattoo shops and a custom autobody shop, I created a portfolio to try and get into illustration, and I went to school for graphic design. Nothing seemed to fit, until I realized maybe I should just focus on fine art as my craft. Initially, this was fruitless, because I didn't have any way to market myself and the galleries near me rarely ever showed surreal art. It wasn't until I was working as a housemaid at a particularly snobby rich lady's mansion that I really kicked into high gear and spent almost all of my free time creating art and posting it on social media.

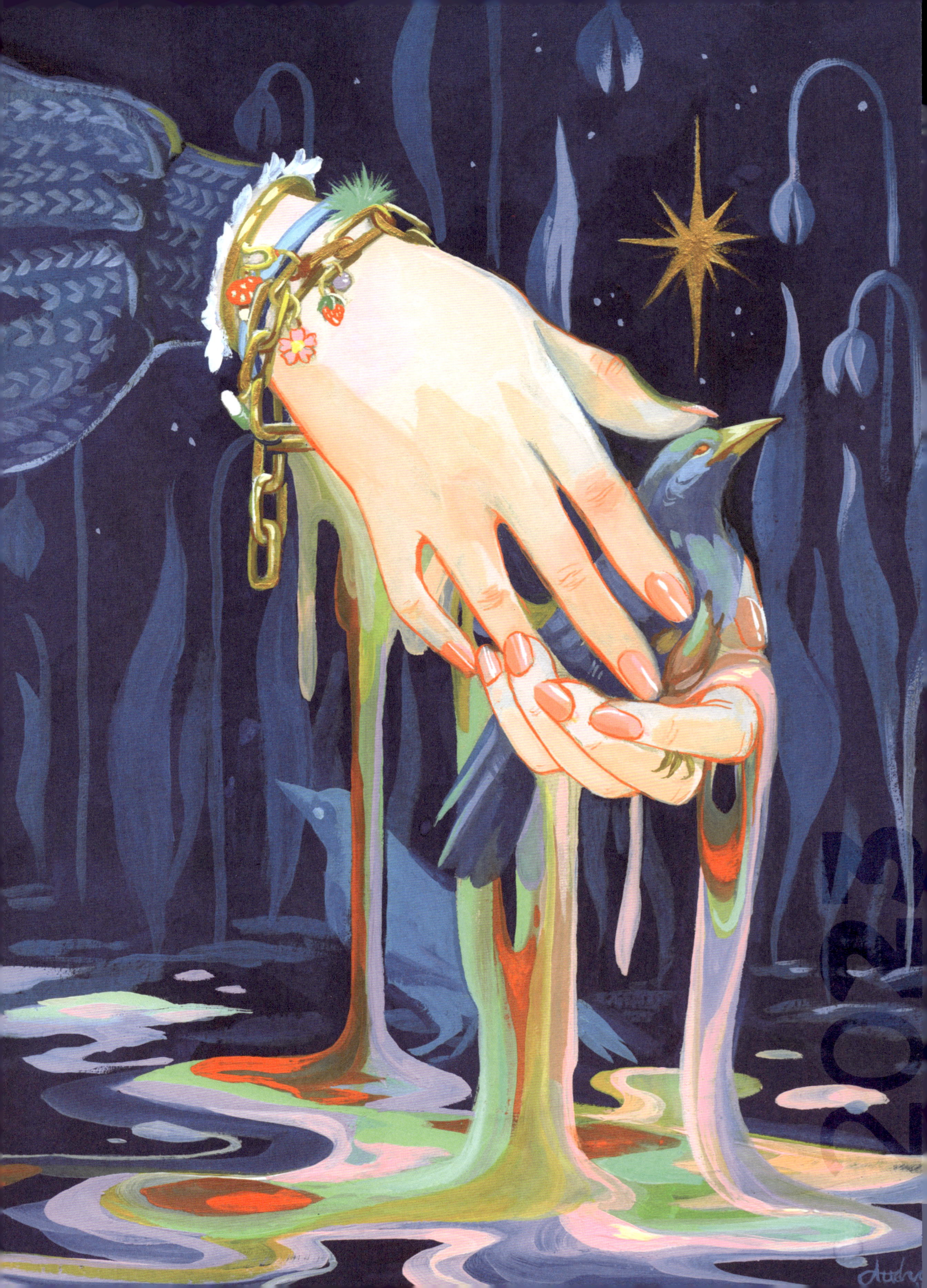

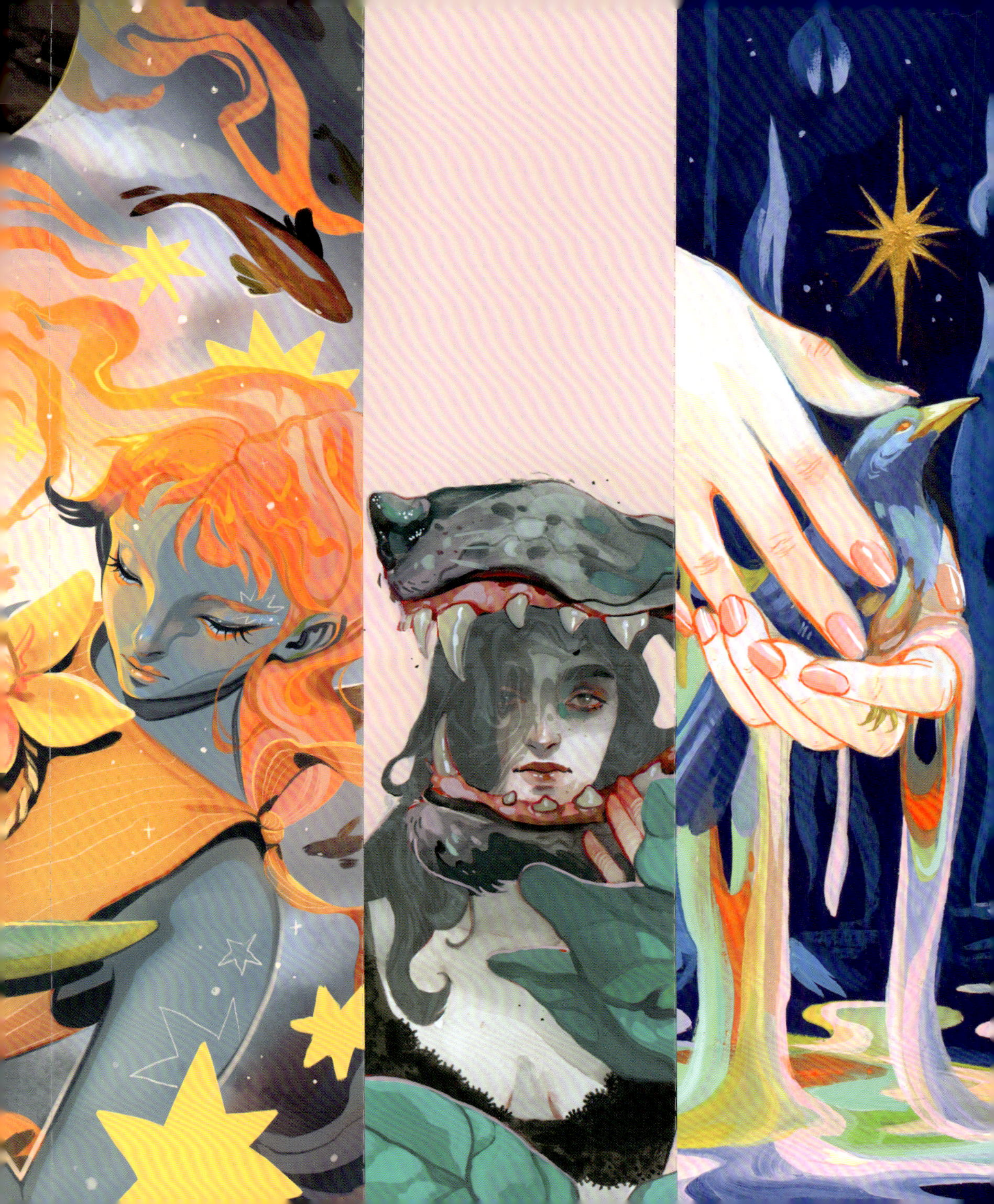

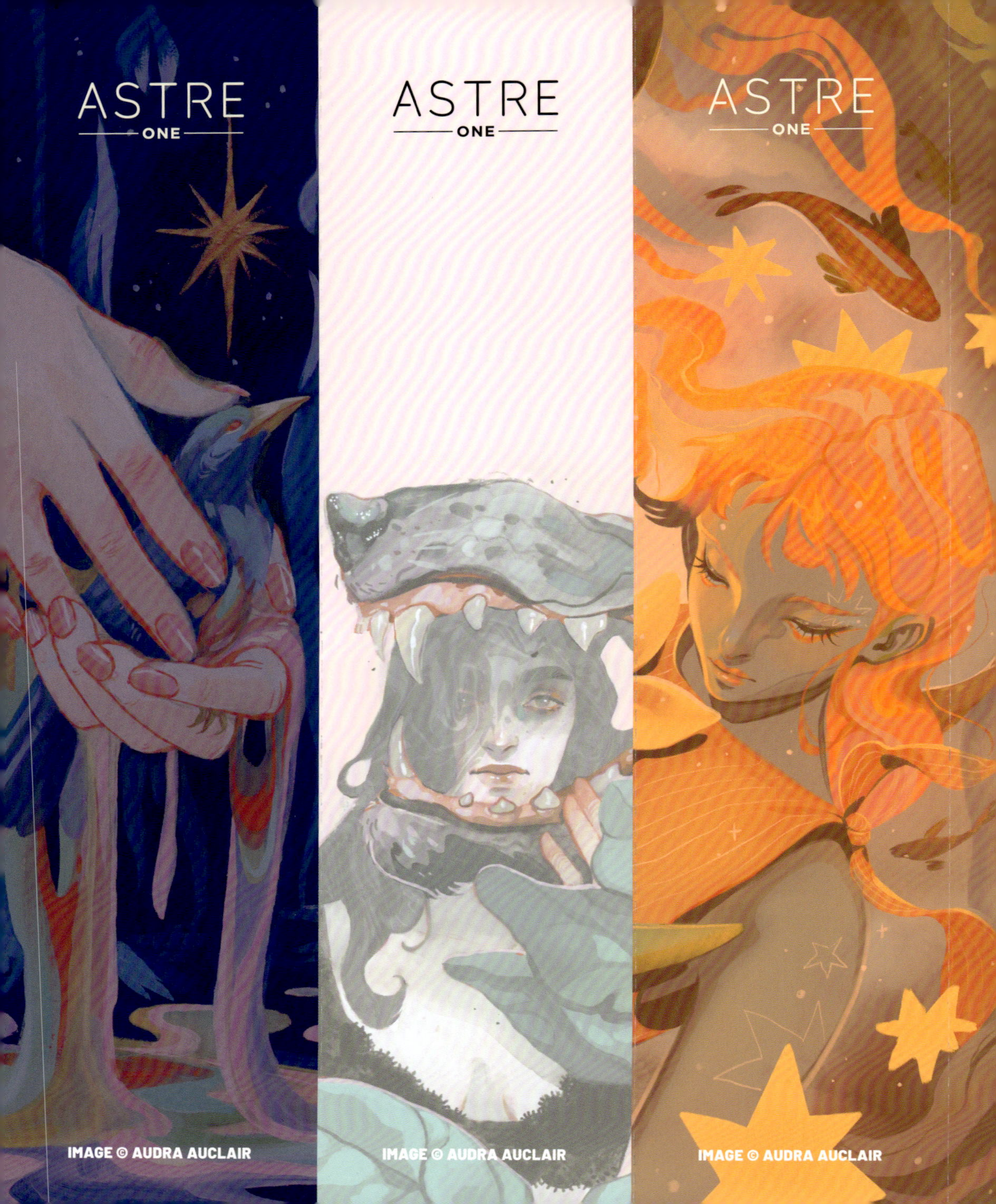
ASTRE
ONE
ASTRE
ONE
ASTRE
ONE
IMAGE © AUDRA AUCLAIR
IMAGE © AUDRA AUCLAIR
IMAGE © AUDRA AUCLAIR

My partner and I agreed on a plan, where I would have a limited amount of time to focus solely on making a living from my art. With a lot of hard work and support, I was able to start making enough to support myself financially. I spent some time creating art and life videos on YouTube and began selling my original prints online. I bought a scanner so I could start scanning my work and I asked for a printer for Christmas – that really helped me sustain myself. Since then, it's been a rollercoaster. I've shown and shipped my work all over the world, and created several books and products, and continue to do so today.

I've never stopped wanting to learn new mediums. I've recently picked up crocheting and I've spent a lot of time learning about sculpture, animation, sewing, and needle felting. I hope to learn how to make stained glass, jewellery, and ceramics. I would also love to learn carpentry and try my hand at woodburning. My earlier works were mostly watercolour, ink, and acrylic, but after I discovered gouache I fell in love with it. I've dabbled in oil painting, but I don't like the faff that comes with it.

Away from work, one of my favourite things to do is swim in lakes and rivers, so I try to do that whenever I get the chance. I like going on walks through the forest or at night, pretty much anywhere the sun isn't. I also love watching and learning about birds. My new hobby, crocheting, has given me a lot of peace, especially since I can do it while watching movies and cuddling my cats.

I read a lot before I fall asleep in order to calm my mind. I am a nerd at heart, so I play a lot of video games with my partner Lopi and my family. I spend an embarrassing amount of time playing *Minecraft* with them and watching HermitCraft videos. I've been playing *Minecraft* for about fourteen years now. I love it because it's a way to spend time with people and create fantastical places that I could 'live' in. I like to use a planner to keep track of things and store memories – it also gives me an excuse to continue collecting washi tapes.

Over time, I have grown to expect more from myself – I strive for perfection and detail more than I once did. In my early twenties I could make several paintings in a day (although I think the original *Under the Surface* actually took longer). From a marketing perspective, that speed was an important factor in my growth, because I was able to constantly churn out content for Instagram. But with time, mental health, and my heart's changing tides, it was clear that this pace just wasn't sustainable. I wanted to slow down and focus on improving my skills.

For instance, I used to avoid doing backgrounds but now I enjoy them, possibly because I took up plein-air painting. I spend much more time on bigger pieces with more colour because I now often use gouache and it's amazing for creating backgrounds. I used to try to follow trends so that my work felt 'current' – in fact, I think I still do, to some extent, but less than I once did. Even as I have evolved and begun to take my time with my work, I think the core of what I'm saying has remained much the same. Nowadays, I have a healthy mix of different projects on the go: I create small 'aesthetic' pieces because they are low-pressure and enjoyable, I make the odd fan art-related painting, and I draw subjects with clothing more often now that I'm more confident I can make something good.

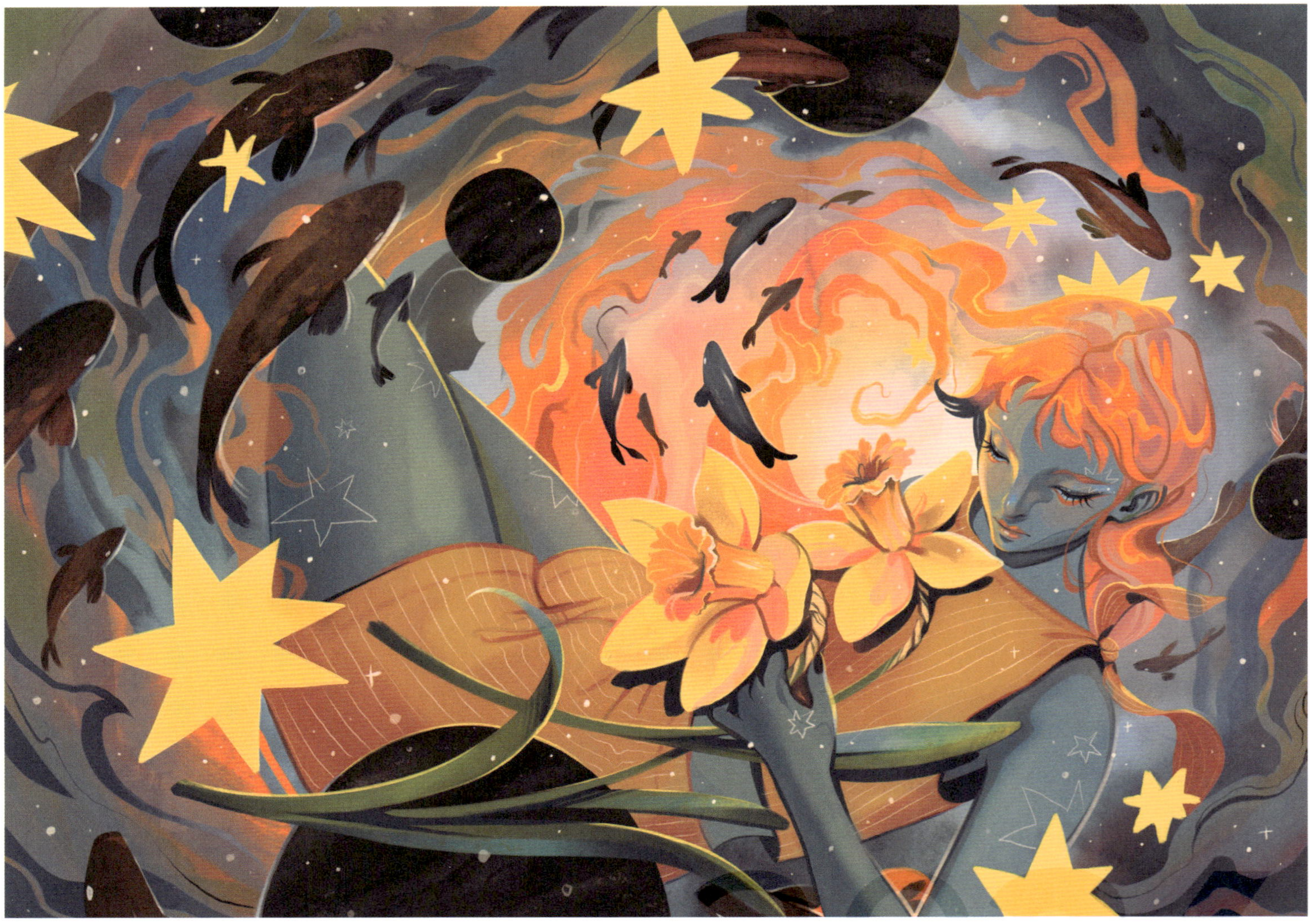

Every now and then, I'll take the time to make something that is deeper and bigger. These are the sorts of paintings that I would focus on exclusively if I lived in the past, at a time when art wasn't expected to be made in a day or a week. I always think about how the *Mona Lisa* was painted over the course of sixteen years – imagine having all that time to work on one piece. Now that I'm a little older and the ego of my youth has subsided, I take more enjoyment from spending a long time on these more detailed paintings, instead of creating quick works for the algorithm. Ultimately, I guess the source of the satisfaction I derive from my work has changed – I no longer look to Instagram for the creative validation my soul needs. These days, it's more important for to feel proud of myself for putting my all into what I'm creating. I strive to create pieces that will hold up against the test of time and my increasingly critical eye.

When deciding what to paint, I try not to limit myself to particular themes or emotions. Some works are just for decorative purposes, some are to inspire a feeling or ambience, and some are meant to convey something I feel, or something someone I know is feeling. If I were no longer here and someone looked at my art, I hope they would be able to piece together bits of my life based on my paintings. My work might be inspired by happiness, love, depression, loss, anger, and so on. I was in a dark space for a while where most of my work would hint at that sadness but, lately, now that I've been feeling better, I'm trying to convey a lot more hope in my work. 🅰

ABOVE:

Holding on close | *This painting represents my relationship with my cat, Nymbus. I wanted to express his amazingness and toxicity while keeping with the aesthetic of the painting, so I came up with the idea of using the toxic but beautiful daffodil. Nymbus has undiagnosed anxiety from his deafness and can be aggressive, but he is otherwise the most cuddly, soft, and sweet cat. I almost always hold him on my chest and he purrs so deeply that it heals me when I'm low*

RIGHT:

Sonnet | *In the past, I would often purge my negative emotions through art, but with age I find myself wanting to reflect instead on the positive things in my life. This painting is about the thing I'm most grateful for, and that is my partner, Lopi. I wanted to express how his love makes me feel. He has remained a guiding light through my darkest times (one of which lasted many years) and he maintains the world around me in any way he can to make me happy*

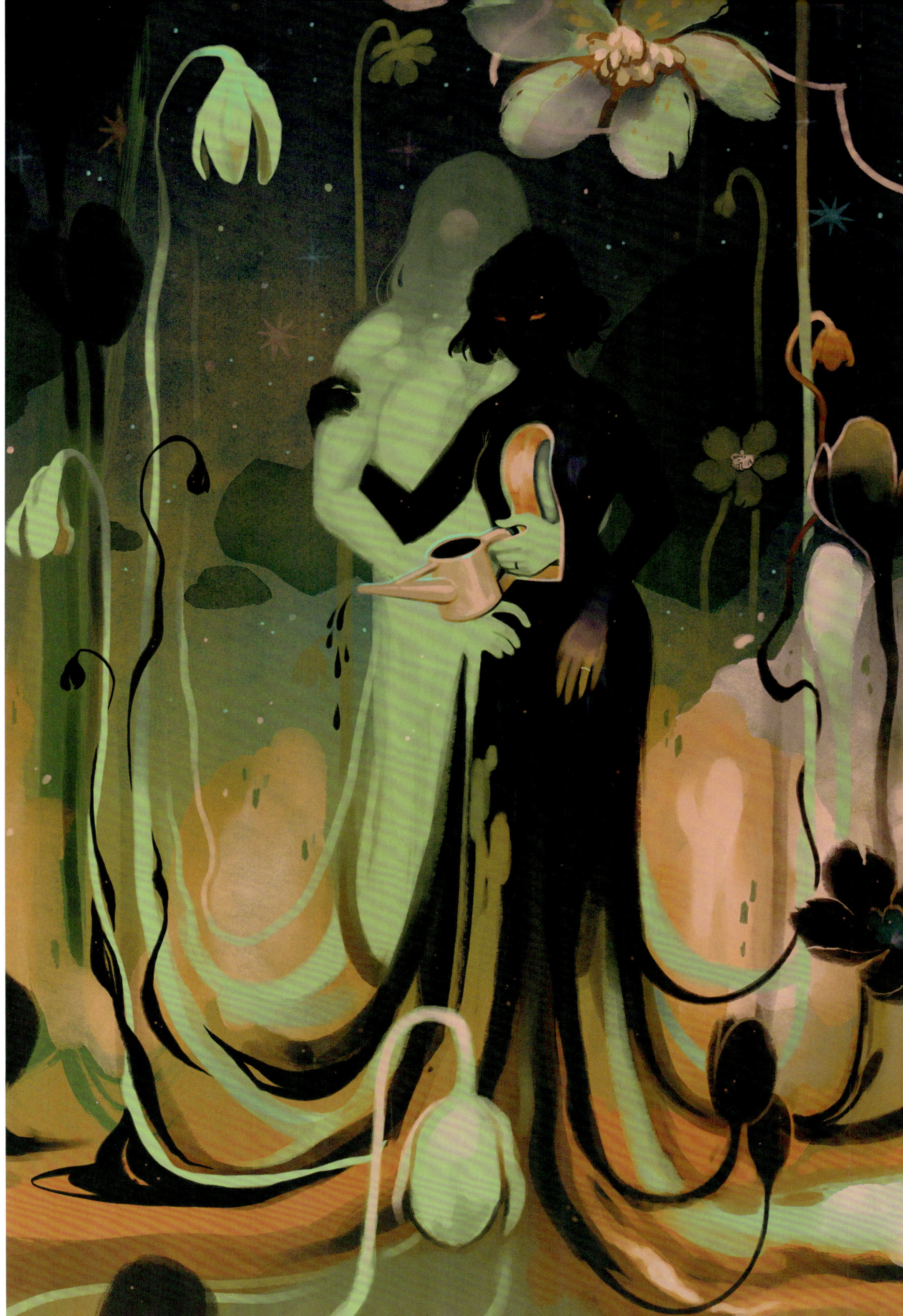

UNDER SUBURBAN SKIES

BY MICHAŁ SAWTYRUK

Like many others, I began drawing as a child and carried that passion forward into adulthood. By luck, I discovered the Platige Image VFX course in Warsaw, which would eventually lead me to my role as a concept artist. I've been developing concepts for commercials and animated films since 2012, collaborating with companies such as BMW, DreamWorks, Procreate, Netflix Animation, and many more. Alongside my professional work, I pursue my own personal projects and experiment with creating short animations.

RIGHT:
Suburbs | While walking at night, I noticed a light spreading across a suburban street. The street was empty and quiet, with no moving cars or passers-by in the area. I immediately thought of a stranger walking through the middle of the scene, almost like a shadow

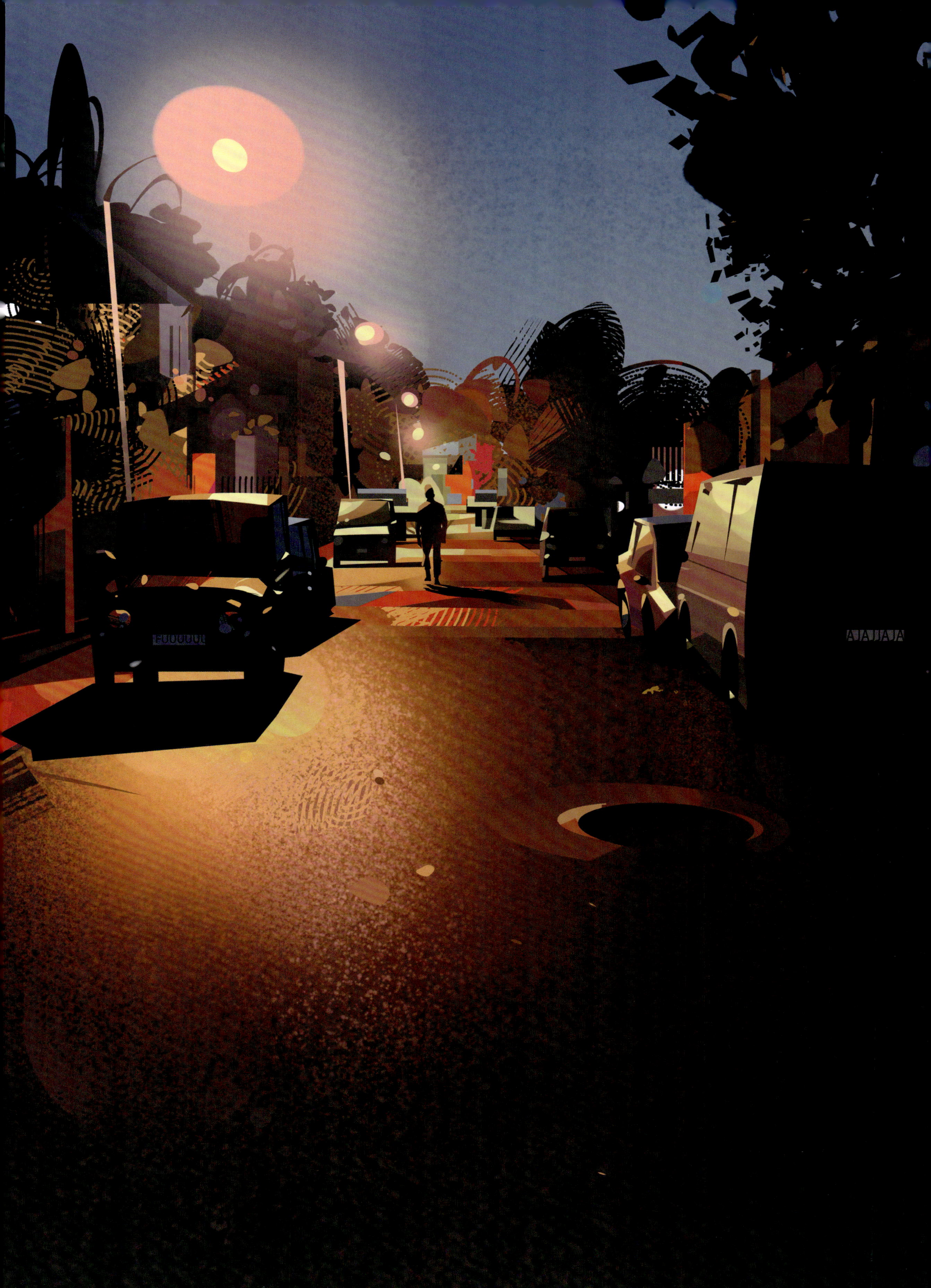

When I was starting out as an artist, I fixated on achieving a specific style, trying to make the paintings look a certain way. Gradually, my process has become more intuitive – I don't think about the overall style and instead focus on simplification and creating an aesthetic I personally find pleasing. Drawing has become somehow integrated into my unconscious decision-making – it's part of me and keeps changing while I change. I think it has gradually shifted towards a greater reduction in detail in my work. Nowadays, I often contemplate how to make something as simple and readable as possible, which has coincided with my life becoming busier.

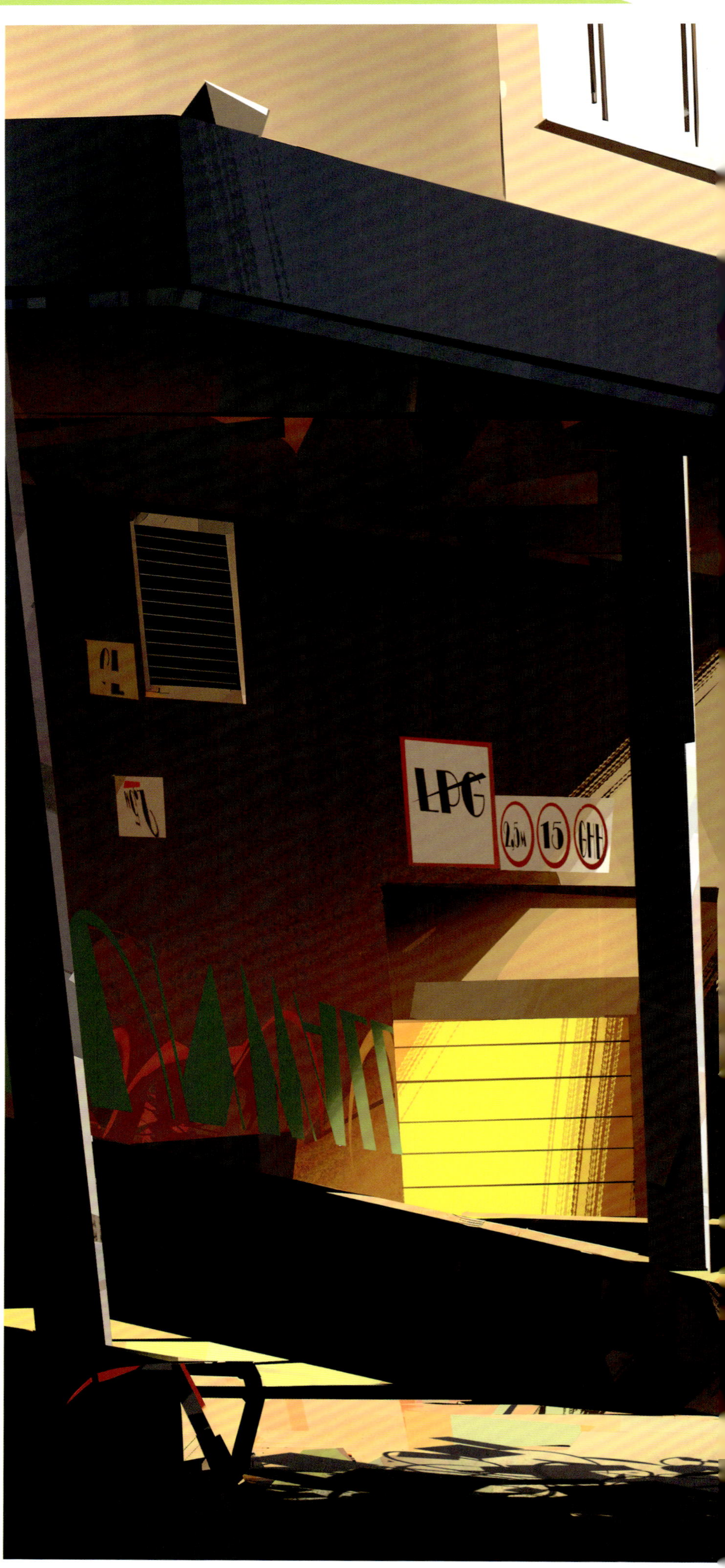

Car park | A view of a car park and garage entrance. I decided to capture this because I was intrigued by the play of light and shadow, and the vector-like shapes of the garage entrance and formed shadows. The colours of the light had to be warm and saturated

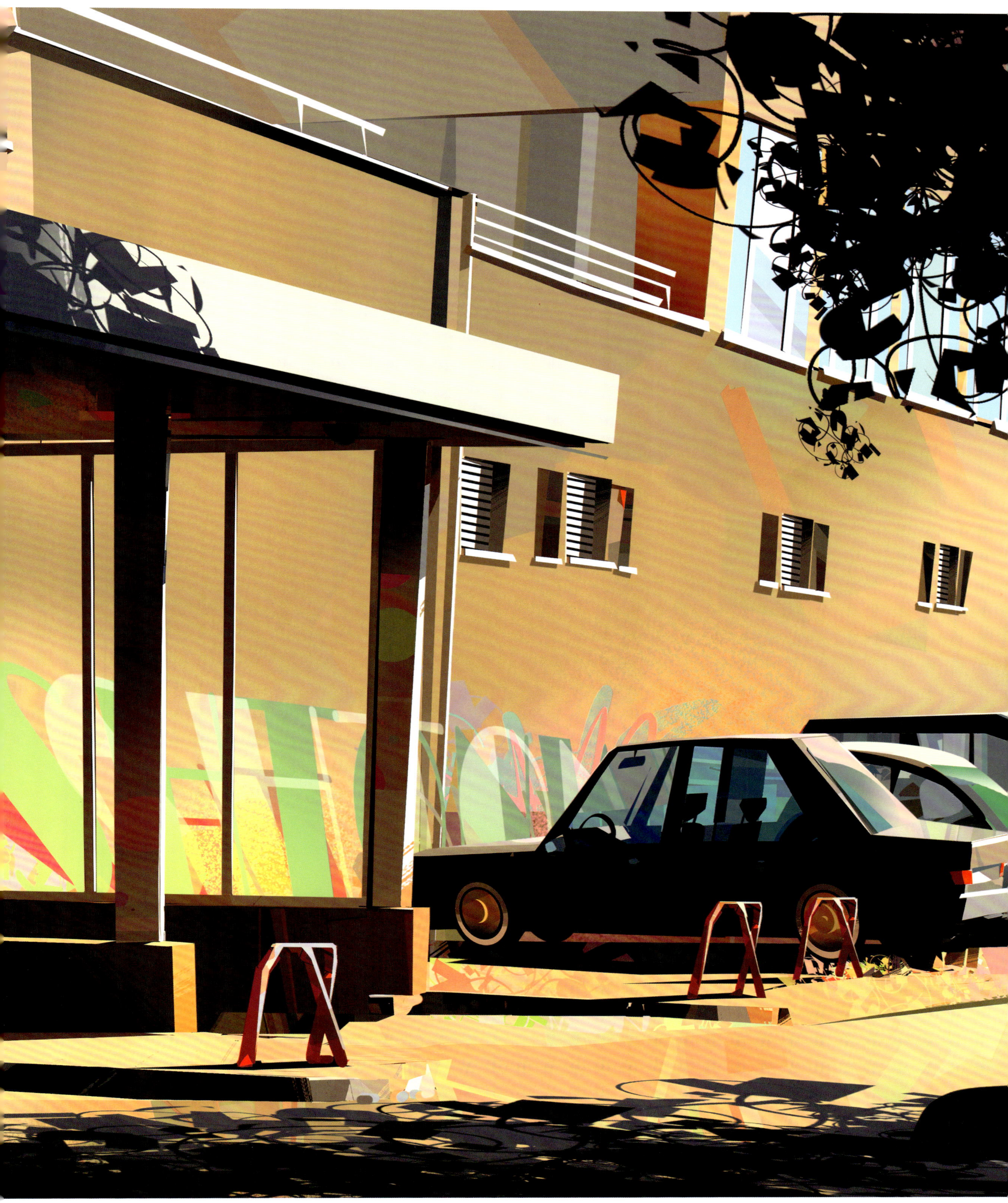

Kitchen | A picture based on a morning view in the kitchen of a holiday cottage. I wanted to capture the contrast between the extremely bright window and the dark interior, and the light spreading inside

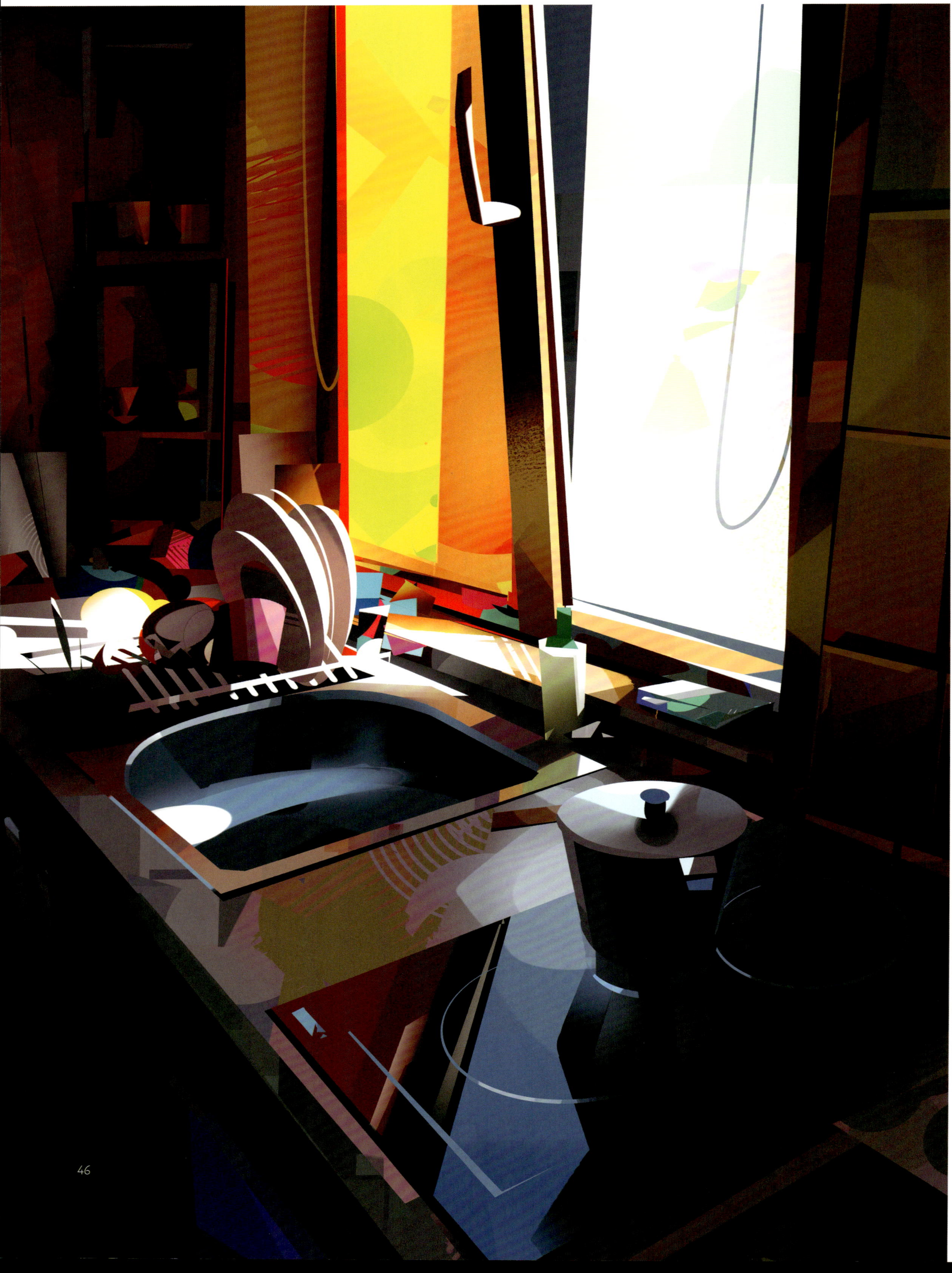

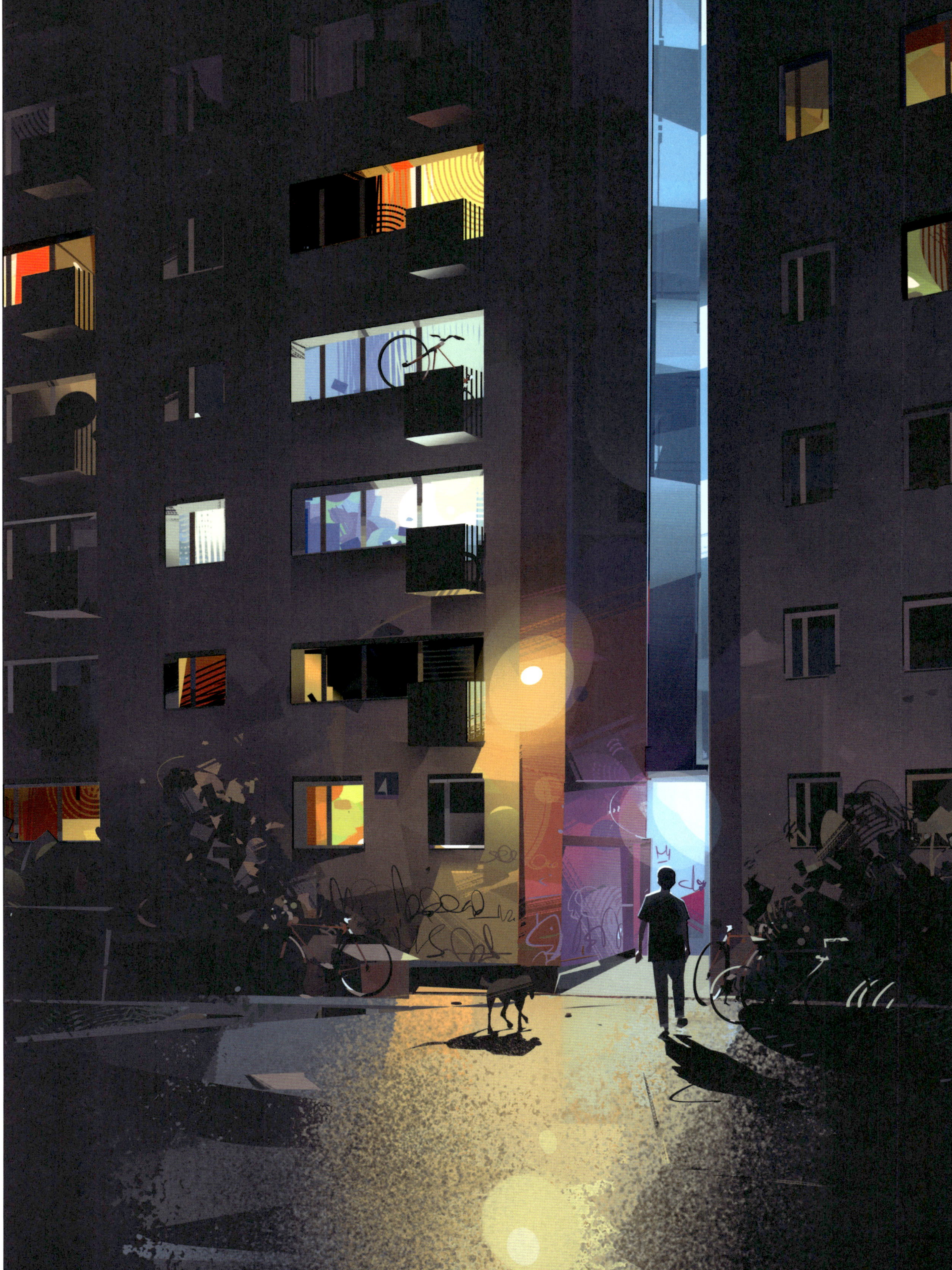

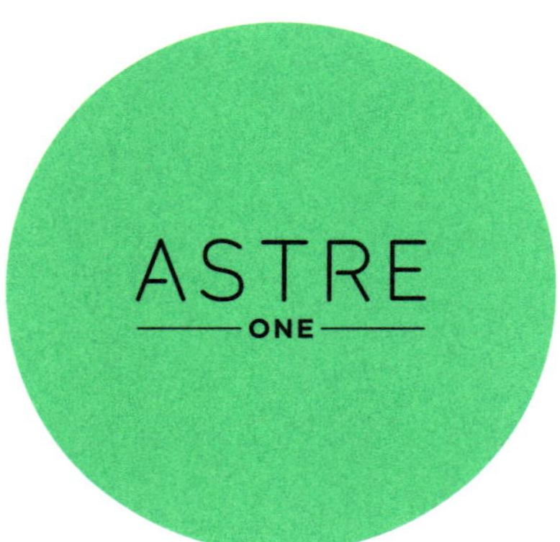

BLOCK OF FLATS BY MICHAŁ SAWTYRUK

ASTRE ORIGINAL PRINT

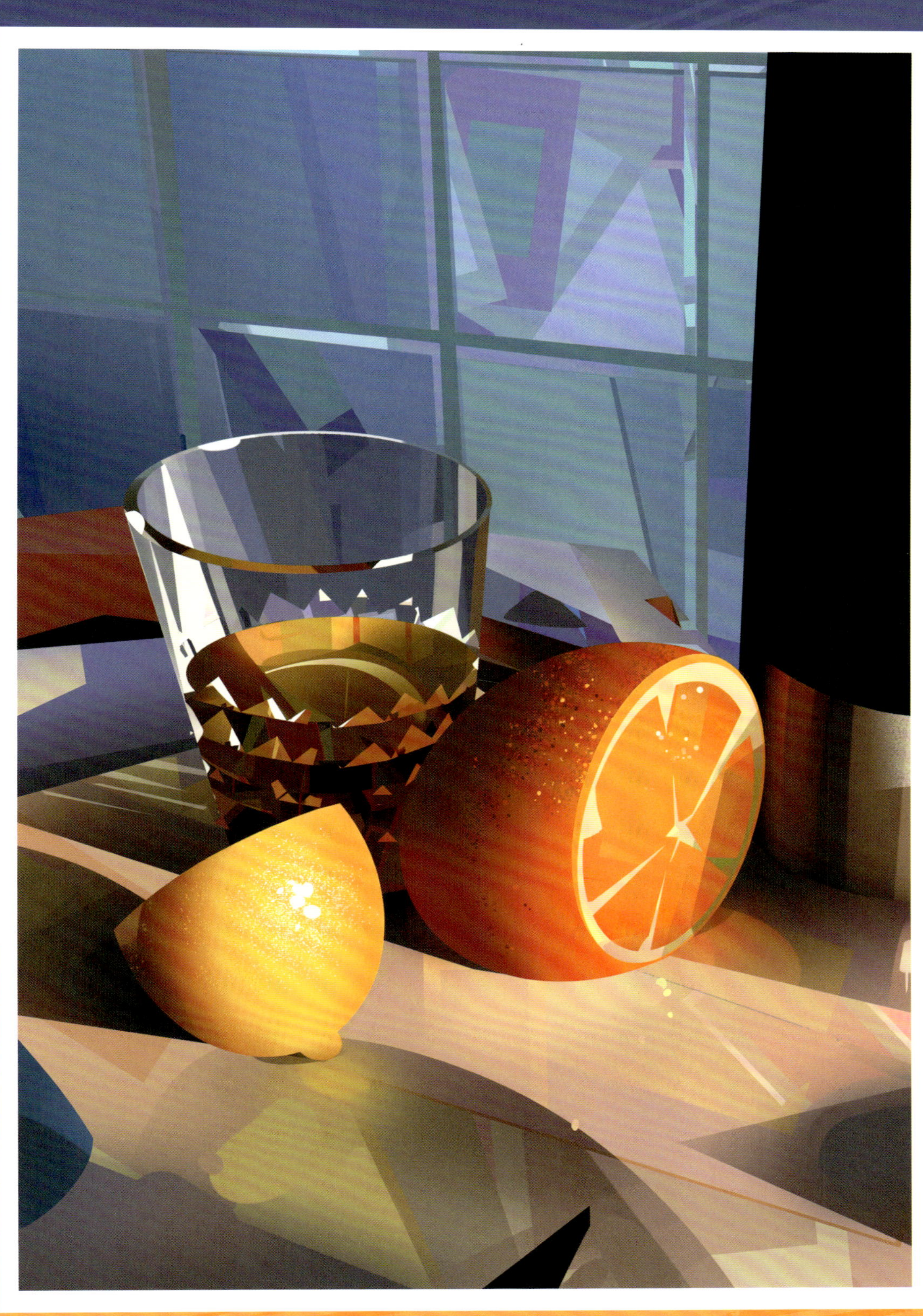

Drink | *I was intrigued by the light refracting in this glass and the shape and colour composition of the scene. I tried to paint this in a simplified manner, reducing the detail to a minimum*

The works of Alberto Mielgo, Robh Ruppel, and Neil Campbell Ross have influenced how I simplify and perceive images. I was always amazed by Alberto Mielgo's early short 2D animations – they made me realize I could go other ways with my paintings and experiment with animation myself.

I love doing anything that brings me to a meditative state and takes me out of the daily churn of thinking, such as listening to music, riding a bike, or just taking a walk. Music is great because of its ephemeral nature – it only exists in the moment. I also love actively spending time with my kids. I take a lot of photos, whether it's just for me or as a reference for a new sketch. ◮

> **"I LOVE ANYTHING THAT BRINGS ME TO A MEDITATIVE STATE AND TAKES ME OUT OF THE DAILY CHURN OF THINKING"**

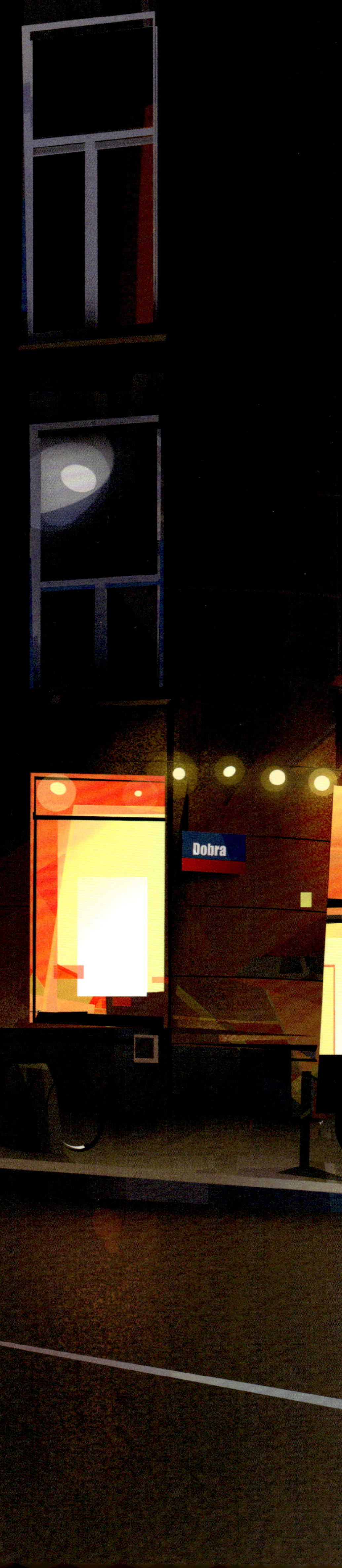

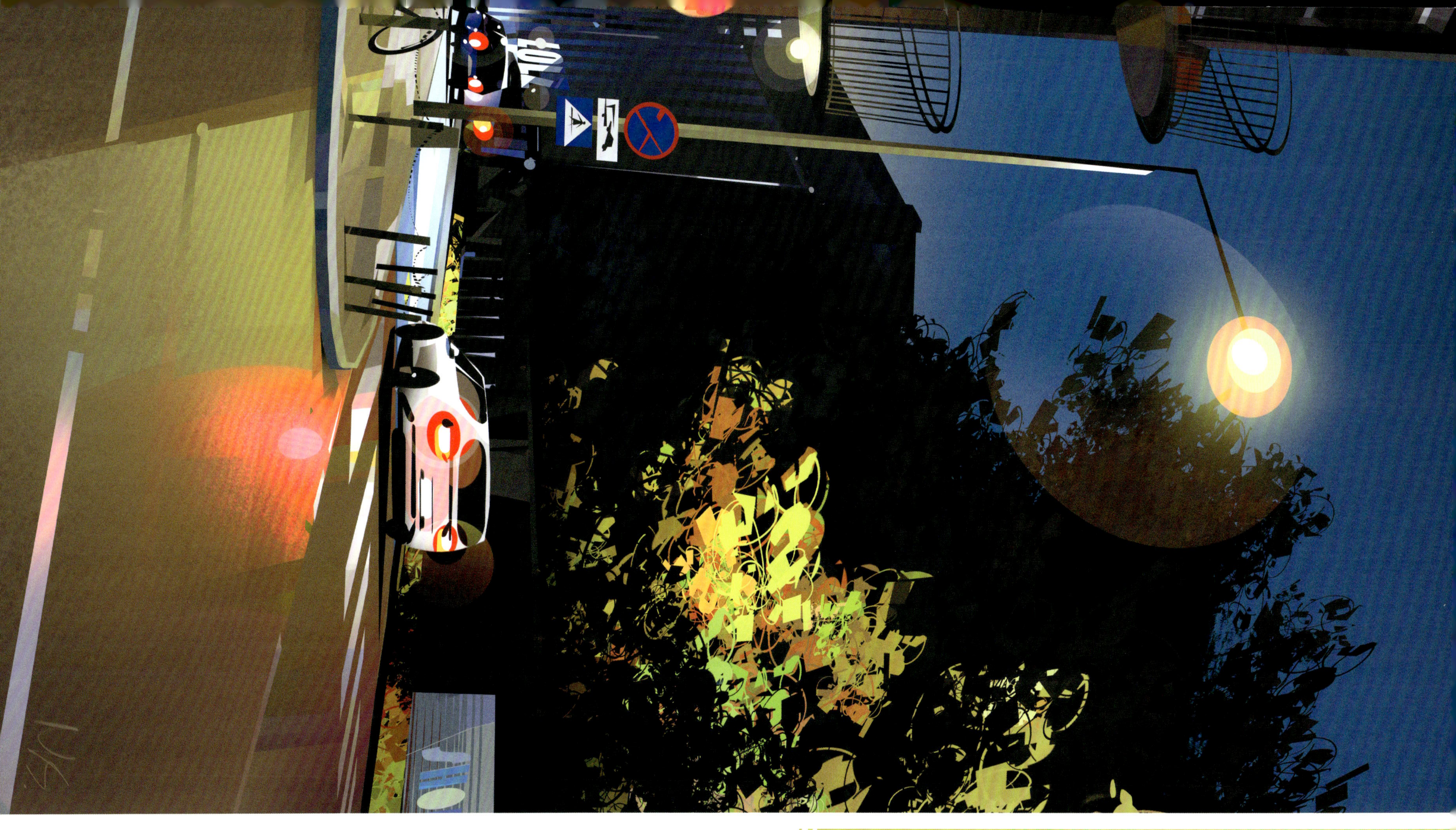

Dobra Street | This is a painting based on a street corner in Powiśle, a neighbourhood in Warsaw. I like capturing photos of streets at night on my phone. When I have a free moment, I jump on a bike and go for a ride, with no destination in mind. Sometimes, I try to get lost and find a place I have never seen before and look for something inspiring, such as an interesting light and shadow composition, contrast, or a particular rhythm to the scene

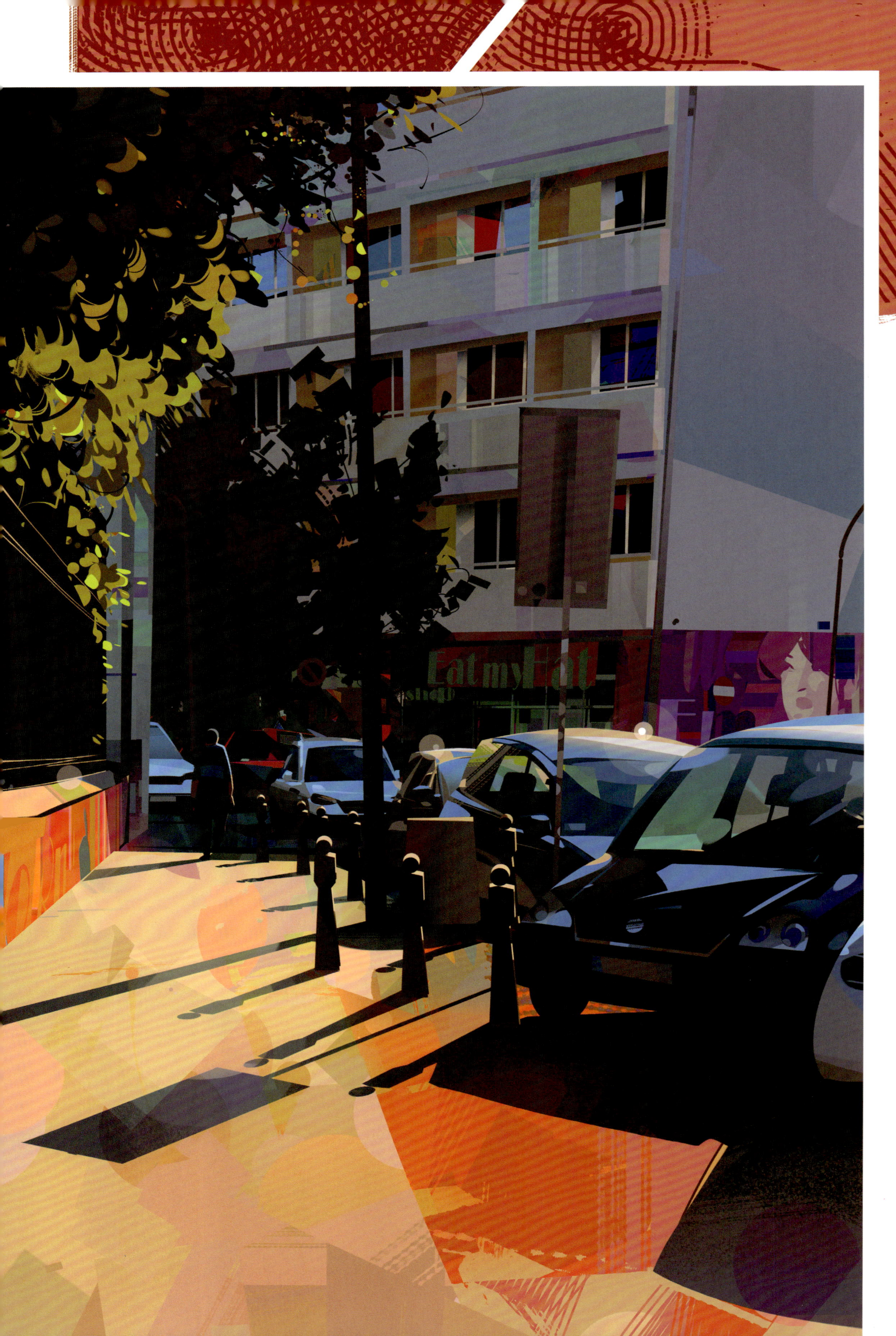

Eat my Fat

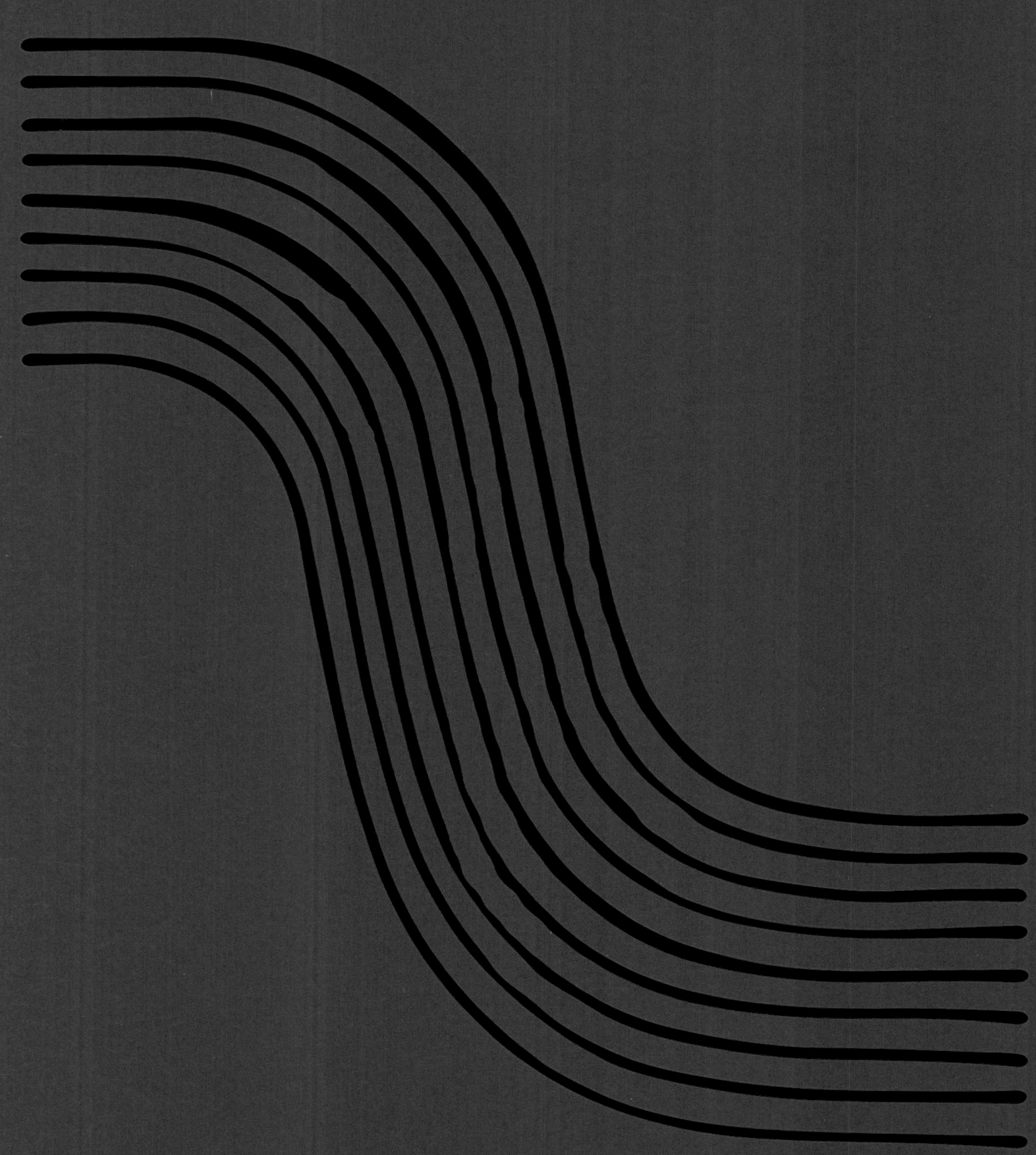

Parked cars | This is a quiet spot, out of the way in the centre of Warsaw – a few steps away there is a lot of noise. The contrast between the interesting shapes of the shadows and the illuminated sections of the drawing effectively builds the composition of the image.

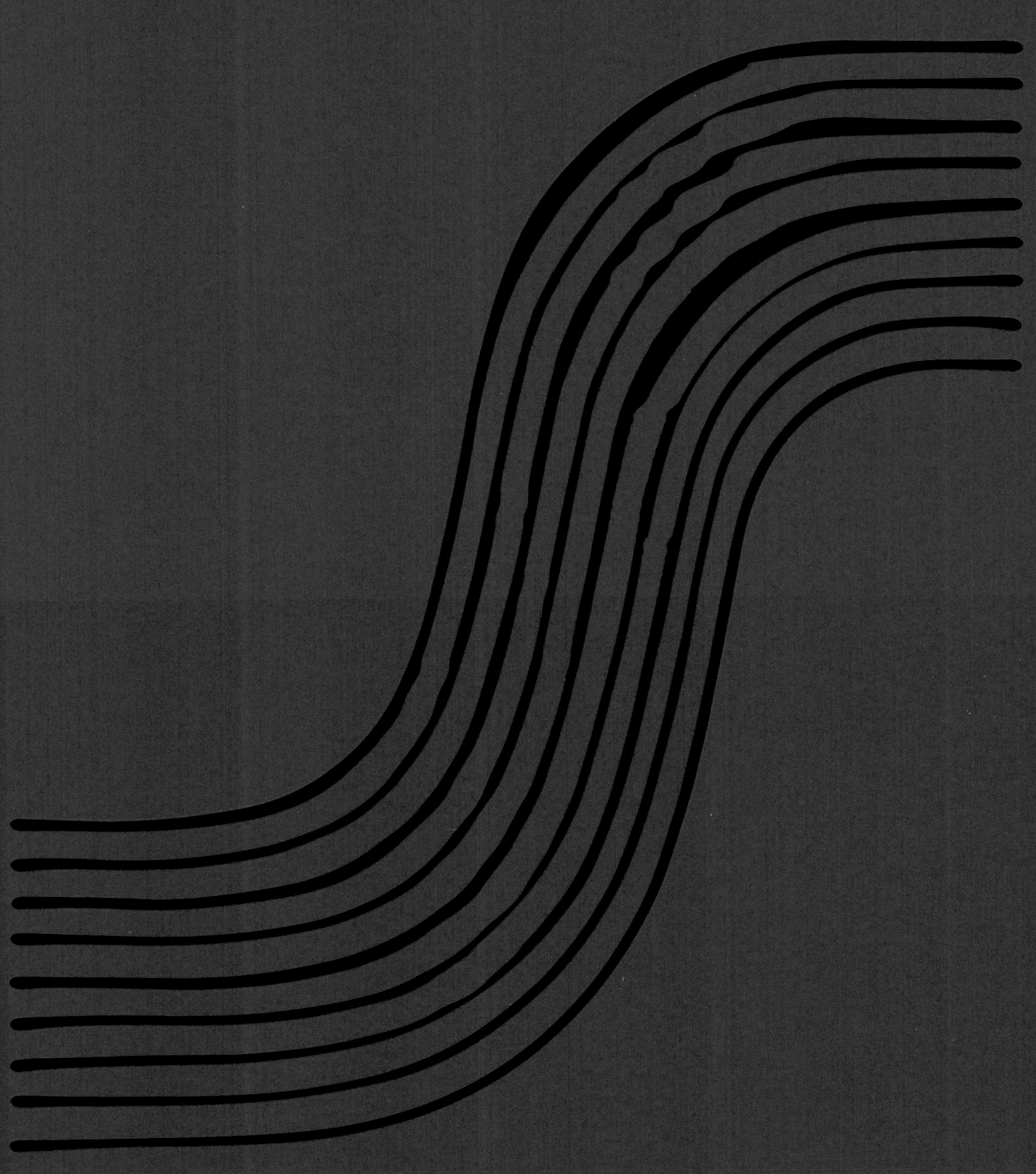

RIGHT:
Profile sketch | A simple sketch of a portrait in profile. I really
wanted to simplify the shapes and the hair textures, which are
the main elements of the image. The face is hidden in shadow

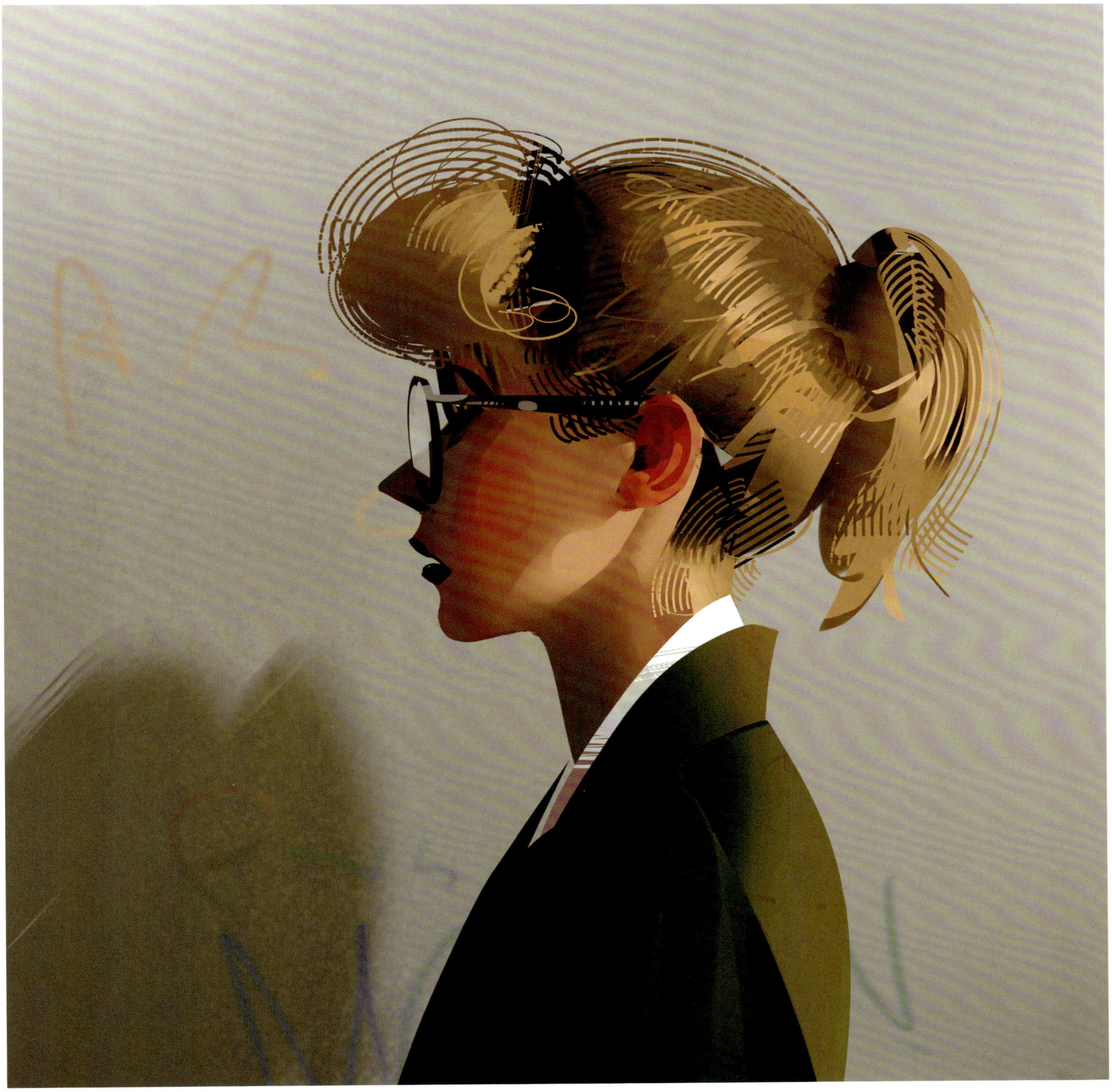

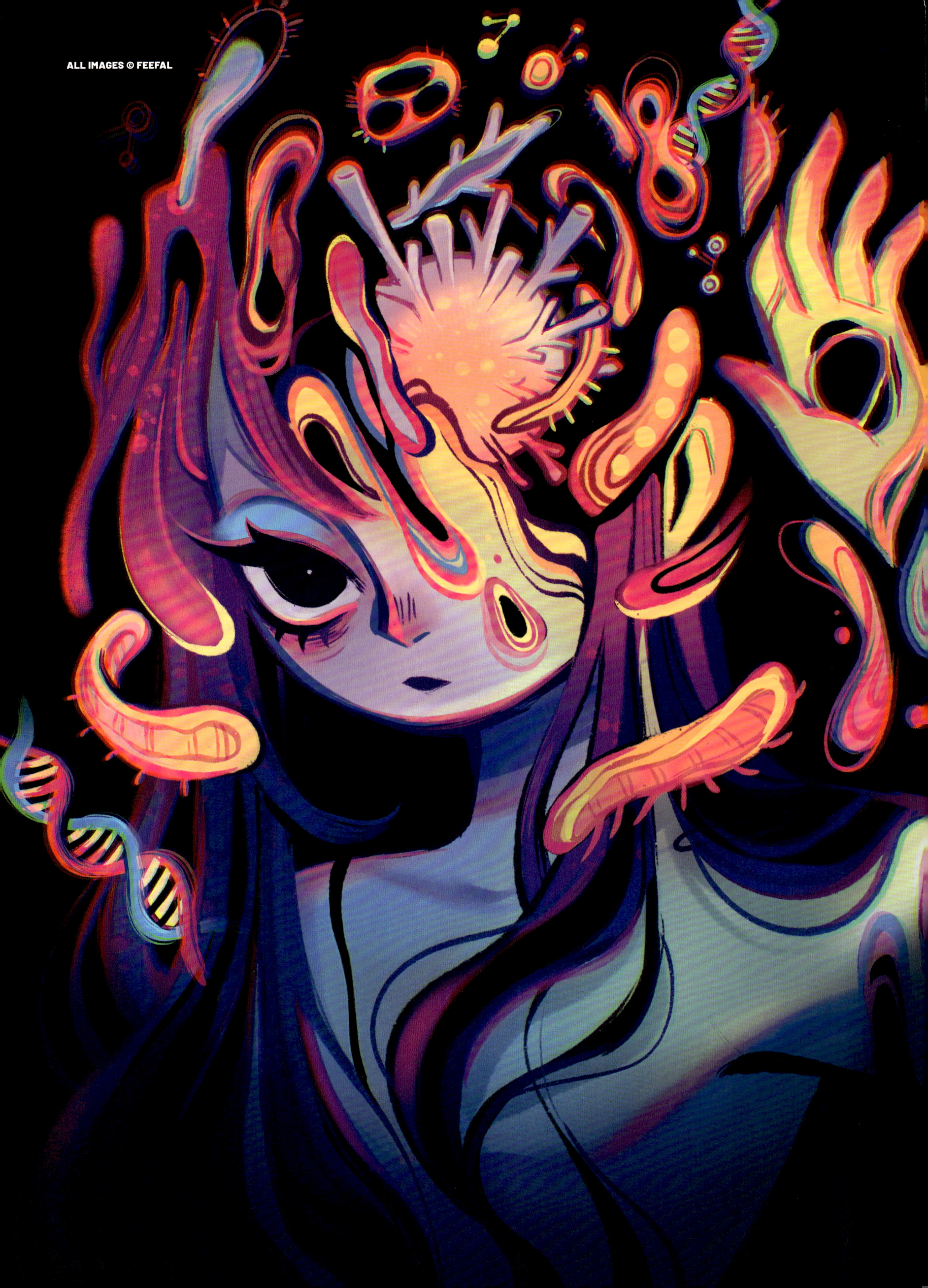

I have a fascination with biology and the developmental stages of how creatures come to be. It seems so strange to me how a clump of cells can transform into a fully fledged living being. I wanted to create a piece that represented the development of life and all the awkward middle stages in between infancy and maturity.

I find it wild that cells are the building blocks of all life and that they each possess their very own complex functions and ways of existing. For instance, us animals have our set of organs that enable us to live and cells have organelles that are specifically engineered to steer, decide, add oxygen, protect, and filter out filth. By comparing them to humans and translating their functions into mammalian characteristics, I'm able to get a firmer grasp on how they work. I've almost started seeing them as cute little animals at this point.

To show my love of biology in an interesting and fun way, I decided to focus my piece around frog embryology. Frogs showcase a particularly fascinating process, since we can clearly see how they metamorphose through their various stages of development. I had to figure out a way to put that into a setting that wouldn't be so science-focused and stiff. My art is quite cute and whimsical in nature, so naturally I have to bring some fantastical elements into the mix. I used Procreate to create this piece, using my favourite brush, the Dry Ink brush, which comes preinstalled.

I associate frogs with witches, since they're a popular choice for familiars. So, I figured it would be cute to have a witch who specializes in frogs, and have her guide them through the various stages of life. She holds an orb of frog embryos like a crystal ball in her right hand and with her other hand she gently guides them into adulthood, until they're ready to accompany her on her magical quests.

I love the themes of death and rebirth – they always find their way into my work in some form. Death can be a bit spooky and dark, but it's also beautiful and wonderful in myriad ways. I view it as a gentle reminder to appreciate my time on this lovely planet – before I eventually rot and some new form of life claims my particles. The vastness of space and the meaning of the universe are quite overwhelming, so I find it comforting to be reminded of how small and insignificant my role in this world is and how I really only have this short glimpse of existence before my time runs out. That's why I can't help but make these dark themes seem cute in my work – I just find it all so endearing.

I do a lot of research on the internet, browsing through articles and studying various topics related to whatever I'm working on. I really enjoy looking at scientific illustrations of body parts and plants, as well as illustrated diagrams. Seeing how other artists manage this blend between illustrative art and science helps me to do the same. If I make something that's inspired by science, it's really important that I get my facts right. I always aim to stay true to the science while bending reality in interesting ways. Balancing these two elements can be quite difficult, but it's also what makes the end result so interesting.

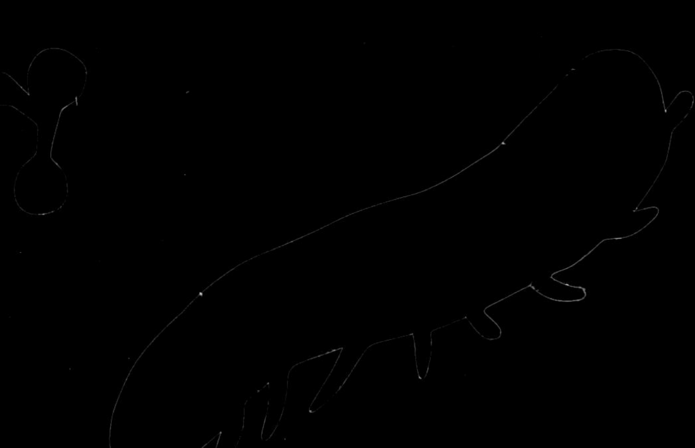

I created my art Instagram in 2016, where I came up with the username 'feefal' on a whim. I had just dropped out of art school and felt very insecure about my work, but I gained so much comfort and confidence by sharing and talking with other artists via the internet. I received the acceptance I had yearned for my whole life, and I slowly let go of the shame and embarrassment I felt over my work. Since then, I've worked as a character designer, toy designer, illustrator, and in a bunch of other roles, too. I prefer to work on my own projects rather than take on freelance work – I'm very fortunate to have a platform that enables me to pursue those interests. The fact that I get to illustrate my hyperfixations for a living is an absolute dream come true.

My style has been inspired by all sorts of anime and cartoons – they're something I grew up with, and I still find exaggerated anatomy and colourful aesthetics compelling. However, my biggest undeniable influence is the whole internet art scene in general. I've been inspired by so many artists who share their work online, ever since I first got access to the world wide web. The work of Loish, Yuumei, and maruti_bitamin are favourites of mine.

I like creating artwork that's a play or a spin on a topic. Something that you can look at and see a narrative within, whether that's a story being told visually or a literal infographic. If I create a larger illustration, I want it to be like a glimpse into a story being played out in some alternative fantasy realm! I tend to shy away from depicting strong emotions, because they're just not something I prioritize or feel compelled by. Art is something I consume and pursue because it's cool and interesting, but it doesn't really evoke any feelings inside me apart from excitement and curiosity. That actually sounds a little cold when I type it out, but that has always been my relationship with art.

Since my job requires me to sit sedentary in a room for the majority of the day, I really make an effort to go out and explore the outside world on my off days. I am naturally quite lazy and unmotivated as a person, but I have discovered that my work suffers greatly if I don't actively engage in hobbies and pursue knowledge. So, just for that reason alone, I feel a great need to read, go on hikes, and generally just try new things! I like finding new stories to read, new fruits to try, and previously unknown areas to explore. If I have the time, I enjoy taking the local transit to a station I've never been to before and exploring a new neighbourhood. △

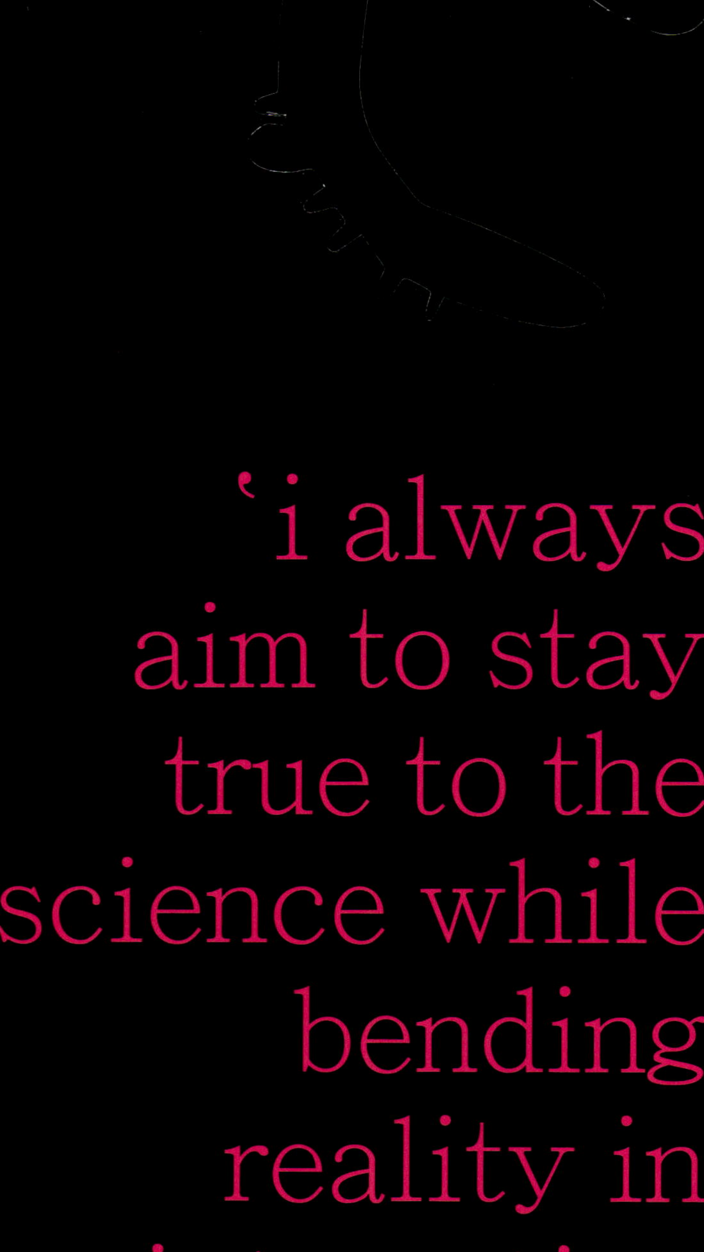

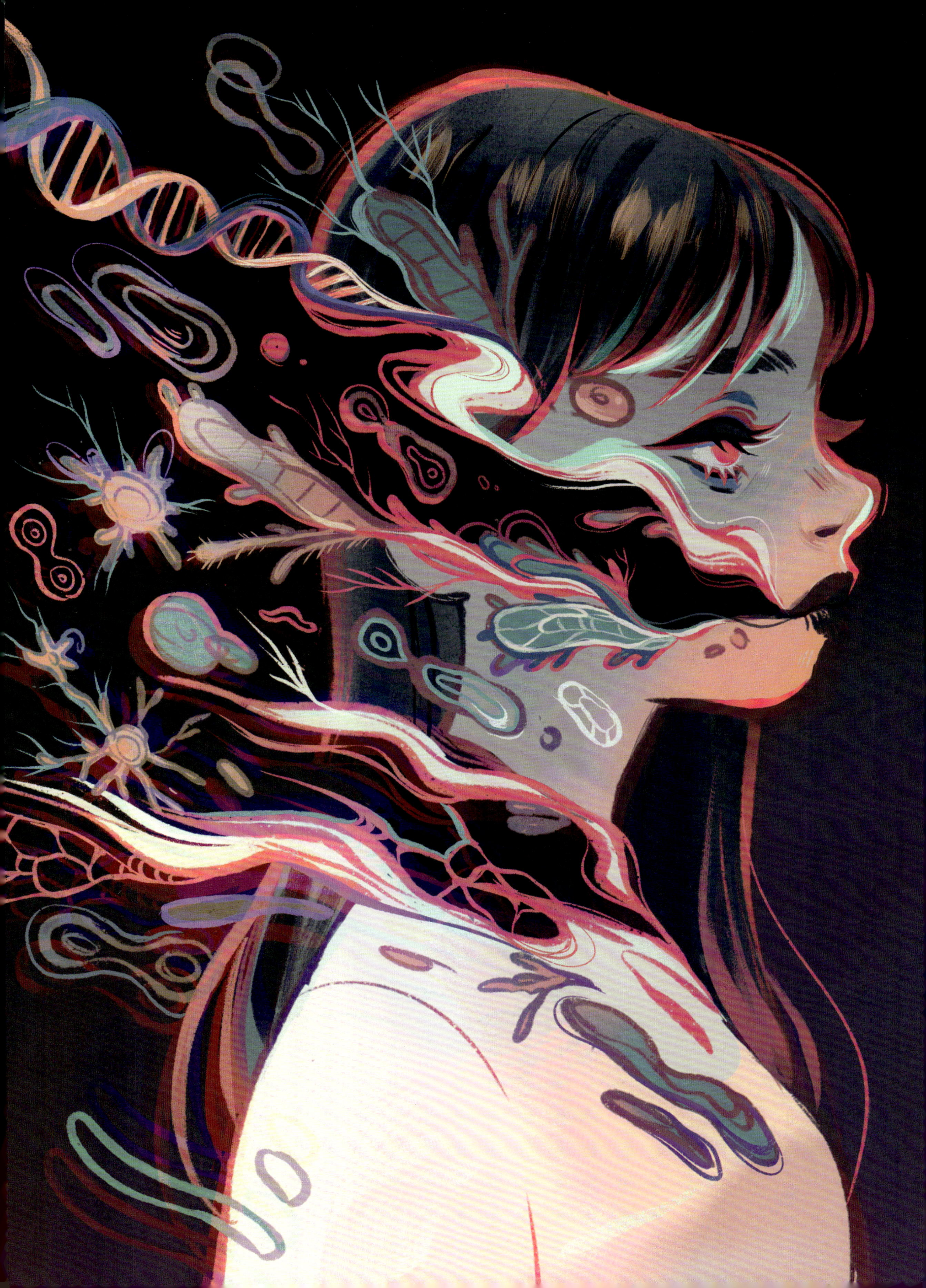

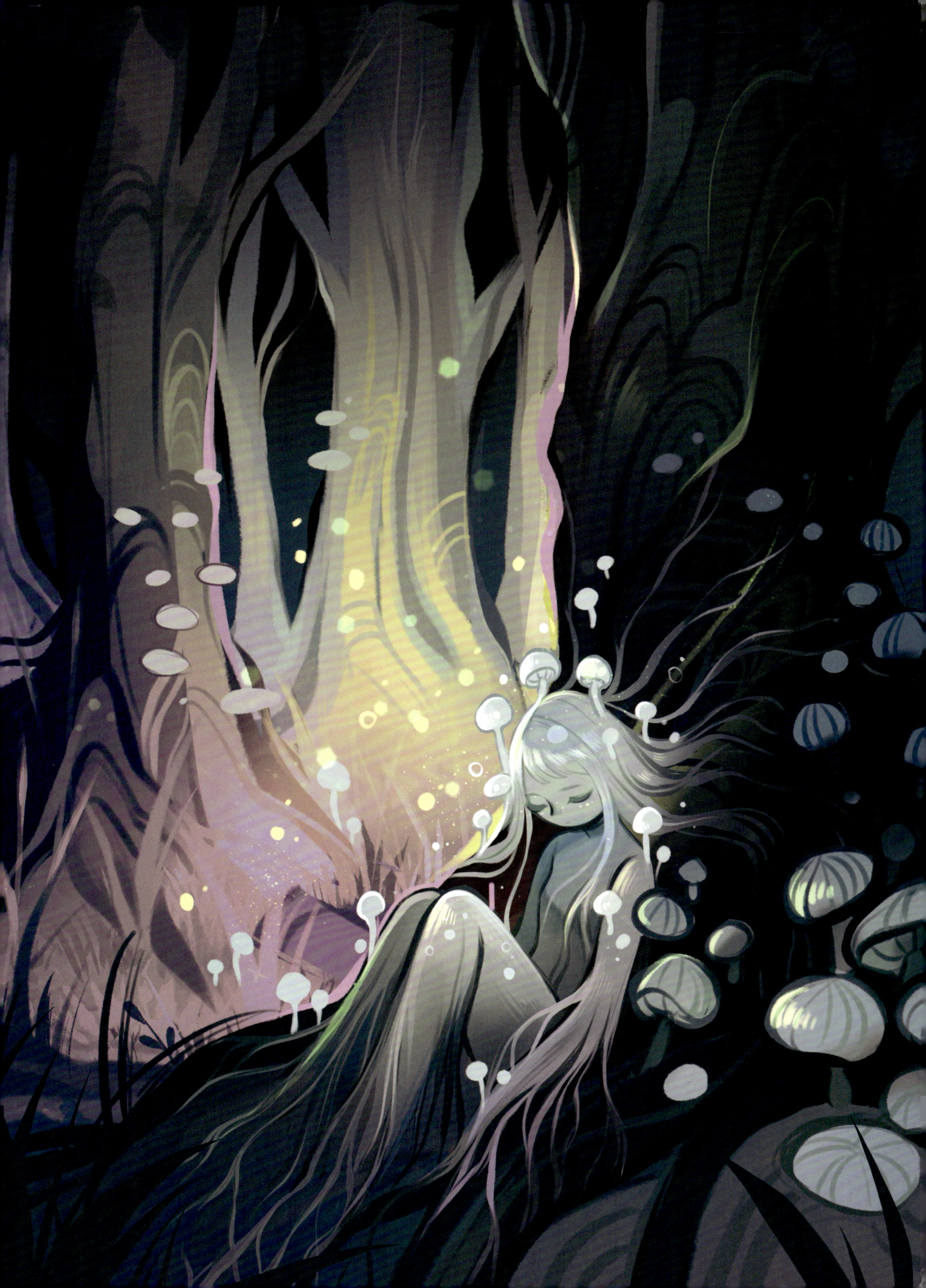

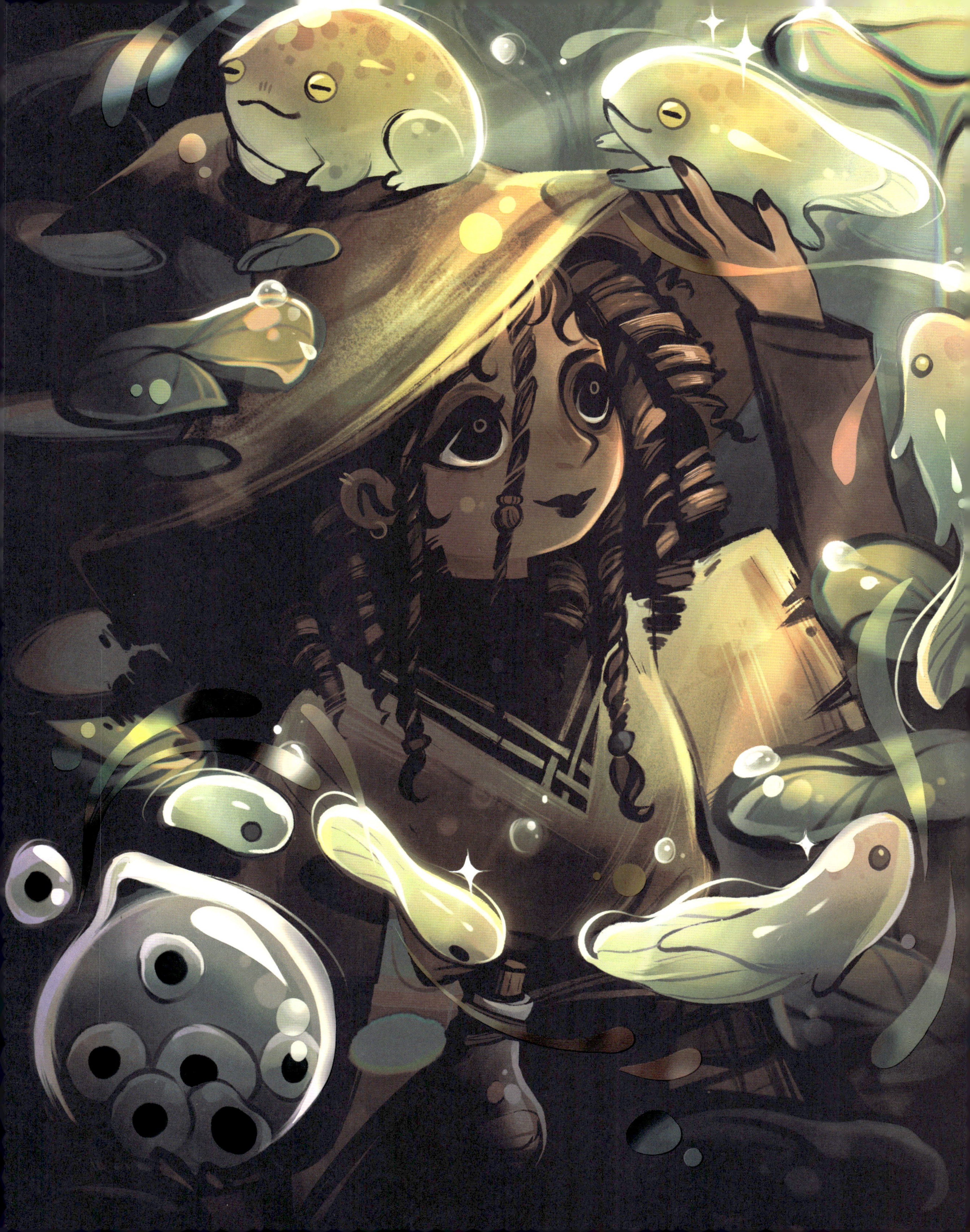

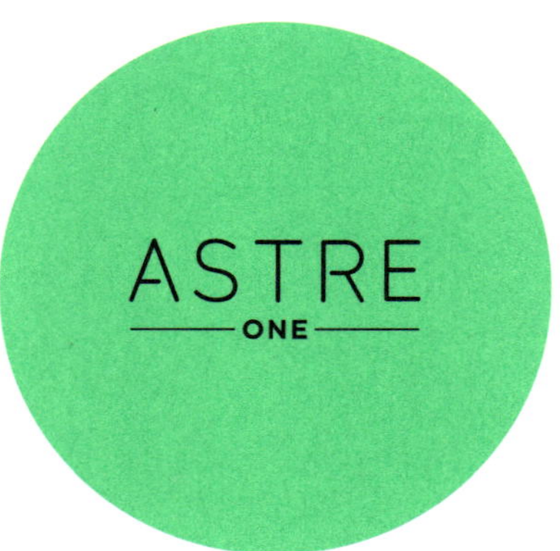

WITCH OF FROG BY FEEFAL

— ASTRE ORIGINAL PRINT —

'death can be
beautiful and
wonderful in
myriad ways'

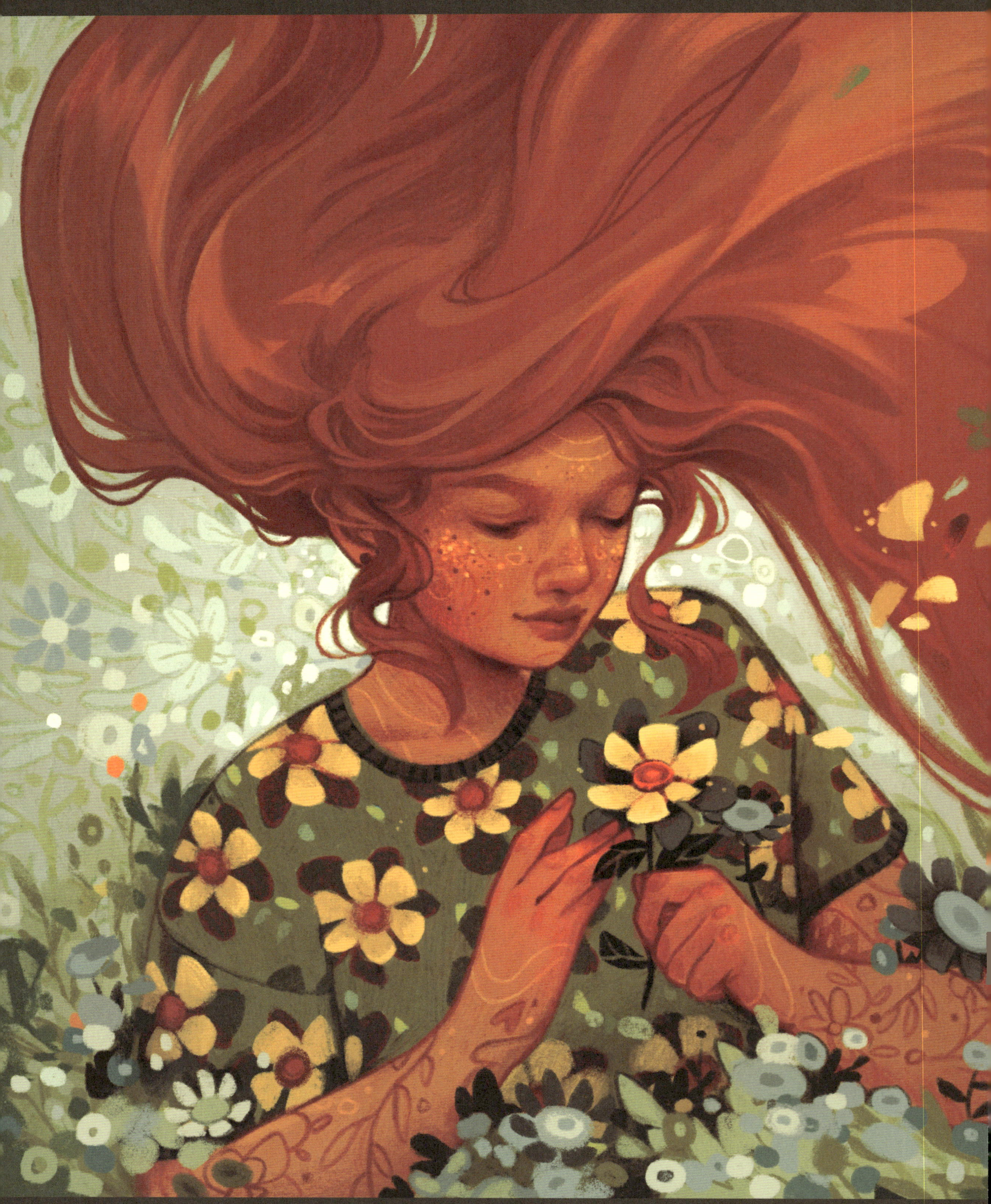

flowing nature

By Chantal Horeis

I'm often asked who the biggest influences on my art style are, and it's a question I struggle to answer. I feel like influences on my work happen organically and passively. I have heard a few people mention Gustav Klimt when they look at my work. I love Klimt, though I can't say I've ever consciously tried to copy his style. If you appreciate something visually, sometimes it just sticks with you. I've always looked up to Loish, so I am sure there is some influence there as well, especially since I draw a lot of female-presenting characters. Rebecca Green and Sha'an d'Anthes (aka furrylittlepeach) have influenced the naïve and raw art style that I use in some of my work. At the other end of the spectrum, I find the elegance and expressiveness of J.A.W. Cooper's work to die for. I guess I try to doodle somewhere in between all of these artists' styles, and many more, integrating their magic into mine, often without even knowing.

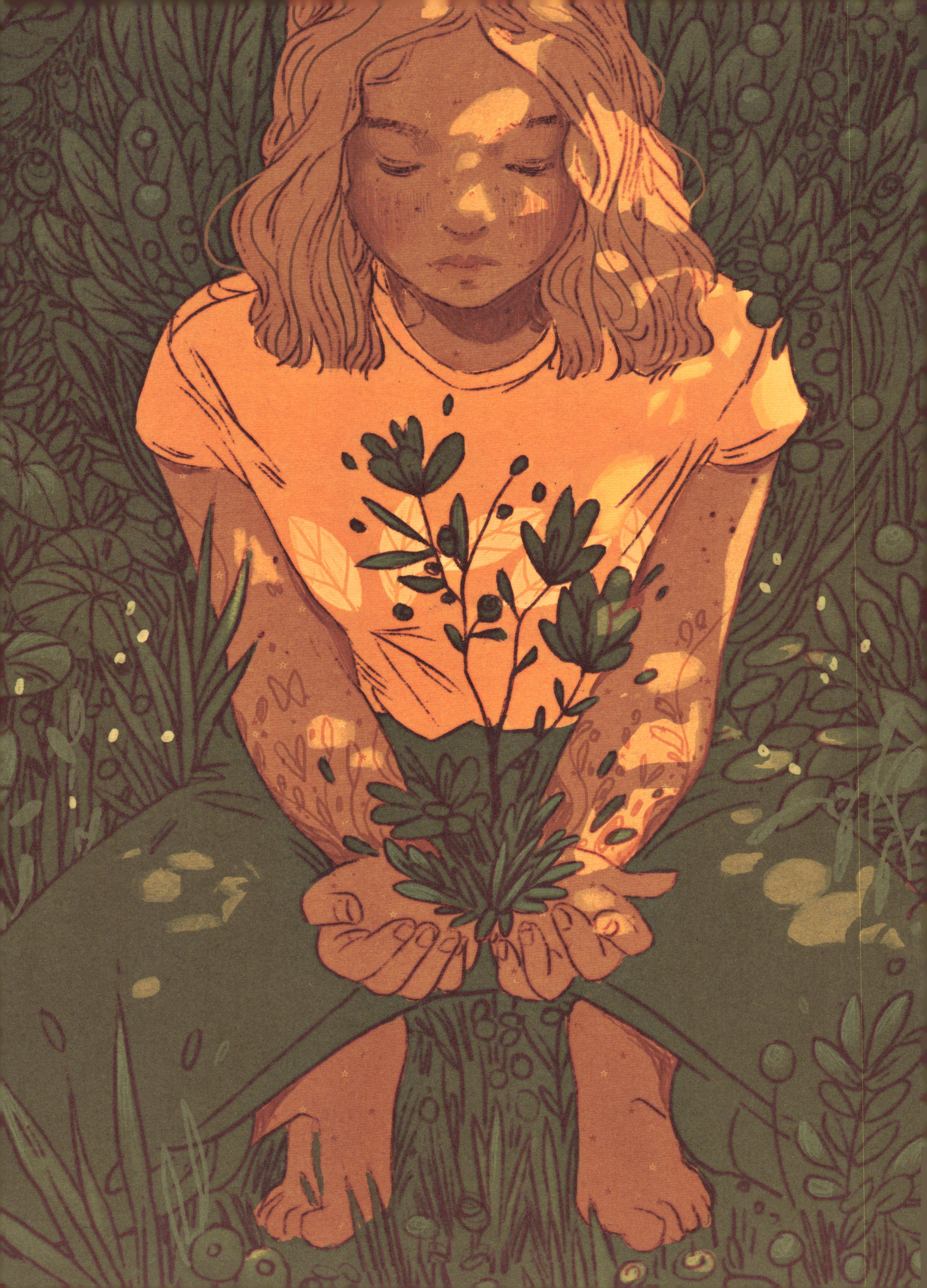

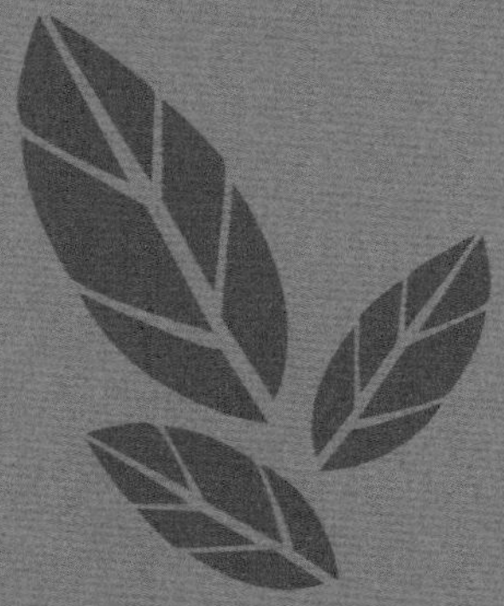

When I started out, I was very focused on what my style would be and the visual elements I wanted people to know me for. I tried to force myself into different restrictive boxes – maybe I would be the artist that drew traditionally and coloured digitally (as if there were only one!), maybe I would only ever work with graphite, or maybe all my characters would look the same way. I was constantly unhappy, eager to try new things, but forever scared that sacrificing consistency would jeopardize any shot I had at making a career out of my art.

I think my style evolved from fighting these inner thoughts and slowly letting go of these artificial restrictions I'd placed upon myself. By letting myself experiment more, I gradually found something unique that connected all my passions together. Flipping through sketchbooks full of my work let me identify common themes and see my style take shape. Over time, I became more and more focused on nature and creating characters that exude calm. I found myself gravitating towards certain colours, too. I think my style is much more playful now because I know I can trust that my personality will always shine through. And if not, maybe I'll find a new part of my voice that wants to be part of it all.

ON PREVIOUS PAGE:
Breeze | *This piece was commissioned by Procreate; they wanted me to create a piece using traditional textures*

LEFT:
Grow | *This piece came together on a very hot June day; I was craving some cool, airy shade, spending my time watering my garden and house plants*

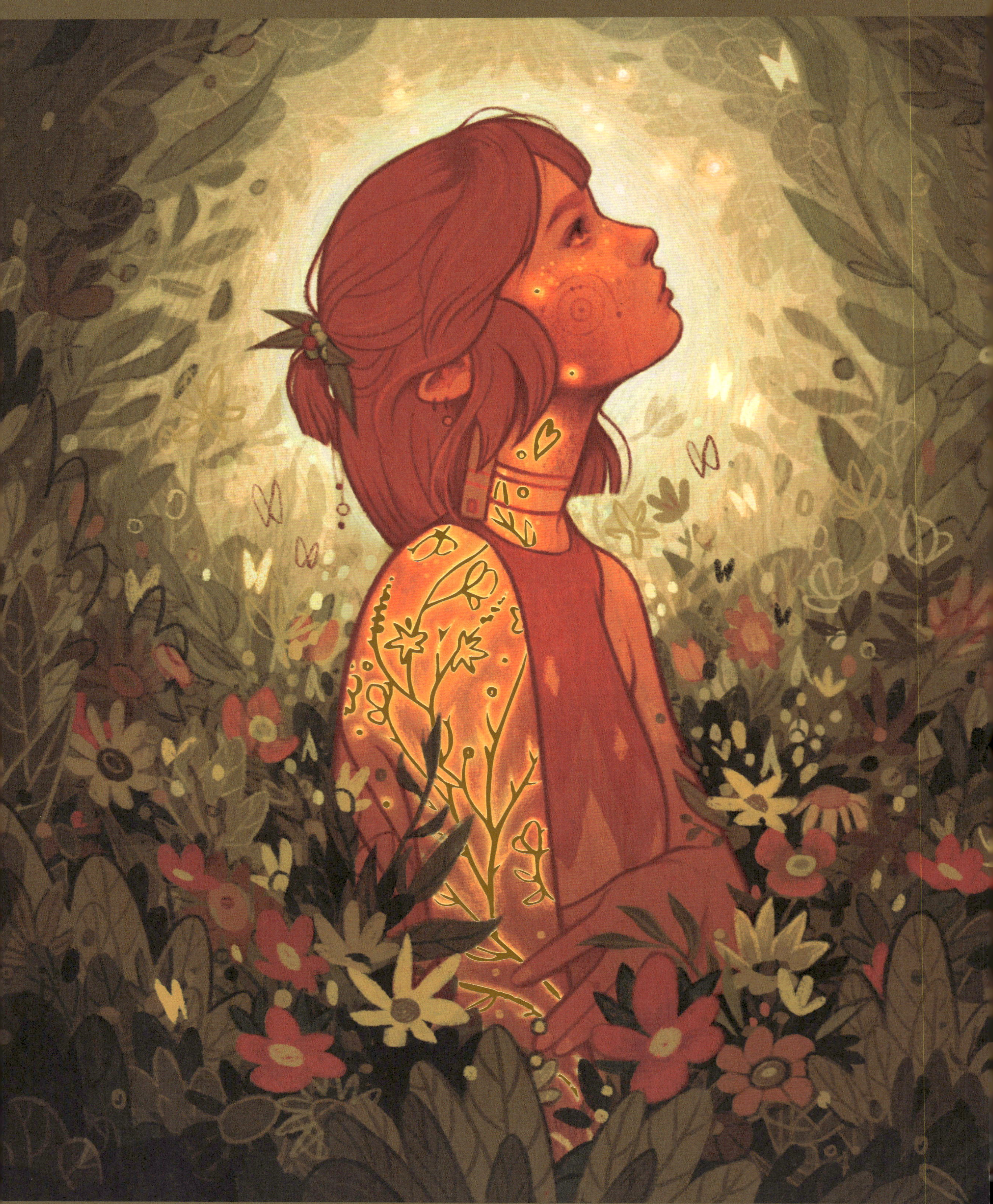

'I gradually found
something unique
that connected all my
passions together'

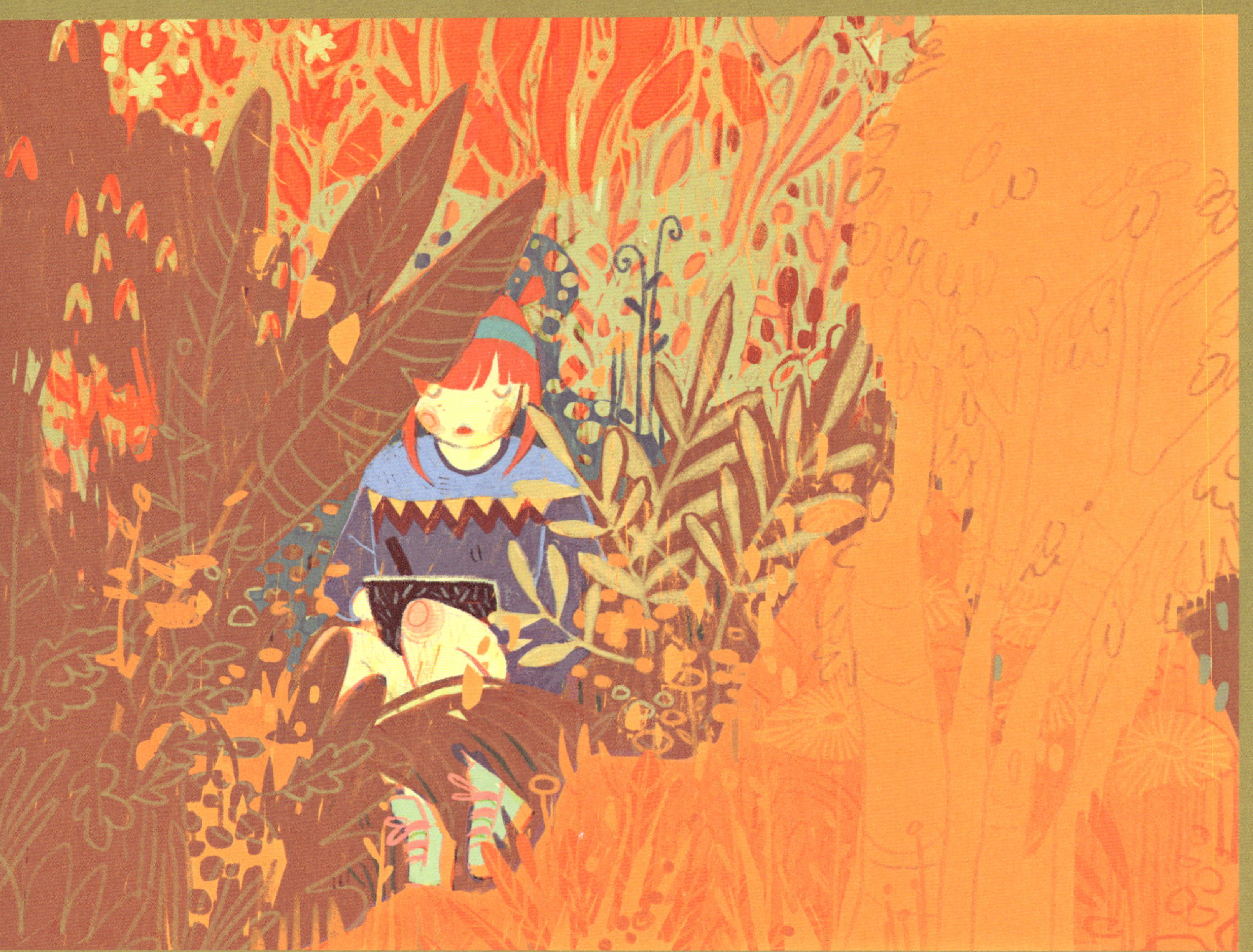

Cosmic Heart is the original piece I've created for ASTRE. I've had the idea for this piece in my head for a while – it came to me with a few other similar concepts, thoughts of distant worlds and longing to be somewhere else. I love stars and flowers so the thought of combining the two was very exciting. The swirls that surround the character were the final element I added. I felt like something was subtly missing, and these final details made the piece complete. I have always loved making round, organic, and swirly gestures whenever I have a pen in my hand, and I find compositions of different textures with different frequencies or densities super appealing.

In *Cosmic Heart*, I wanted to capture what I see when I look at nature. When I walk into a forest, everything is eye candy to me and I find millions of different little chaotic-yet-structured compositions that I would love to take home with me. I live in a house surrounded by nature. We have a tiny piece of forest that is part of our garden and there are many big, beautiful forests and lakes here in Sweden – you never have to go far to find one. I see nature when I look out the window. It's all around me – a feeling I hope *Cosmic Heart* evokes. Nature can be so calming, which I think is something many people are longing for these days.

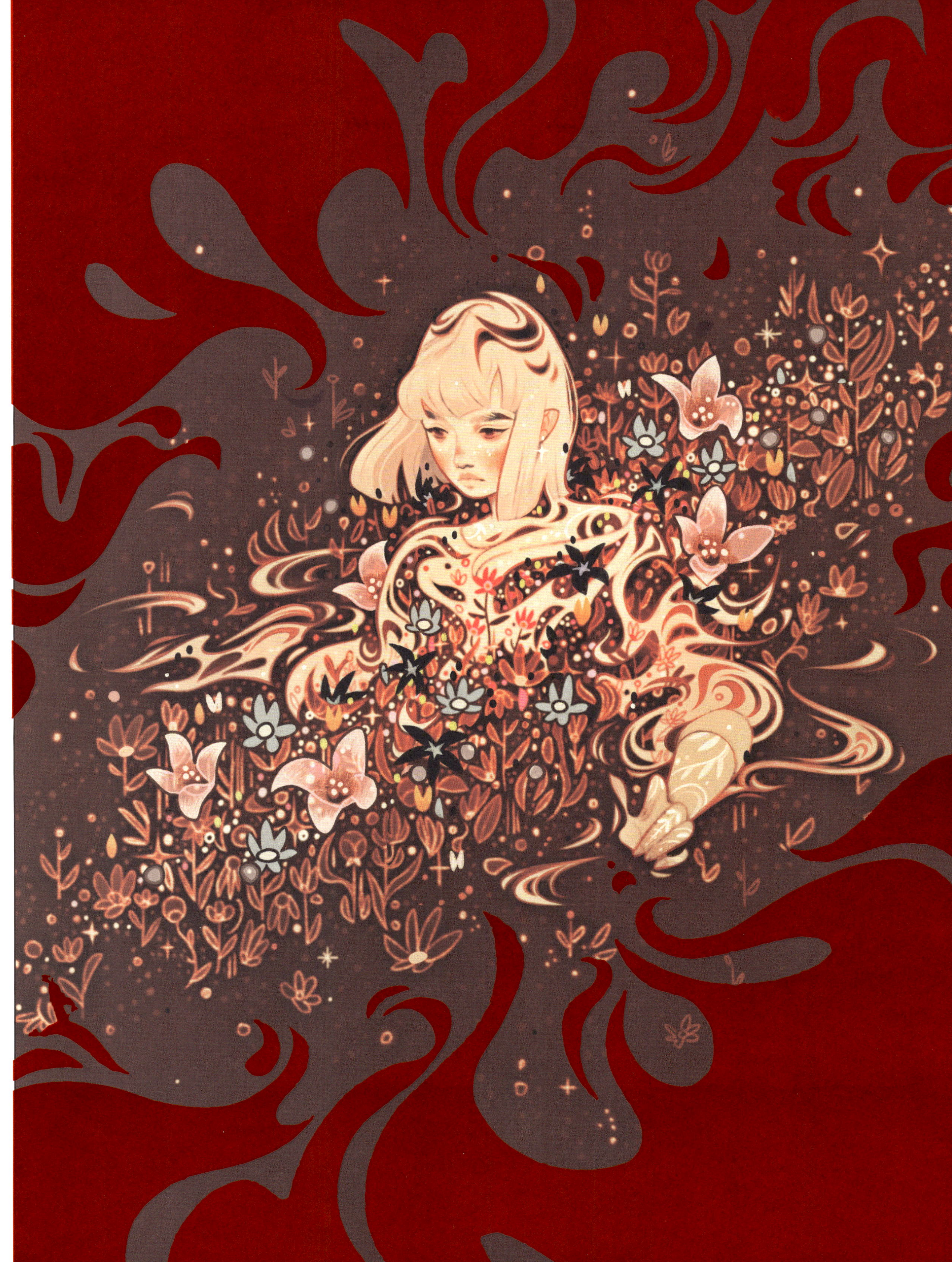

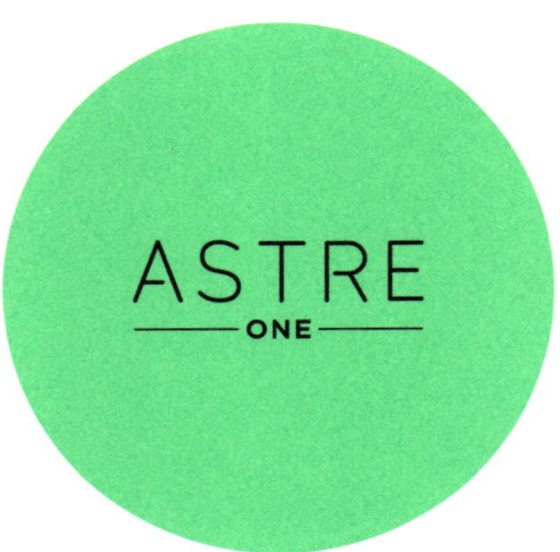

COSMIC HEART BY CHANTAL HOREIS

— ASTRE ORIGINAL PRINT —

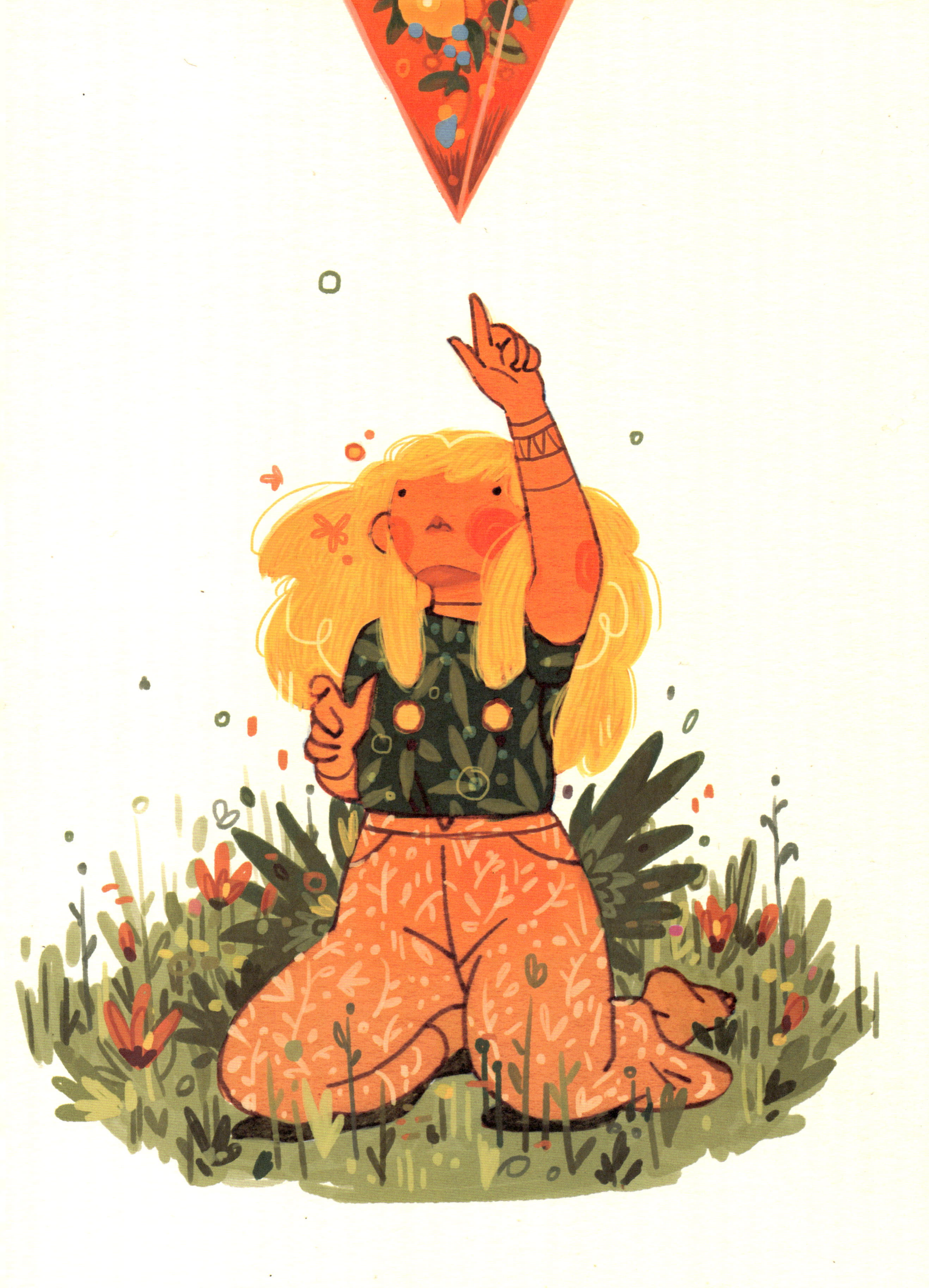

RIGHT:
Serenity | This was a private commission
of a disabled girl enjoying nature

NEXT PAGE:
Grow on me | I think this image represents
everything I love to draw and paint: the
meadow, the plants, the warm colours,
and the strong female character

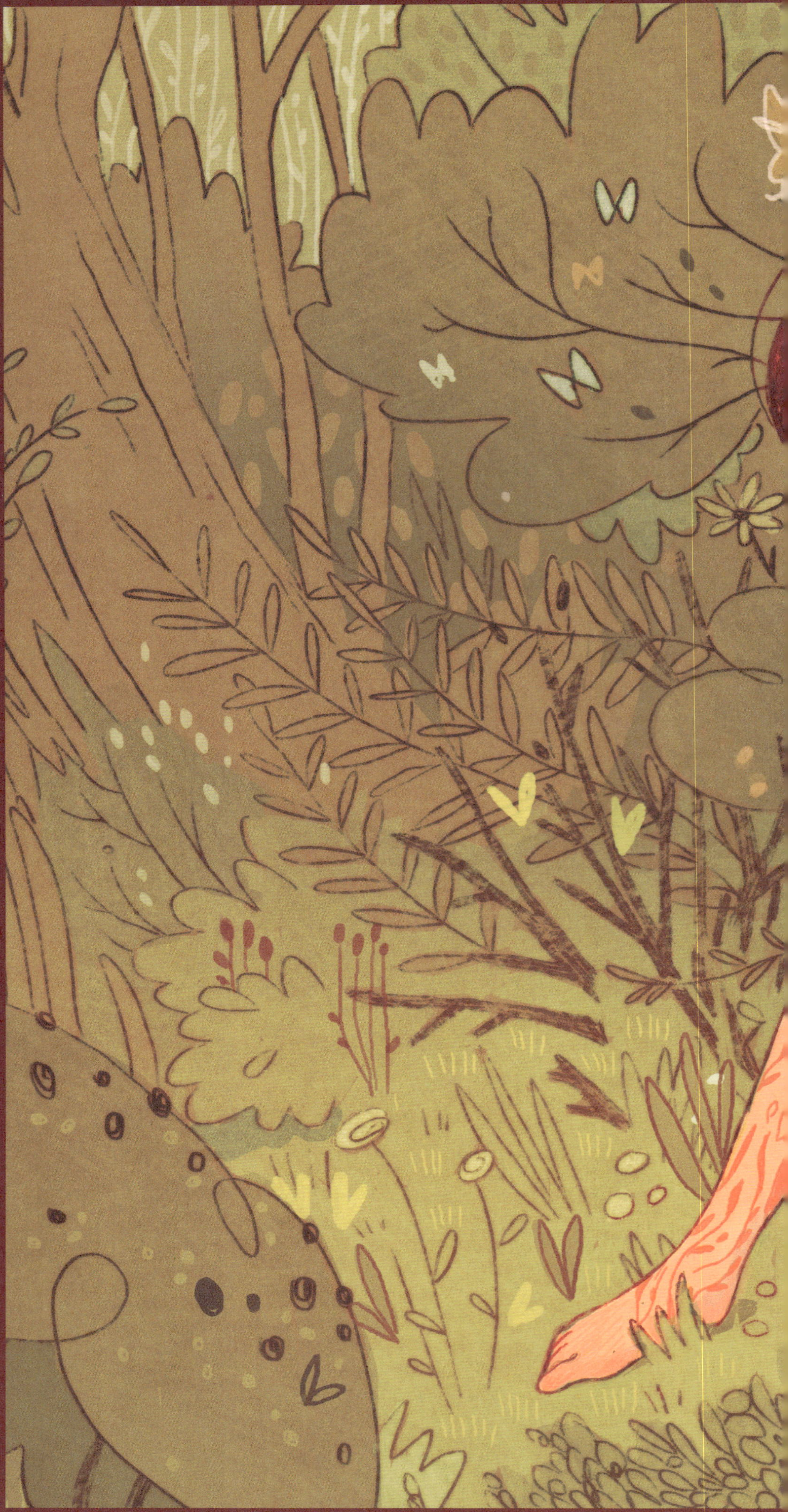

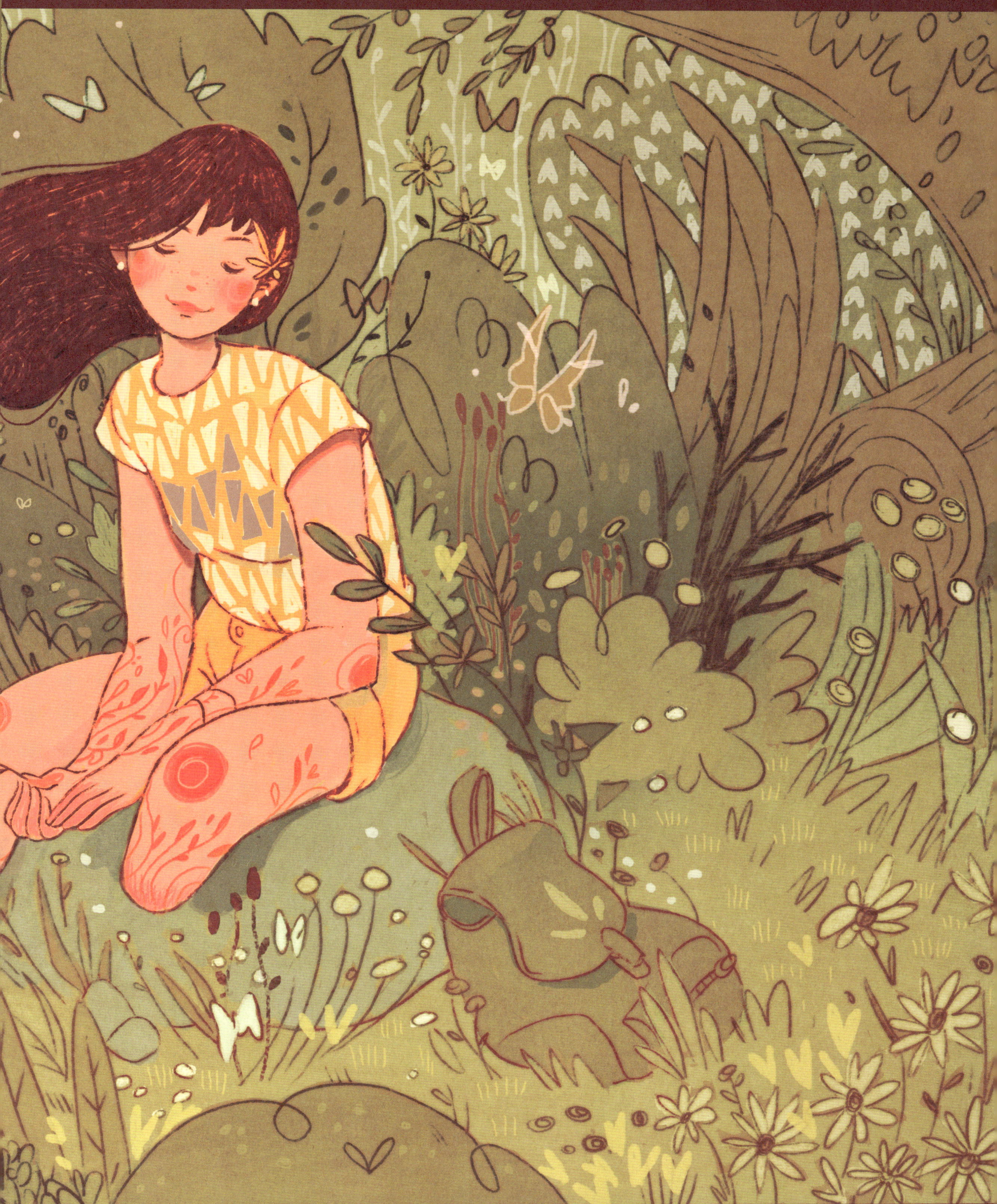

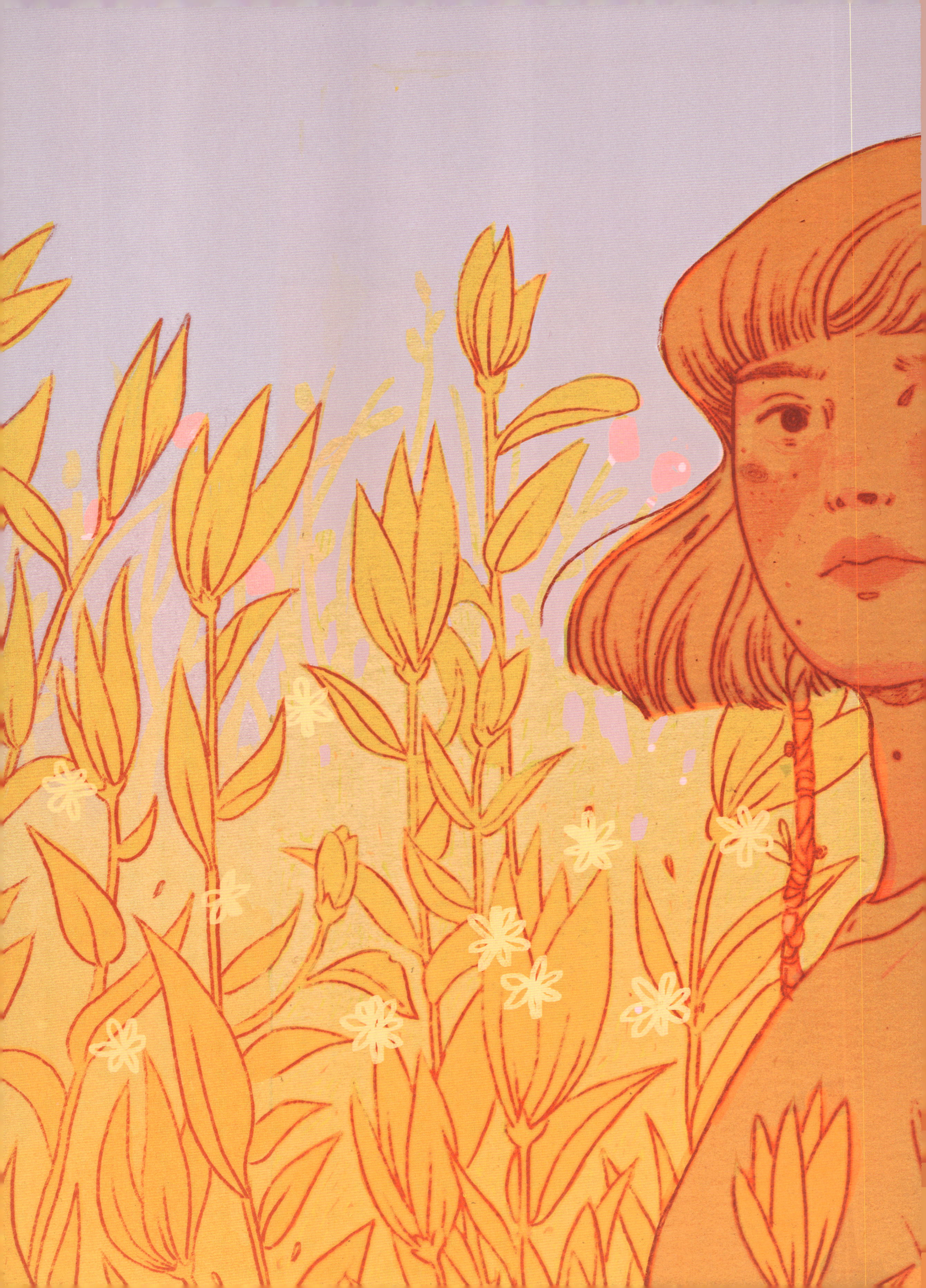

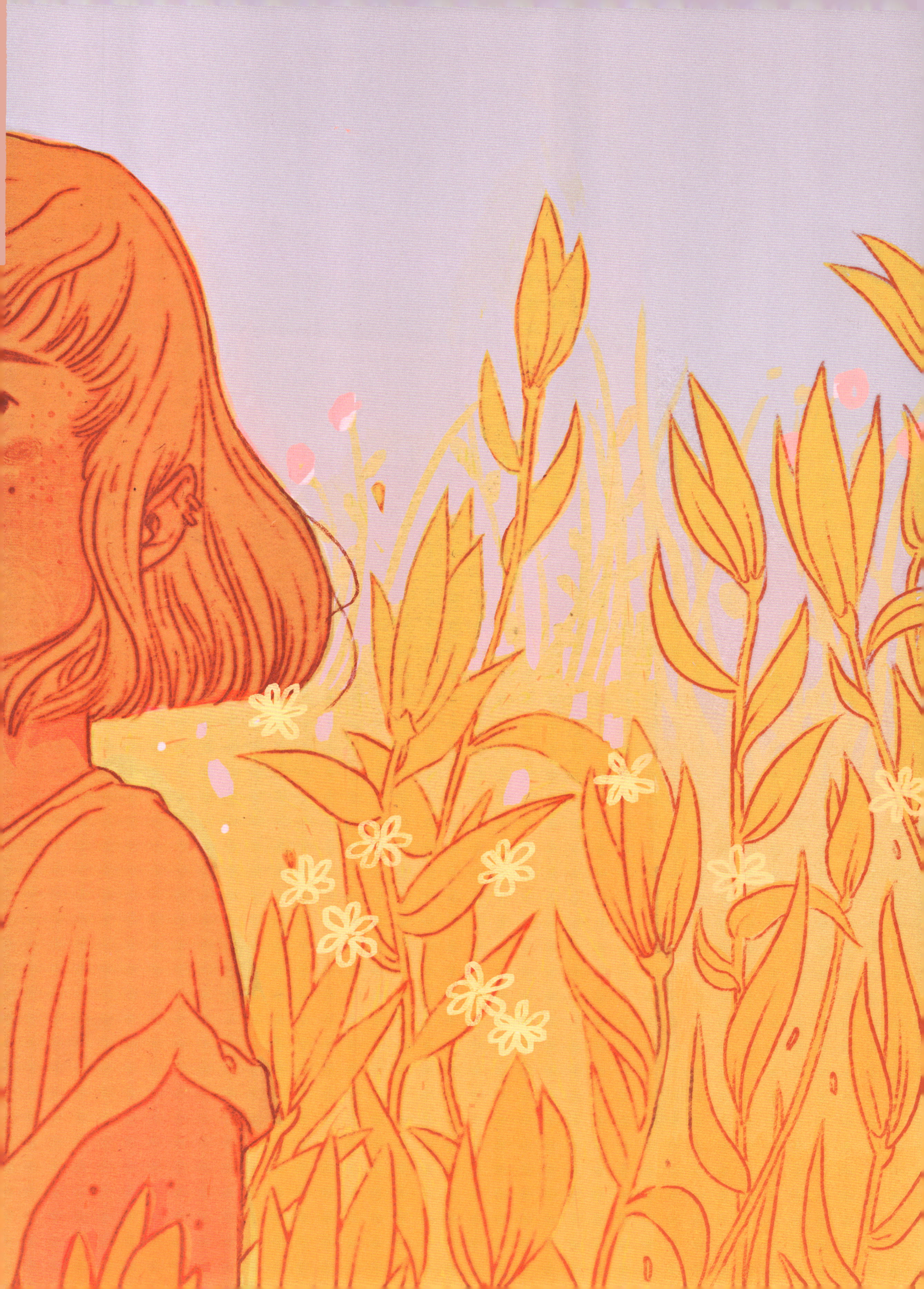

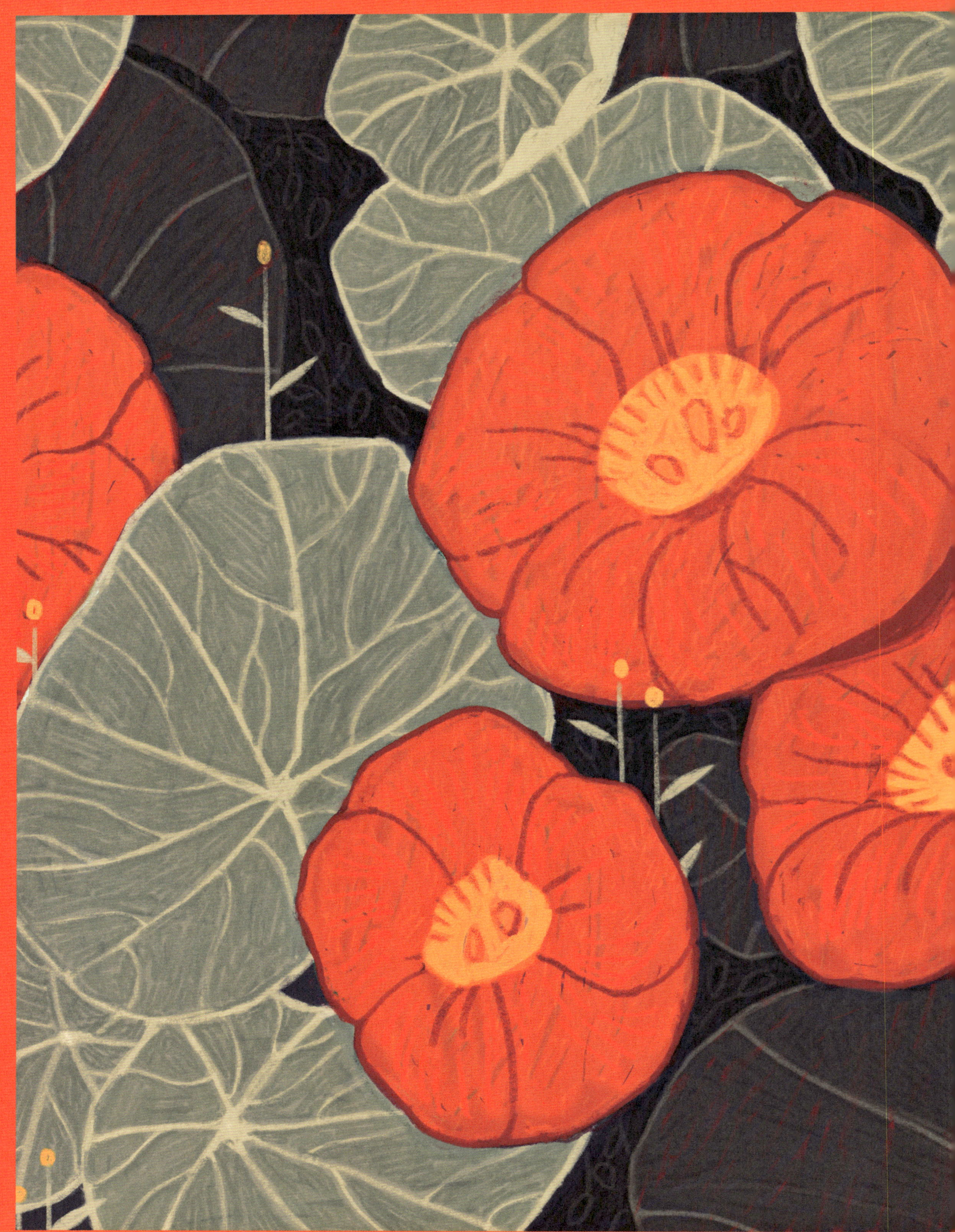

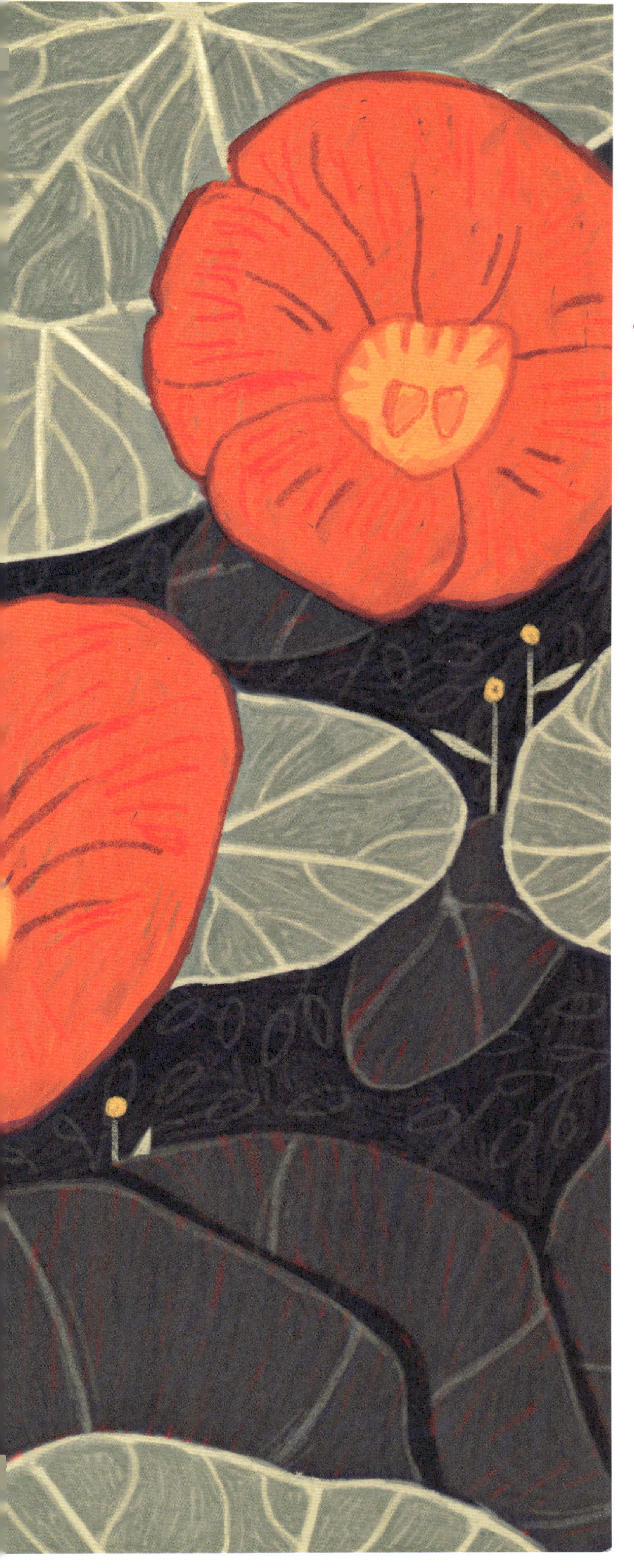

I don't usually study plants or minerals or do any formal sort of research for my nature drawings like this, although it does sound appealing, and I would love to be more knowledgeable one day. I don't have specific books I use as inspiration, either, but I do love to flip through scientific books with illustrations whenever I get my hands on one.

A theme that I explore in a lot of my pieces like *Cosmic Heart* is of characters being completely surrounded by nature – obscured, even swallowed up. This is a theme that comes very naturally to me when I work, without me actively trying to say a specific thing. I think these sorts of images come from a deep longing to connect with nature and maybe one's inner, natural ways. The ongoing climate crisis and modern technologies pose such a great threat to the natural world, and often block our access to these simple pleasures. Of course, this sounds so passive – I know that we are all responsible for the perpetuation of our circumstances. Although I love technology and all the things it has to offer, I also feel the sorrow of what we lose as we move ever further away from a simpler way of life. I know I'm not alone in feeling this way, either.

I hope that art can be an inspiration for people to reconnect with the natural world. Some people do not have easy access to a forest, a lake, or the sea, so art can bring nature to them. But regardless of whether you live in a city or out in the country, I think anyone can see an image, maybe even while looking at their phone, and that person can pause, and be reminded of how nature can make them feel. I think the act of capturing nature in an image is a way of honouring it, too. It's a way of saying, 'I'm showing this to you because I think it's important and valuable. It made me feel something – what do you feel when you look at it?' So, art can hopefully start a conversation, at least, and make someone stop and think. ◪

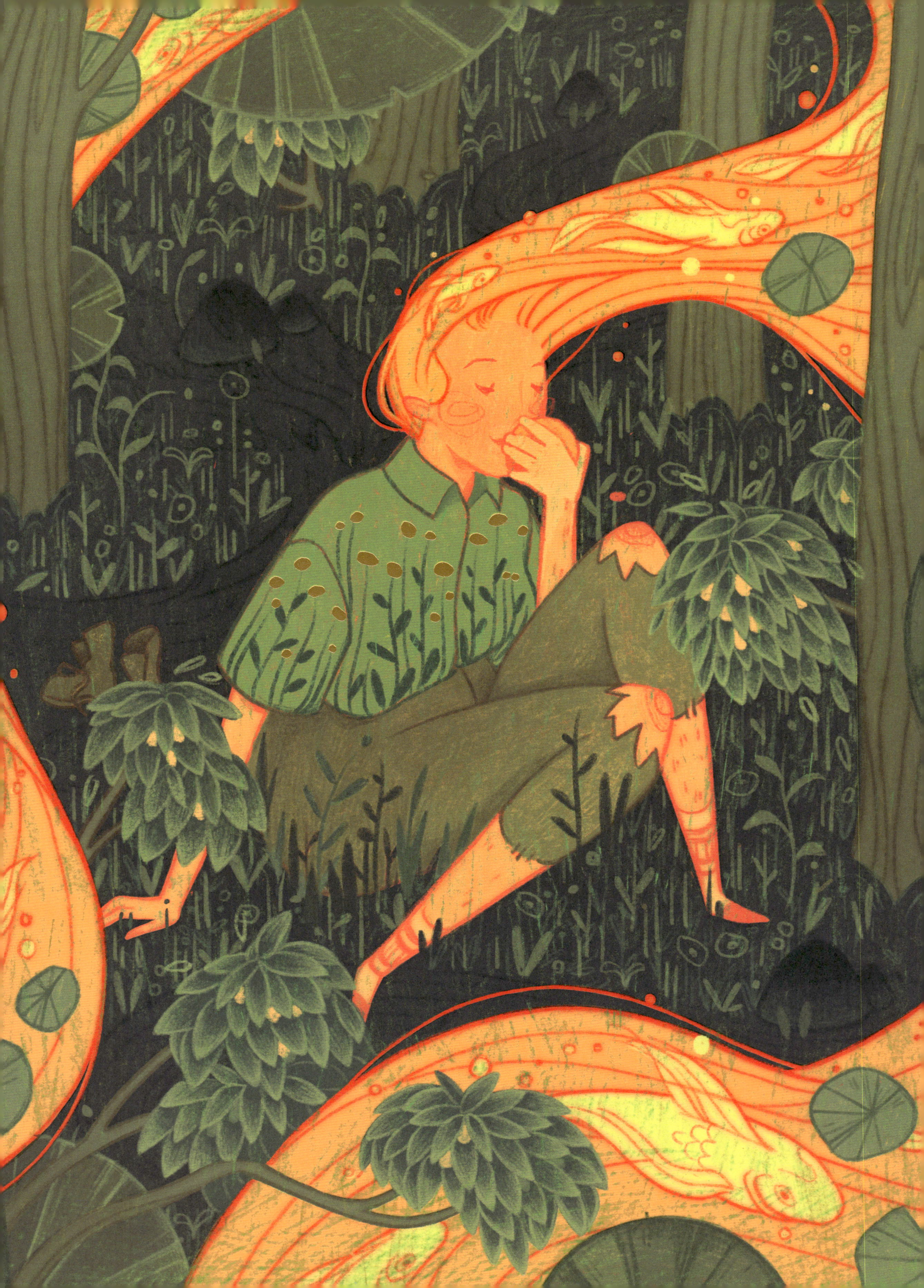

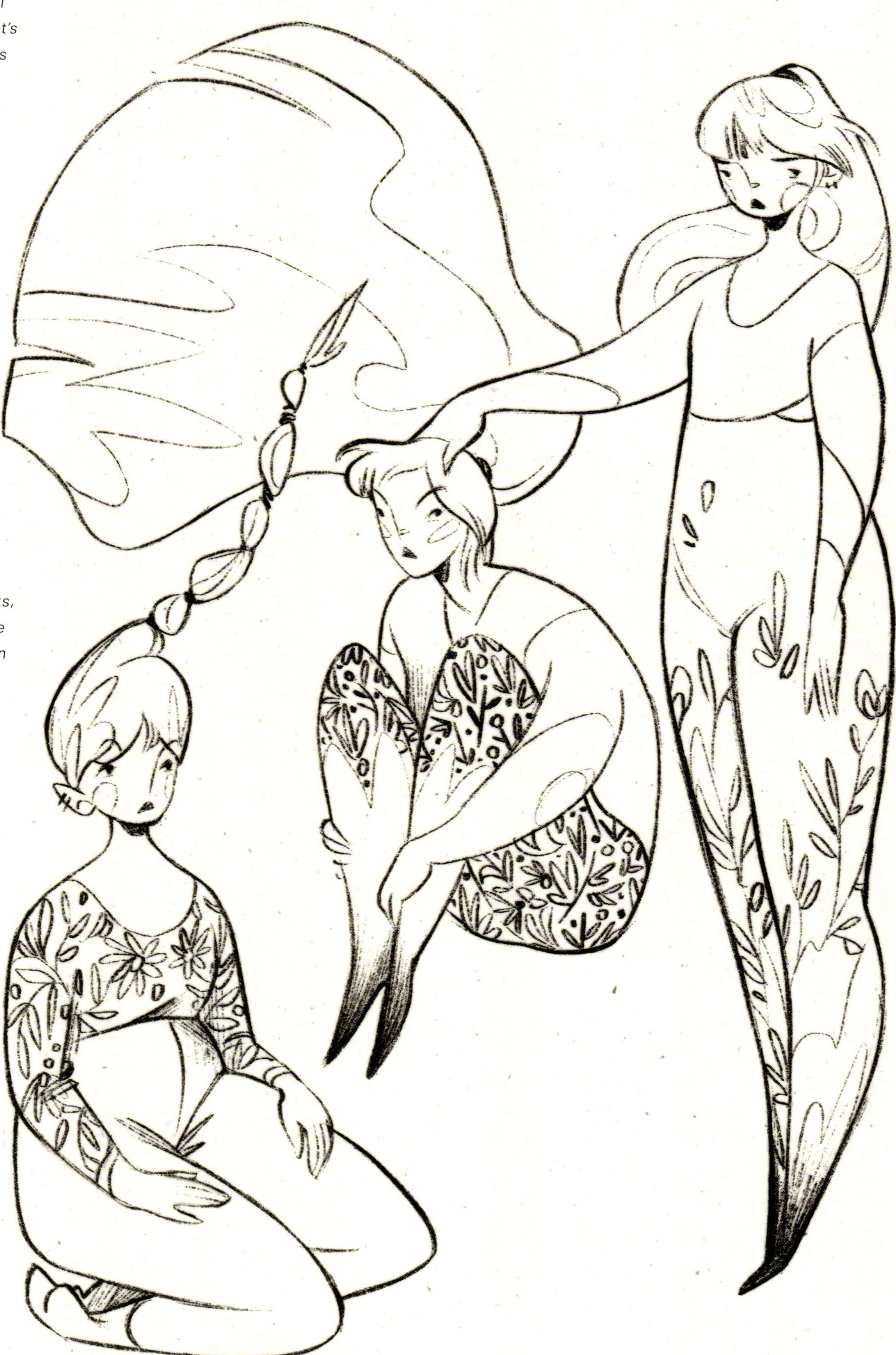

PREVIOUS PAGE:

Flowers | *This was made in Procreate, from beginning to end. I had a photograph of these flowers sitting on my shelf and I just had to draw them. It was a wonderful exercise and with its simplicity it's still one of my favourite artworks I have ever created*

LEFT:

Natureanoid | *This piece was created as part of a bigger project called 'Quaranoids', about different forms of humans that formed during the pandemic quarantine. My contribution was the Natureanoid – a person that coped with this troubled time by spending as much time outdoors as possible*

BELOW:

Ongrowing | *Some character sketches that I created on my iPad. I love to form characters from big, organic shapes, and adorn them with floral ornaments, patterns, and tattoos. This is the most appealing thing to me when drawing – just lots of flowy lines and doodles creating an image*

Beneath the waves

By Eliza Ivanova

My original piece for ASTRE was shaped by the sea – a woman listening to the waves through a conch shell. The ocean has always been close to me, in both distance and heart, and water finds its way into much of my work. The sea's beauty and quiet danger fascinate me – this piece was an attempt to capture that deep longing for a blue horizon.

I began with a pencil sketch, then brought it into Procreate to add colour and refine the details. I explored several sketches before landing on the final design, looking for the right balance between listening and longing. I chose to cover the character's eyes, hiding one sense to amplify another.

I live and work in the Bay Area, where I mostly spend my time on personal projects. I still dabble in the film and animation industries, but lately I've been craving the solitude of fine art. This yearning is emerging in my current work – images of rest and contemplation, reflecting a need to escape the constant noise of the world.

While working on ASTRE, and its philosophy of pushing back against AI art, I was asked to consider what I felt about this new technology. While I appreciate the strides in science and progress, I can't ignore how AI is being used to exploit and erase the creative efforts of artists, with little regard for their original work. The relentless imitation without ackhowledgment or compensation is frustrating. I believe in ethical technology, but for now, AI feels like a tool for theft. ◣

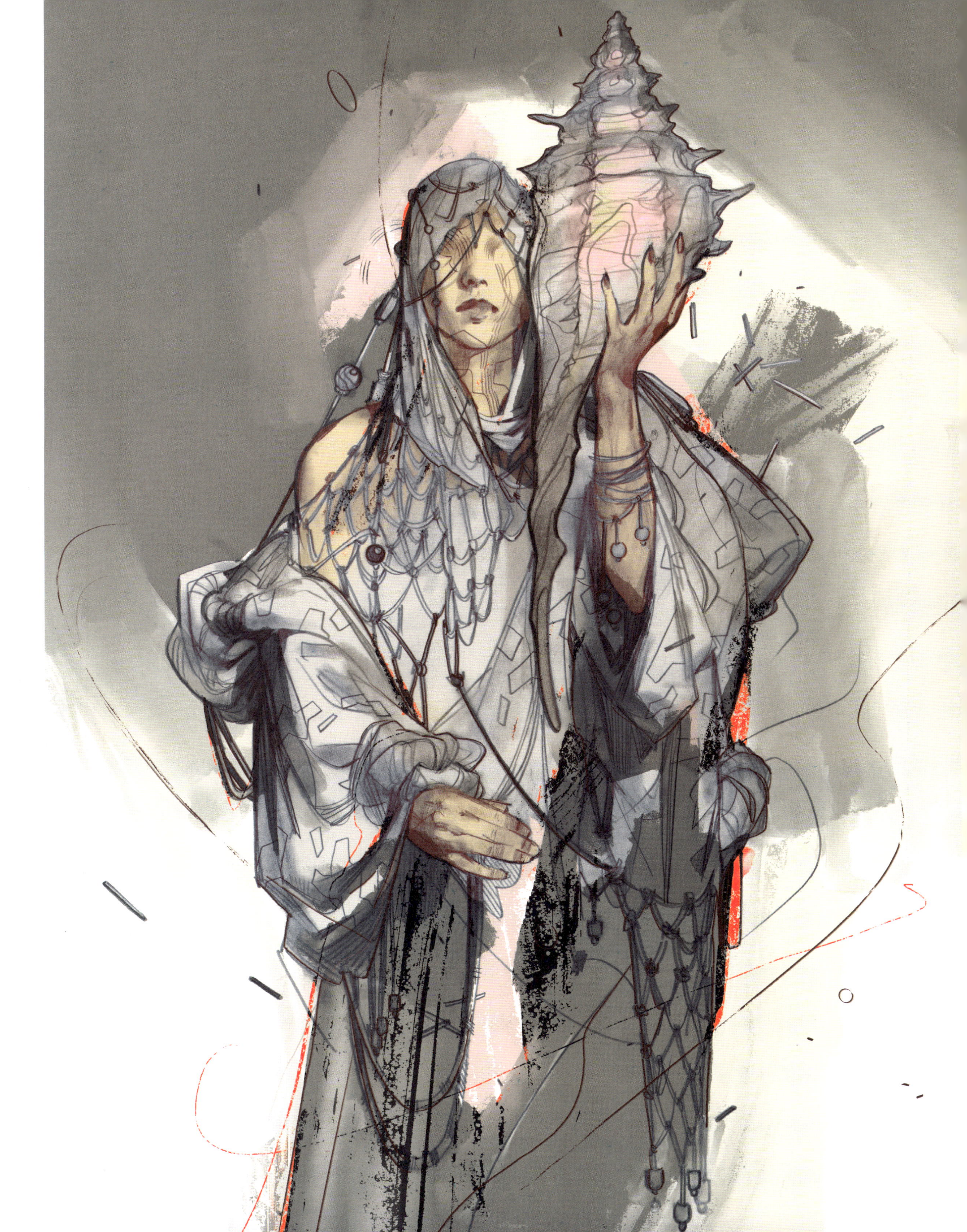

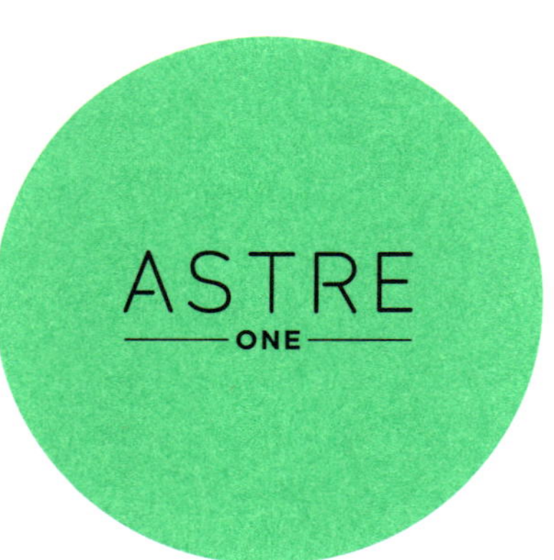

CONCH BY ELIZA IVANOVA

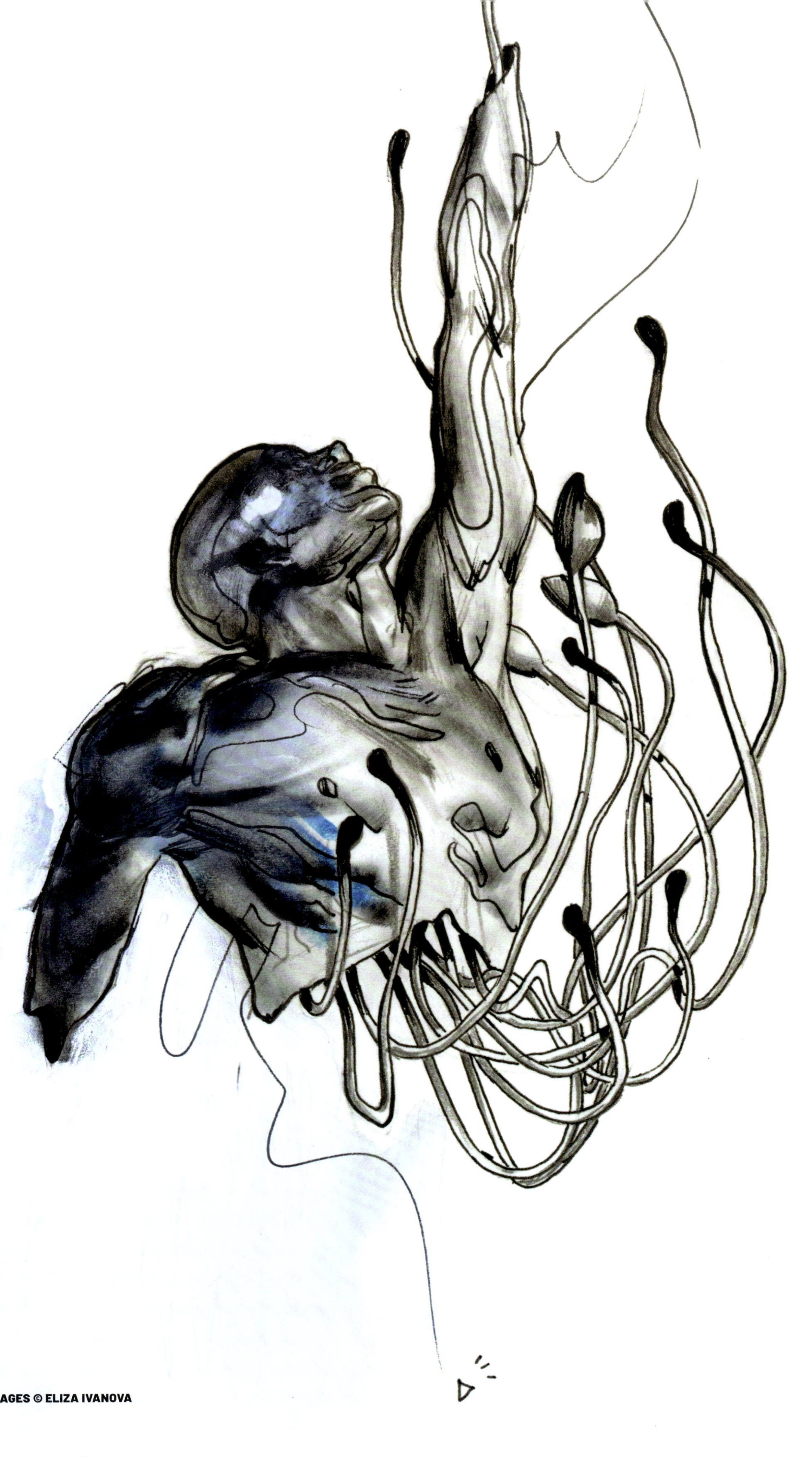

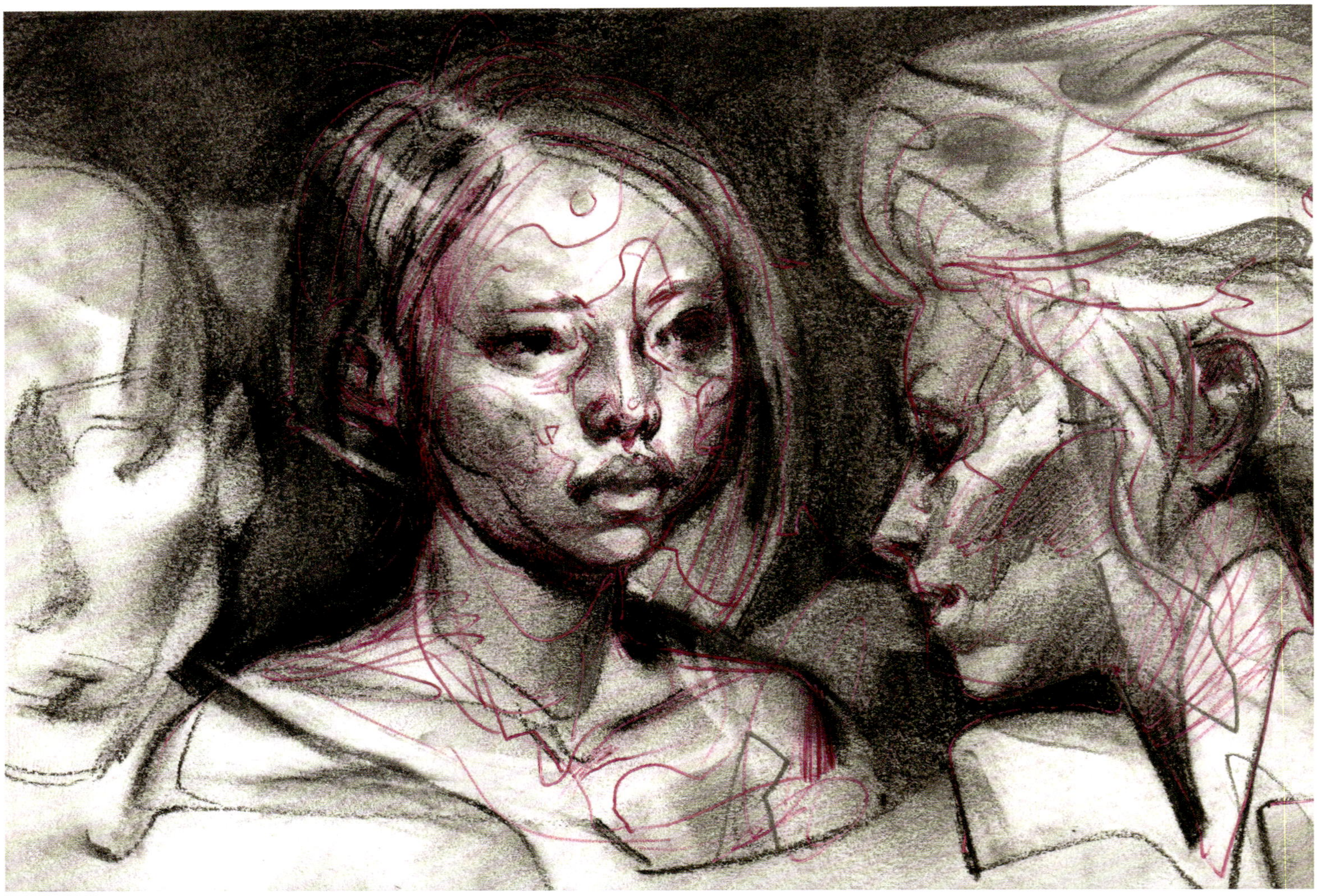

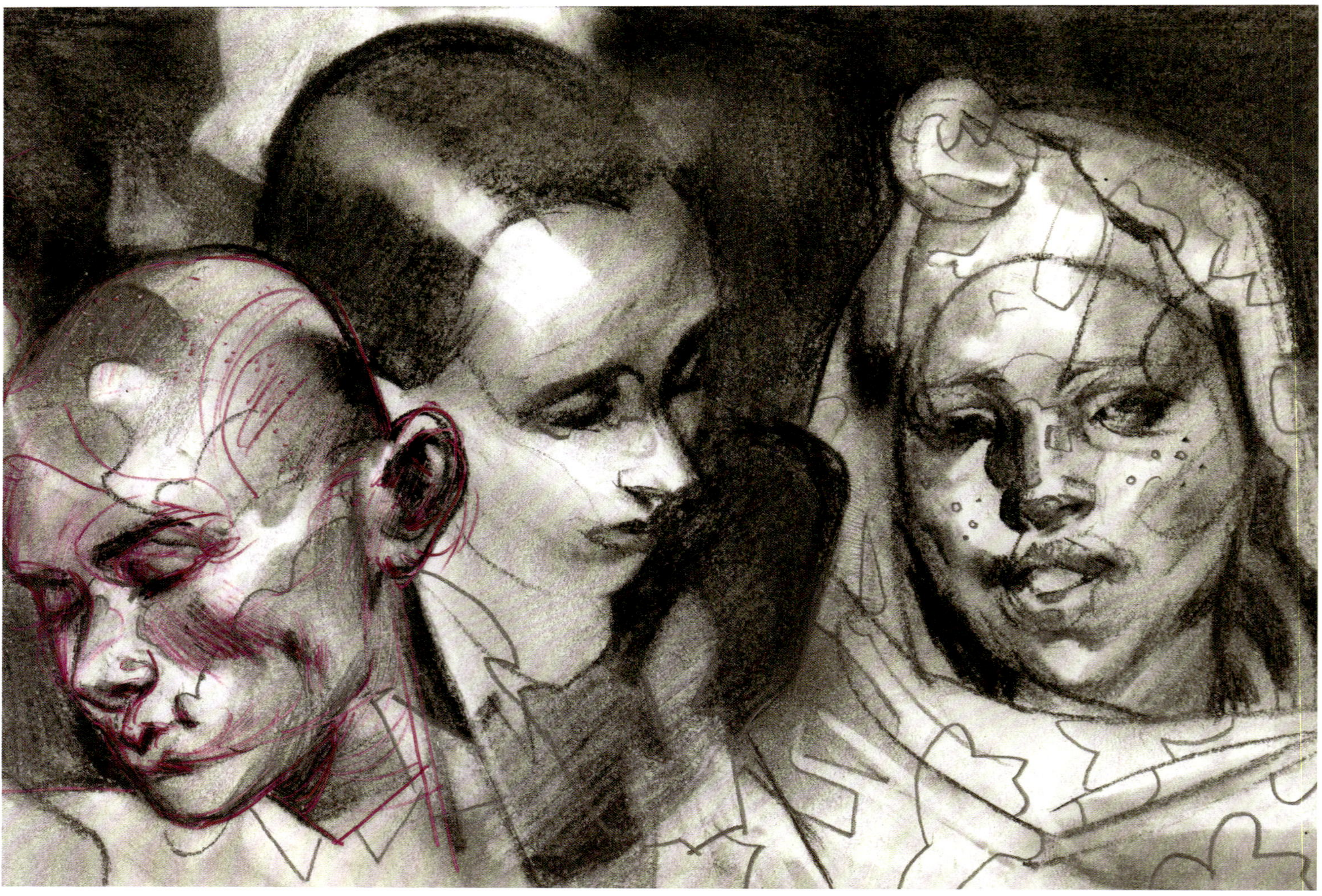

I am fascinated
by everything that
has to do with
the ocean and the
beauty and dread
that it can bring

A history of myth

By Sean Layh

My career as an artist began in earnest in 2021. While I was a keen painter and drawer in my youth, I couldn't find a way turn it into a stable career in the years following school. When the opportunity finally presented itself, nearly two decades later, I was in an unrelated field of work. Since becoming a full-time artist, I have had the honor of exhibiting at the European Museum of Modern Art (MEAM) in Barcelona, and Arcadia Contemporary in New York, as well as being a finalist and semi-finalist in the Portrait Society of America's International competition, in 2023 and 2024 respectively.

In some ways, my art style has barely evolved in my time as an artist. When I started painting as a sixteen-year-old, my first attempt was on a huge canvas, depicting the crucifixion. It was ambitious in scale and composition, as well as dramatic and sombre. I feel like I am doing the same thing nearly twenty-five years later. I guess what has changed, understandably, has been my increased proficiency as a painter and composer of images. My work has probably become a little less naive, but not entirely so. To deal with the subject matter that I love most – whether that is Sophocles, Shakespeare, or some naughty monarch or saint from yesteryear – I need to wilfully turn a blind eye to contemporary sentiments that can view these subjects as outdated. I think my work continues to evolve but in small increments over larger swathes of time.

***All Things Made New** | This painting takes its name from the eponymous book by Diarmaid MacCulloch. While the book deals explicitly with the history of the Protestant Reformation on the religious landscape of Medieval Europe, this painting was designed to more broadly depict the destructive nature of zealotry*

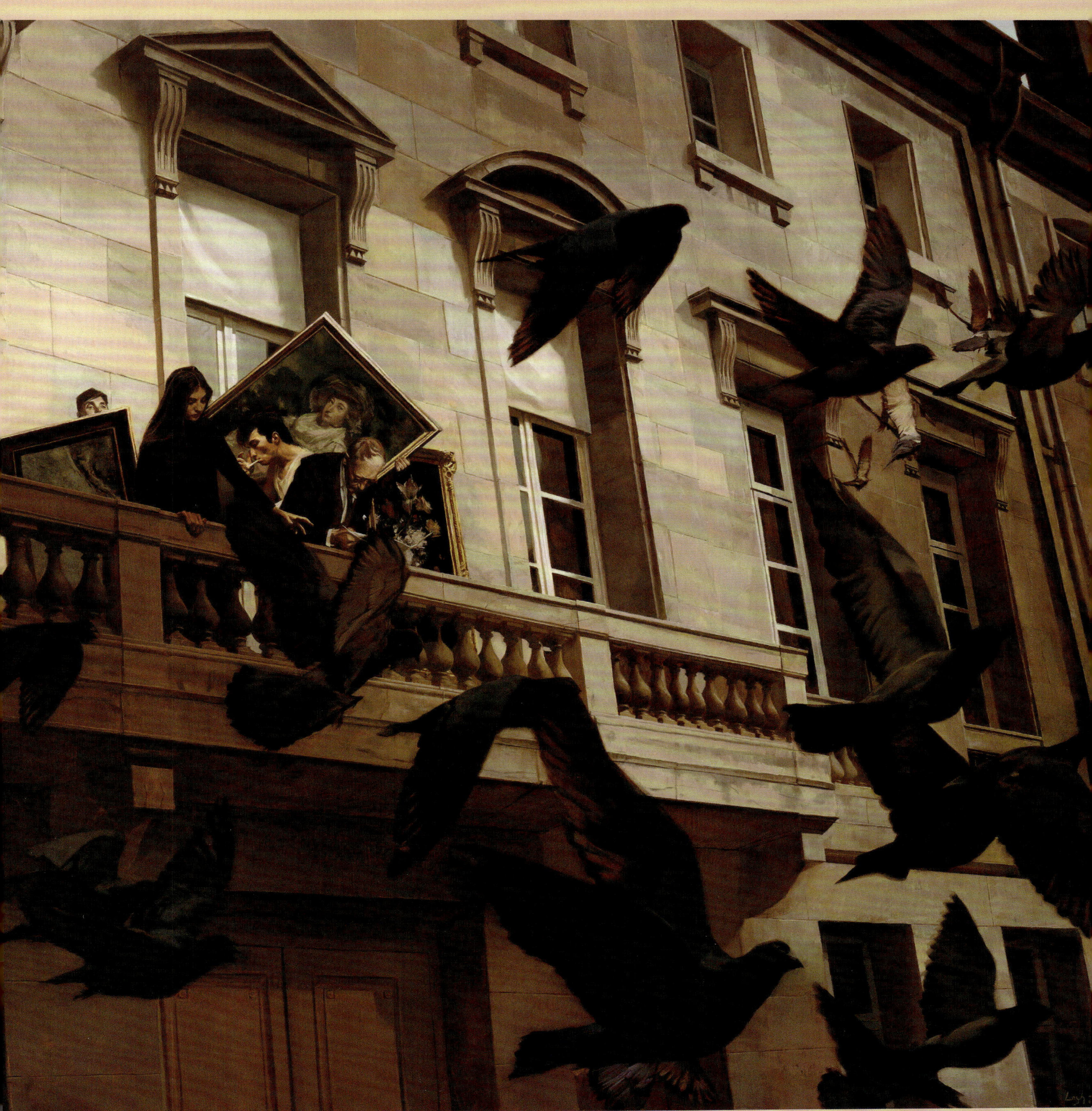

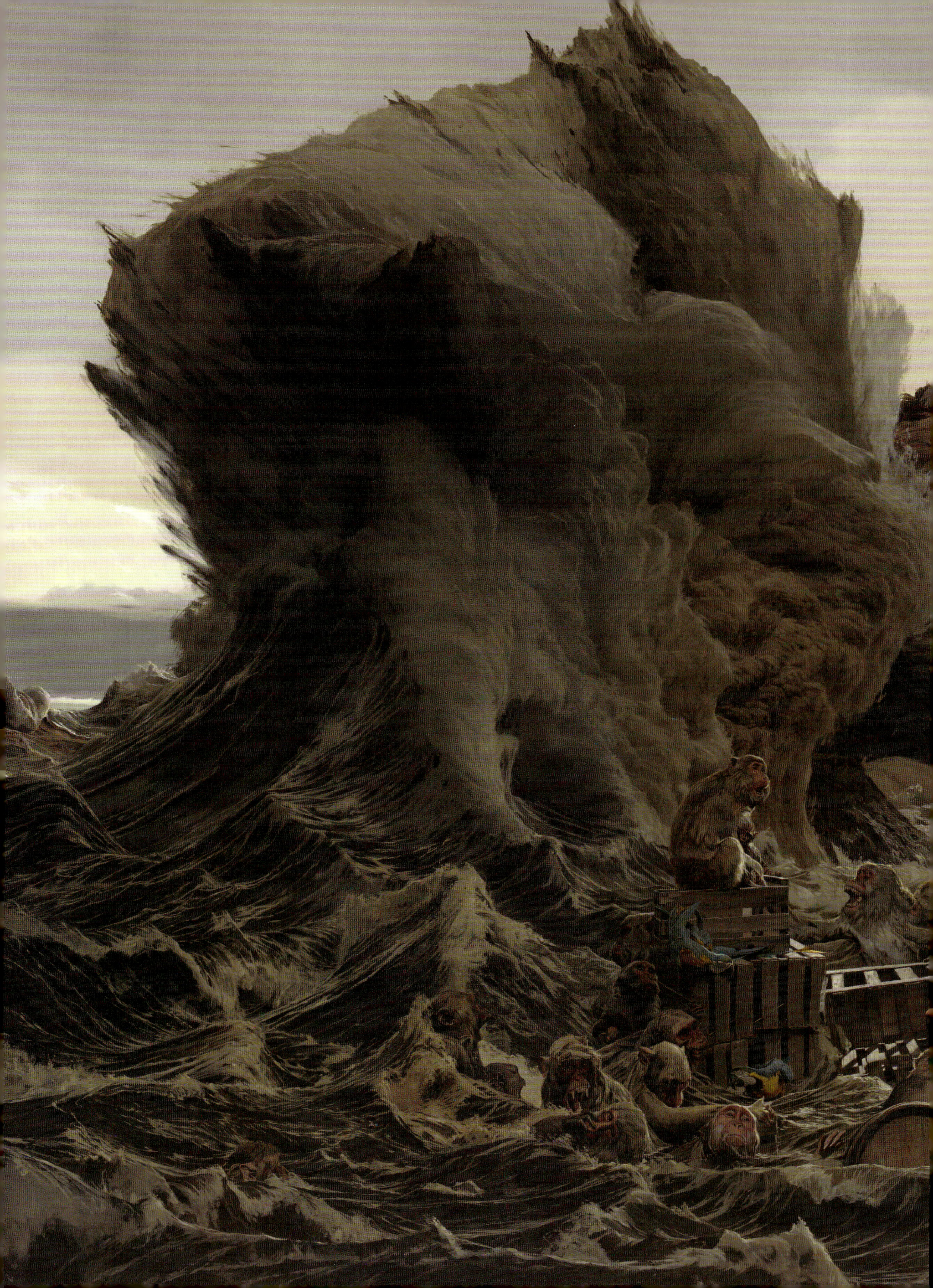

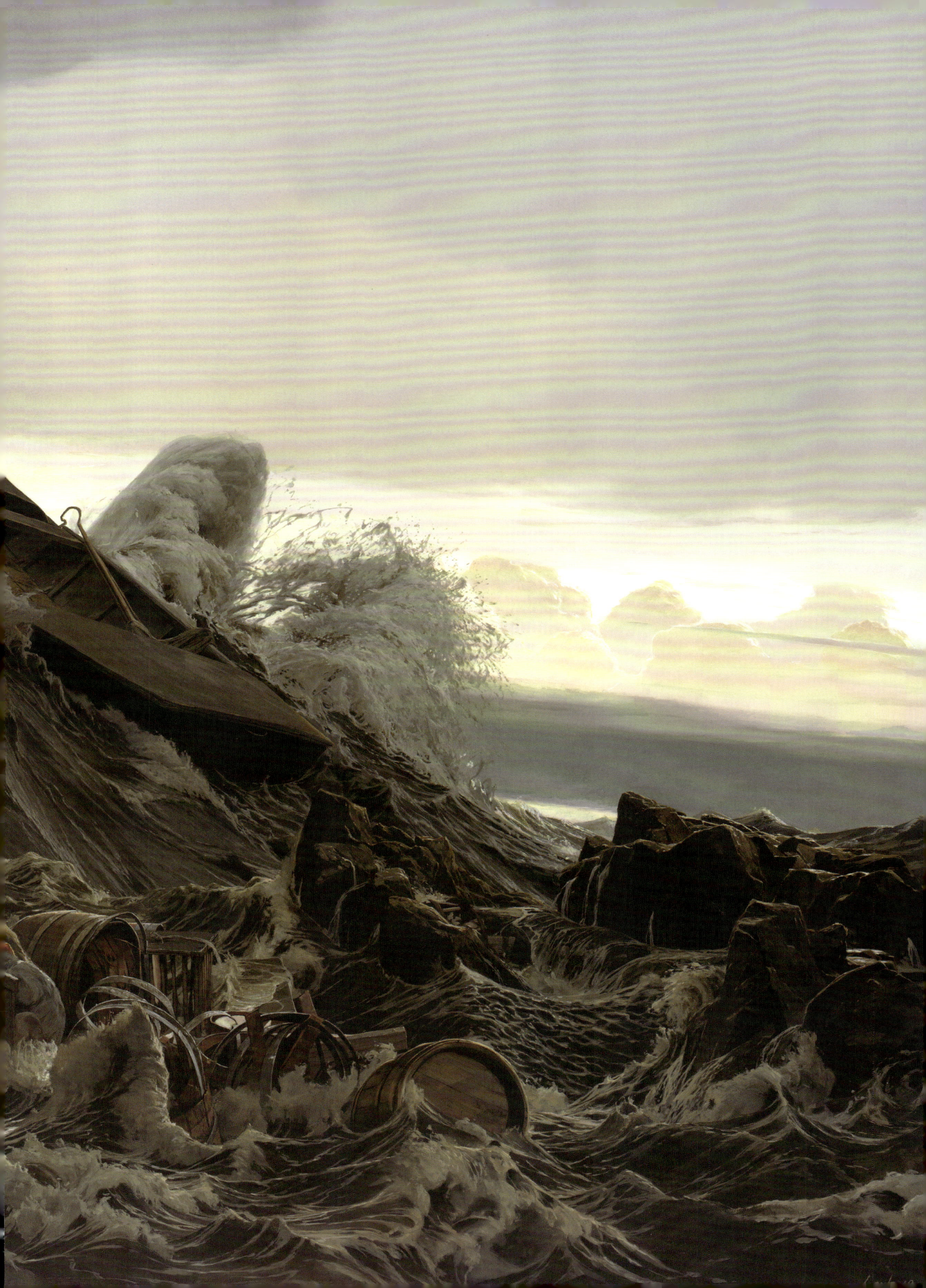

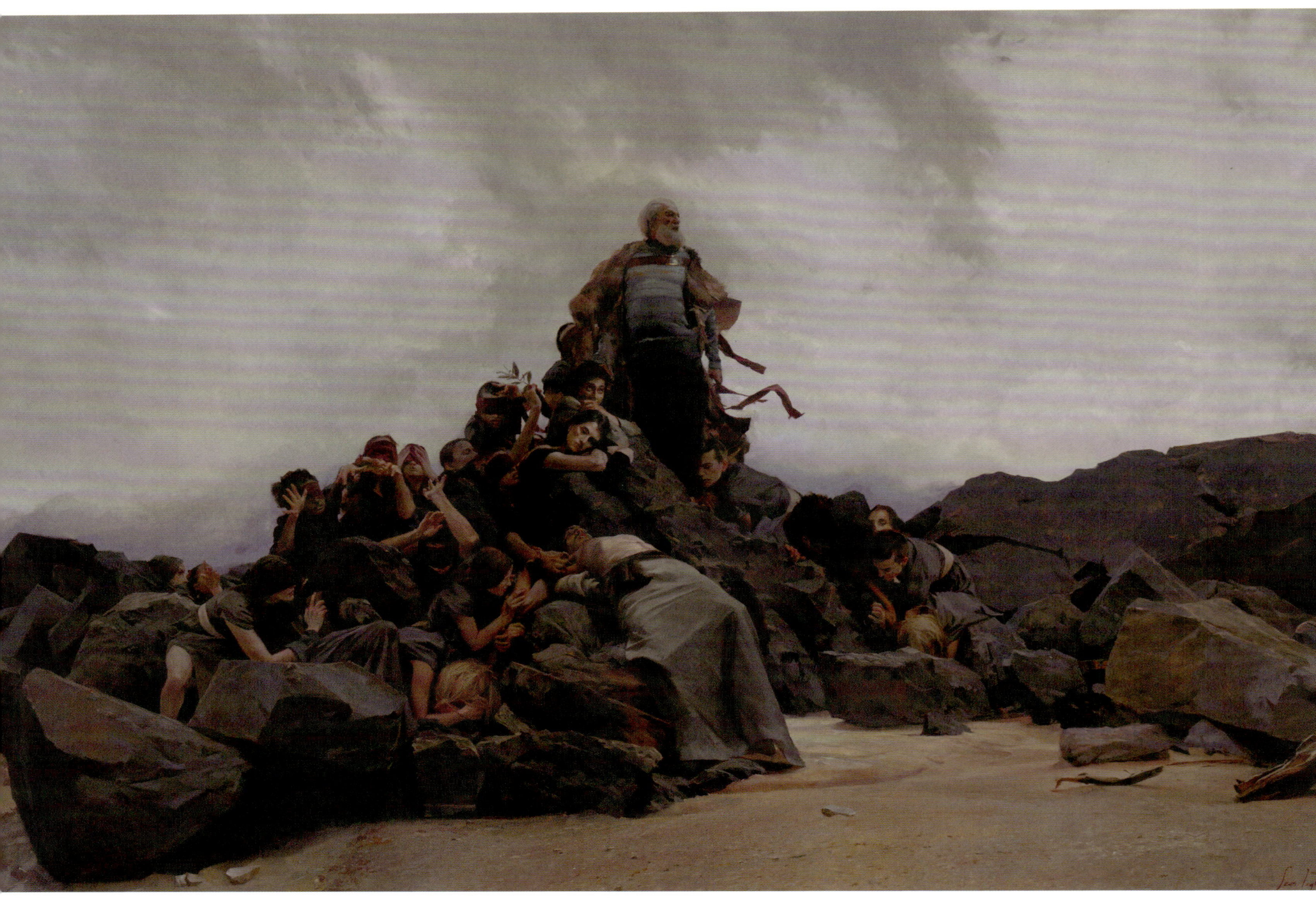

ABOVE:

Oedipus at Colonus | *This painting tells the tale of Oedipus, the erstwhile King of Thebes, as he seeks solace in Colonus during his twilight years. The painting depicts Oedipus' journey towards redemption, his tender relationship with his two sister-daughters, Ismene and Antigone (pictured underneath him), and his estrangement from his two brother-sons*

PREVIOUS PAGE:

The Wreck | *This painting took many years to complete, mainly due to the endless revisions of the monkey figures clinging to the raft. The initial idea behind the design was the story of Iphigenia who was sacrificed by her father Agamemnon to appease Aeolus, the god of winds, and allow his ships to sail to Troy – hence the wind, waves, and solitary woman. However, the design evolved beyond this and turned into a kind of shipwreck scene where exotic animals try and scramble to safety on the high seas*

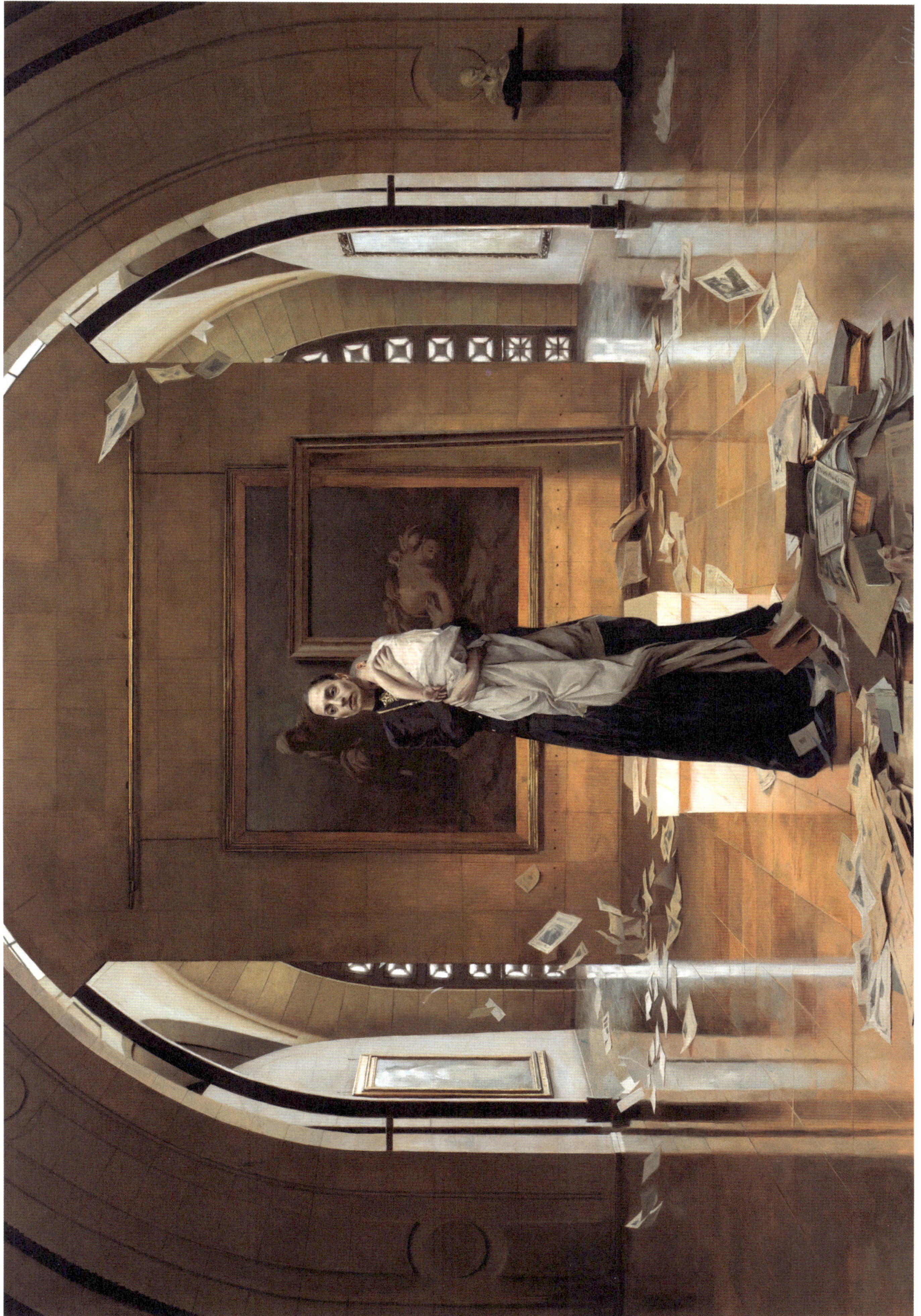

ABOUT THIS PRINT:

Antigone | *The main figure of this piece
is Antigone, as dramatized in the plays
of Sophocles and Euripides. The tale of
Antigone is nested in the larger story of
the curse of the Theban King, Laius. Laius'
curse is hereditary. Famously, Lauis' son,
Oedipus, is cursed to kill his father and marry
his mother. Antigone, Oedipus' daughter,
defies Theban law by burying her brother.
Consequently, she is pronounced a traitor to
the state and buried alive in a mausoleum.
In despair, she kills herself. The main themes
of the play are the conflict between natural
law and profane law, civil disobedience, and
fidelity to the family*

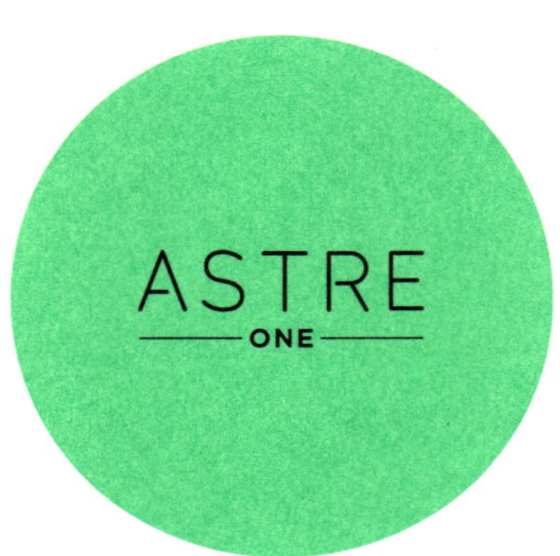

ANTIGONE BY SEAN LAYH

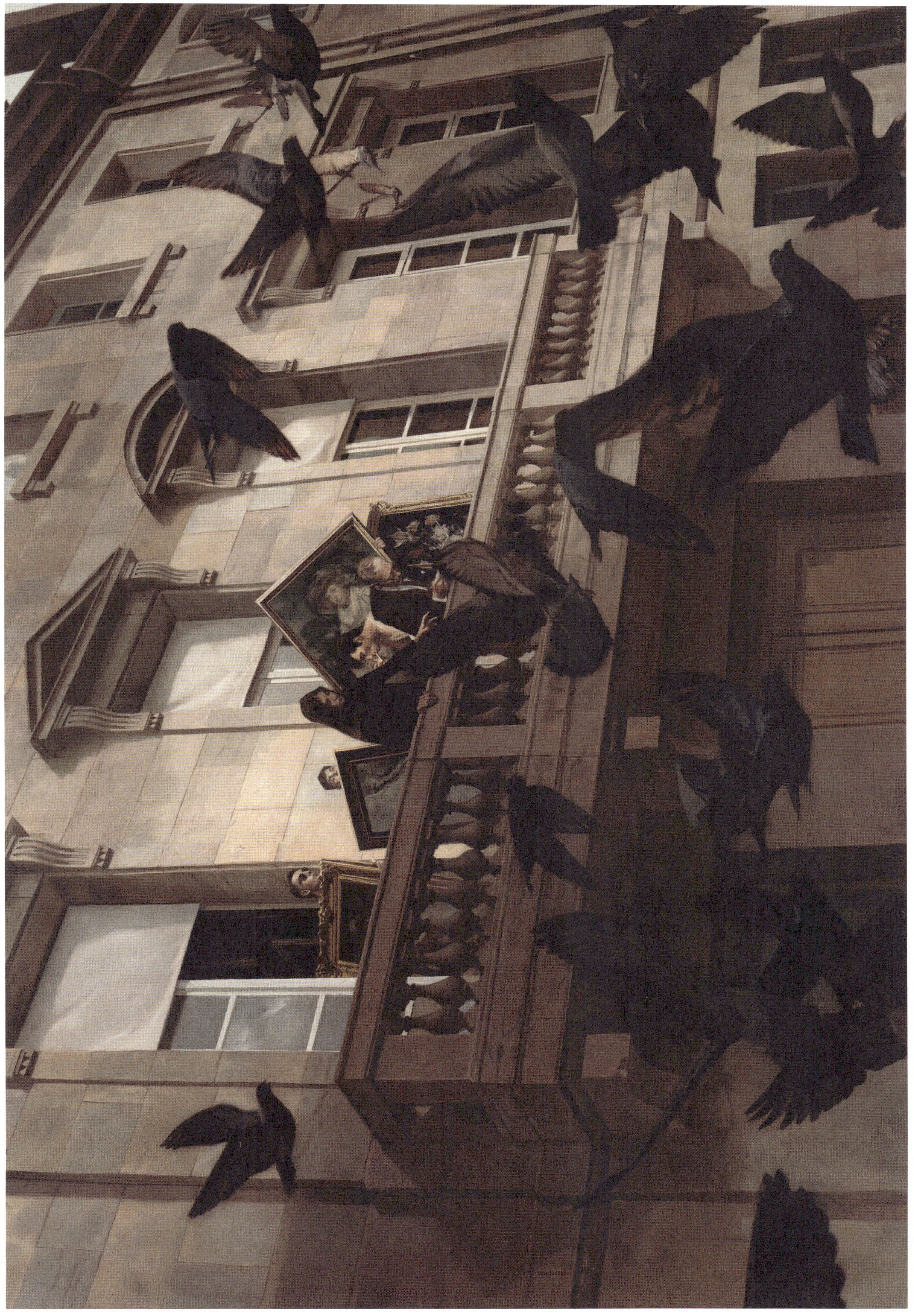

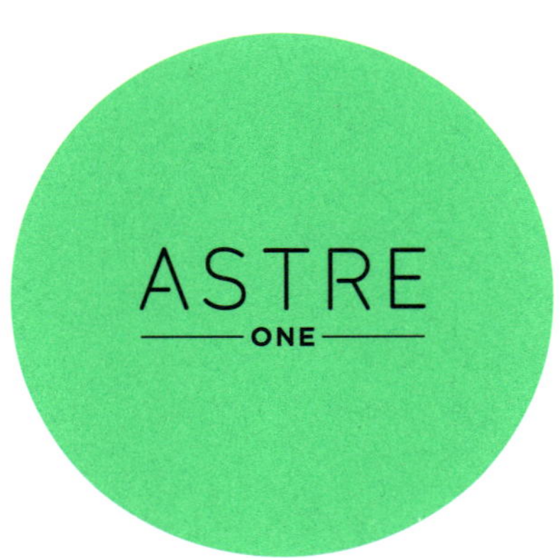

ALL THINGS MADE NEW BY SEAN LAYH

NEXT PAGE:

This Gilded Serpent | The gilded serpent refers to Shakespeare's character Goneril, the villainous daughter of King Lear. Here, she is plotting to poison her sister and co-conspirator, Regan. Although never shown in the play (the plotting and murder happen off stage), I set the drama in a high wind at the break of day

BELOW:

Rockfall | This artwork is a dry-media medley: tinted charcoal, conté, and pastel on paper. Techniques of scuffing and rolling white conté over the surface generated the pleasing effects of distressed quartz in the rock. Unlike many of my pieces, this artwork does not have any narrative source – instead, it simply implies a narrative through the placement of elements within the composition

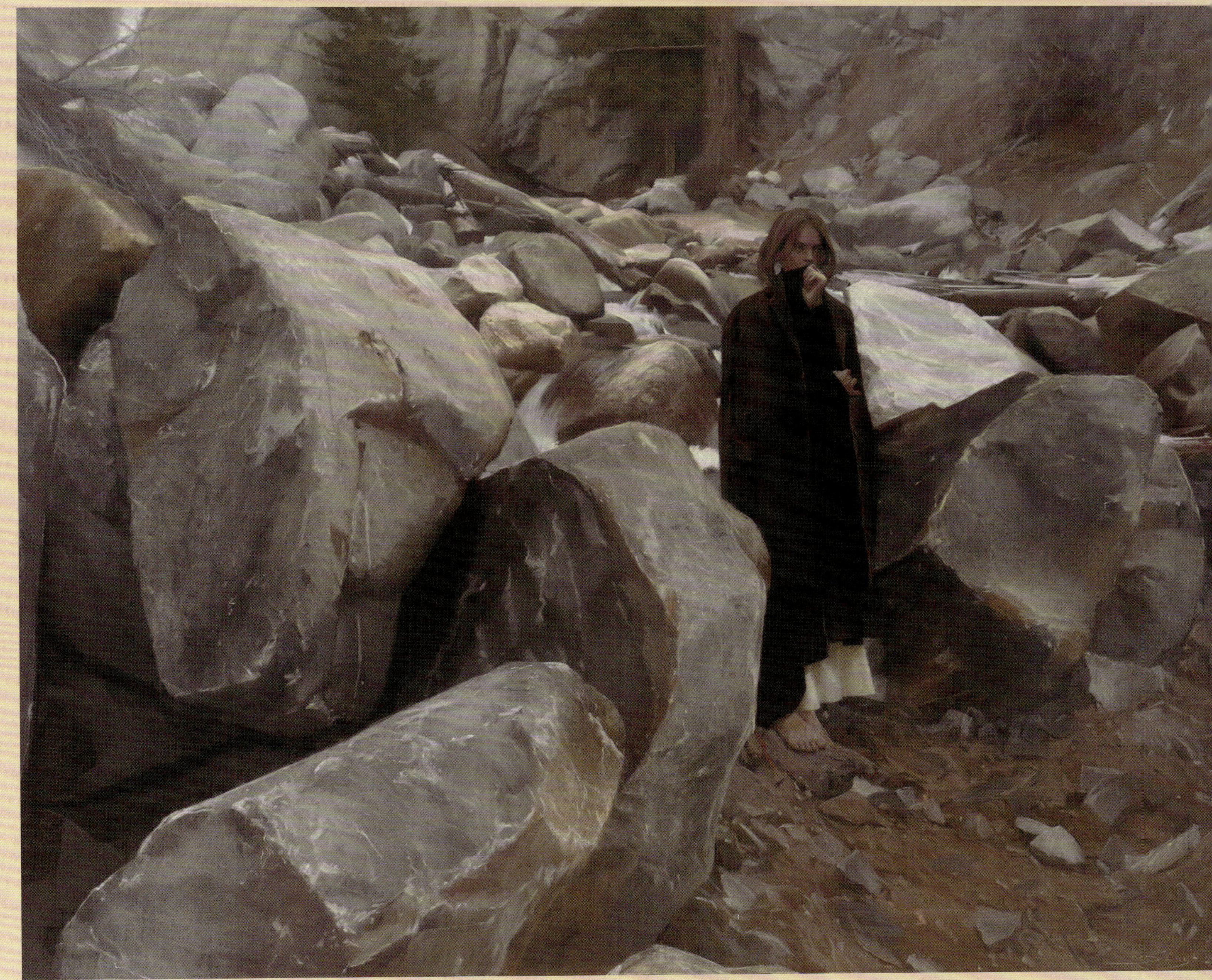

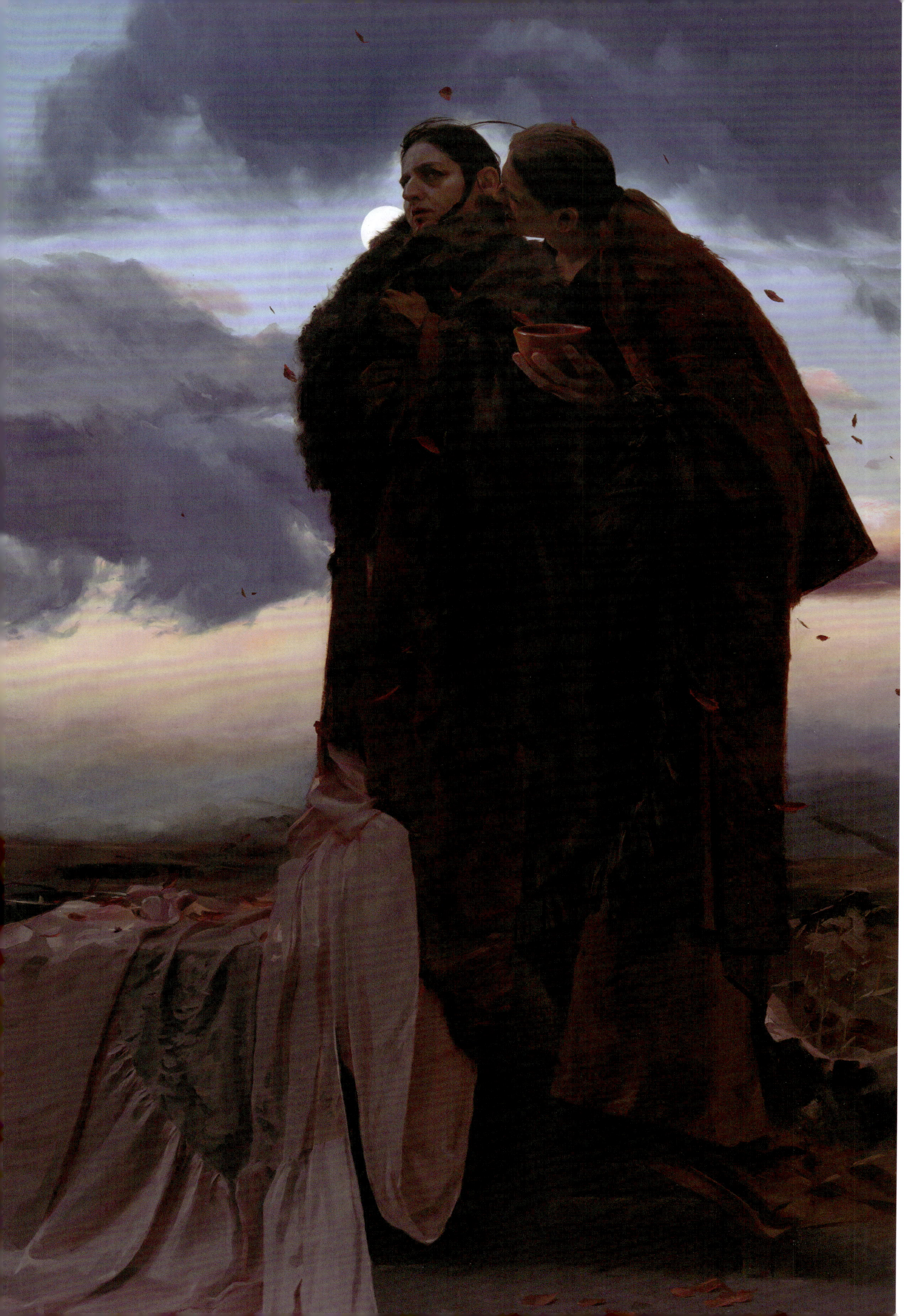

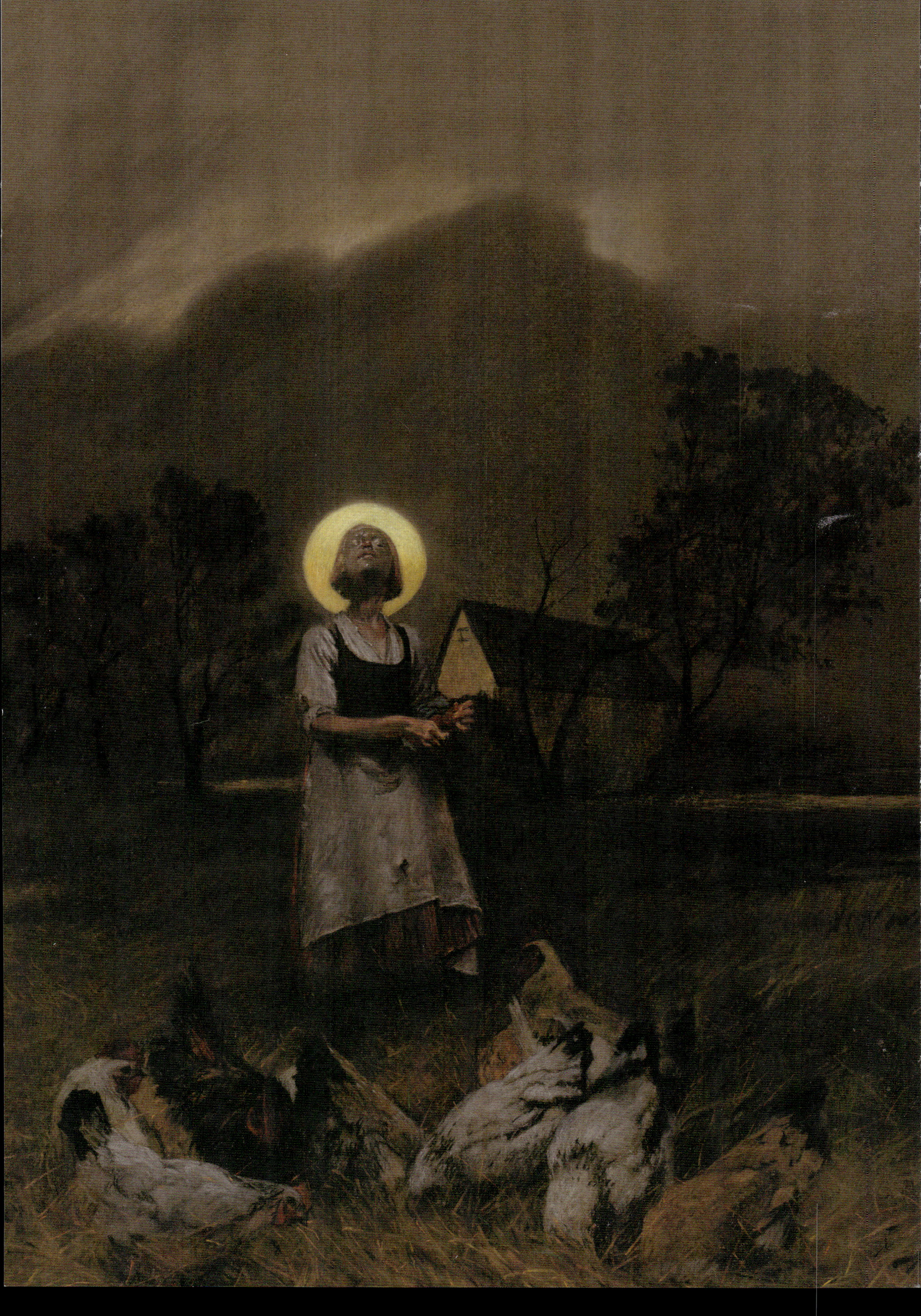

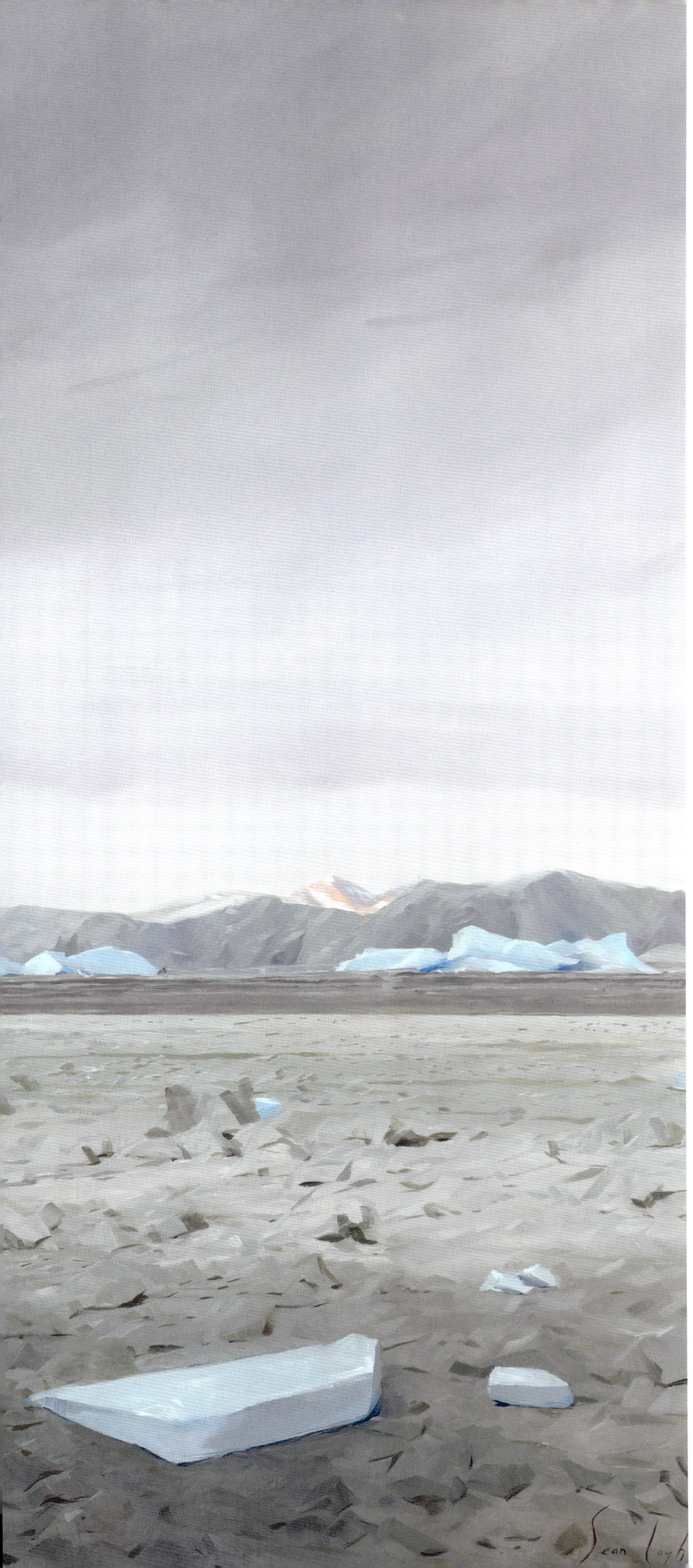

NEXT PAGE

Joan Hears the Voices | This is a dry media work on paper, and depicts the apocryphal moment when the young peasant girl who will become known as Joan of Arc hears the angel's command to lead an army in defence of France against the English. Here, the question is whether the voices are those of the angels, her psyche, or the distant rumbling of an approaching storm

ON THIS PAGE

May We Be Spared | This painting depicts the fateful moment in the Franklin Expedition to traverse the Northwest passage where, after eighteen months stuck in the arctic ice, the remaining crew leave their doomed ships and attempt to escape on foot. Out of the 129 crew, none survived. Reports of cannibalism relayed by the local Inuit were met with outrage and disbelief. It would take over 150 years to discover the lost ships

The biggest influences on my work are the titans of 19th-century representational painters: John William Waterhouse, Lawrence Alma-Tadema, Jules Bastien-Lepage, Arthur Streeton, and Elizabeth Thompson, to name a few. I am fortunate that artworks by each of these painters are viewable just down the road from my studio, at my local National Gallery. This accounts for much of their influence on my work – as I never had a formal education in fine art, being able to view works in person has been so important to my development. Ultimately, I look to these painters as they dealt with the two aspects of art that I care most about: the skill of painting and storytelling.

I produce on average four paintings a year, each one constituting a project in its own right. I have many designs on the go and the main challenge for me is choosing which to dedicate the next three months of my working life to. As a father, much of the rest of my life is dedicated to my family and, when I have the time, my friends. I do try to find time to indulge in reading and observing; two favourite pastimes to which I owe much of my inspiration. ◼

Icarus was the son of Daedalus, the master craftsmen who built the labyrinth of Crete for King Minos. After Theseus escaped the supposedly inescapable maze, Icarus was imprisoned, along with his father, as punishment. Ever resourceful, Daedalus crafted wings from feathers and wax, and took to the skies with his son to escape the maze. However, despite his father's warnings, Icarus flew higher and higher until he was so close to the sun that the wax in his wings melted, and he fell to the ocean, drowning in the depths below.

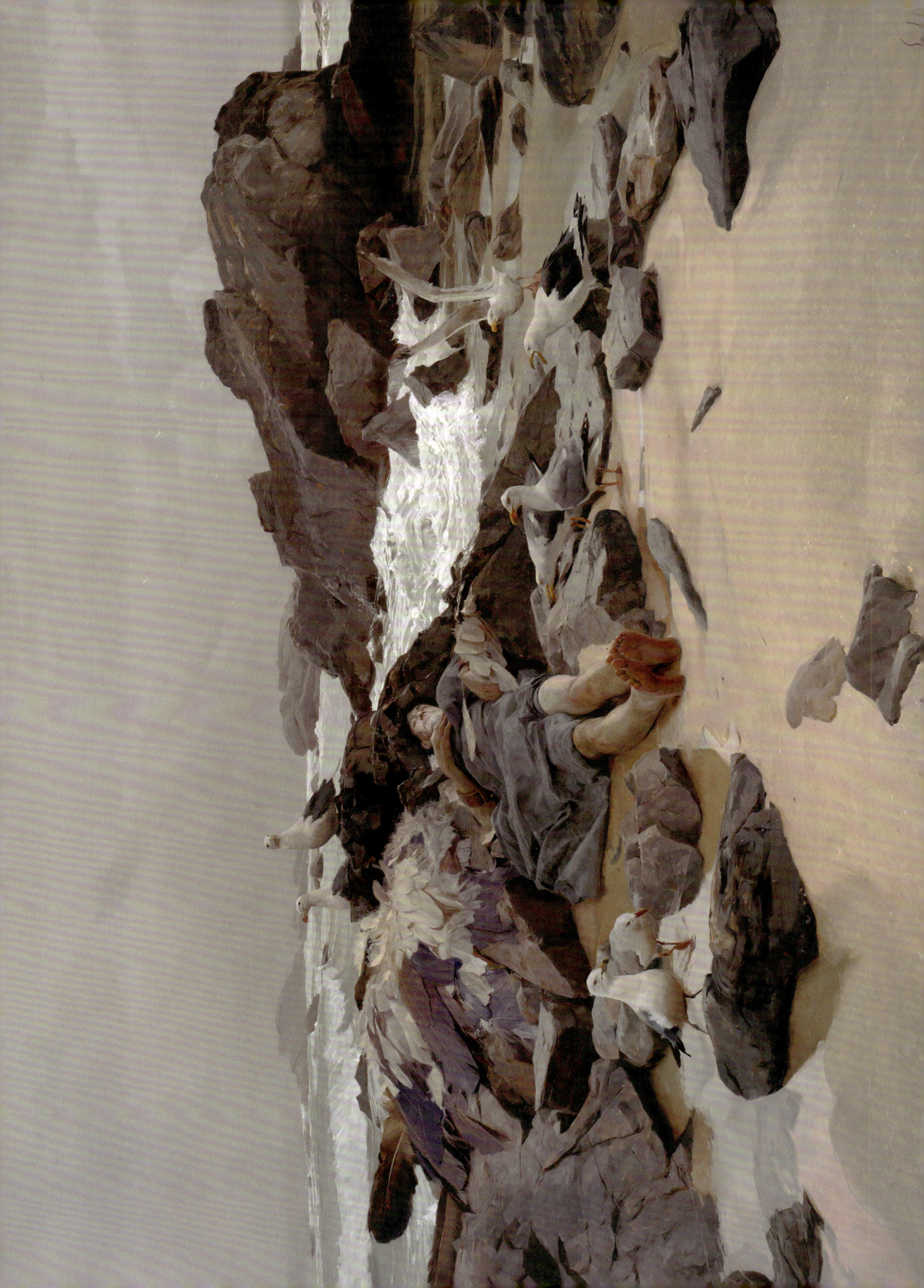

ASTRE

Correspondence: **publishing@3dtotal.com**
Website: **store.3dtotal.com**

Every effort has been made to ensure the credits and contact information listed are present and correct. In the case of any errors that have occurred, the publisher respectfully directs readers to **store.3dtotal.com/pages/information** for any updated information and corrections.

First published in the United Kingdom, 2025, by 3dtotal Publishing.

Address: 3dtotal.com Ltd,
29 Foregate Street, Worcester,
WR1 1DS, United Kingdom.

ISBN: 978-1-915992-03-1

Printed and bound in China by C&C Offset Printing Co., Ltd

Visit **store.3dtotal.com** for a complete list of available publications.

Editor: Sam Draper
Designers: Fiona Tarbet & Matthew Lewis
Proofreader: Marisa Lewis
Lead Editor: Samantha Rigby
Lead Designer: Joseph Cartwright
Studio Manager: Simon Morse
Managing Director: Tom Greenway

Front cover artwork © Andrew Hem

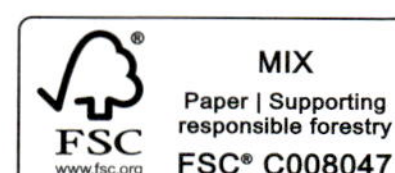

Format: *235 x 325 mm* **Paper (Cover):** *FSC-certified 350 gr/m² white, glossy, art paper*
Paper (Content): *FSC-certified 120 gr/m² wood-free Golden Sun paper*
Paper (Prints): *FSC-certified 180 gr/m² Pingri neutral paper* **Colours:** *Printed in cyan, magenta, yellow, and black* **Pantones:** *Creative Green 802 C and Pantone Rhodamine Red C*
Foils: *DA-288, F6800, F9001, GBA-108, SP01, 931, 401* **Type:** *Sourced from Adobe Fonts*

CONTRIBUTORS

Audra Auclair | *Artist*
Audra is a Canadian artist living in the Pacific Northwest. She combines a diverse range of inspirations and interests to create surreal and fantastical works.
audraauclair.com

Andrew Hem | *Artist & Muralist*
Andrew is a Cambodian-born artist who lives and works in Los Angeles. He works with gouache, oil, and acrylic, mixing the rich styles of his heritage with graffiti-inspired urban art.
andrewhem.com

Chantal Horeis | *Illustrator*
Chantal is based in Stockholm, Sweden. The biggest inspiration for her work is nature in all its forms and colours. She often likes to capture and explore the simple, mundane moments of life.
chantalhoreis.com

Eliza Ivanova | *Owner, CREAOS*
Eliza is an award-winning Bulgarian artist, animator, and filmmaker, currently living and working in San Francisco. She has worked as a 3D animator on multiple projects at Pixar, published four books, and participated in multi-artist publications.
elizaivanova.com

Linnea Kikuchi (Feefal) | *Digital Artist*
Linnea is an illustrator from Sweden with a passion for creating artwork that is rich in dreamlike elements. She takes inspiration from science and biology.
@feefal across the internet

Sean Layh | *Artist*
Sean is a fine artist primarily working in oils and dry media. In 2023, Sean was one of twenty finalists in the 25th Portrait Society of America's International Competition.
seanlayh.com

Janice Sung | *Artist & Painter*
Janice is based in Victoria, Canada and is known for her whimsical paintings that often portray women entwined with animals and nature. She has recently started experimenting with watercolours and gouache.
janicesung.com

Michał Sawtyruk | *Freelance Vis Dev Artist*
Michael is a visual development artist and illustrator currently living in Warsaw. He has worked in the animation and commercial industry for over a decade and creates experimental animated shorts in his spare time.
michalsawtyruk.com

3dtotal Publishing